Fans, Bloggers, and Gamers

Fans, Bloggers, and Gamers

Exploring Participatory Culture

Henry Jenkins

NEW YORK UNIVERSITY PRESS
New York and London

NEW YORK UNIVERSITY PRESS
New York and London
www.nyupress.org

Library of Congress Cataloging-in-Publication Data
Jenkins, Henry, 1958–
Fans, bloggers, and gamers : exploring participatory culture / Henry
Jenkins.
p.   cm.
Includes bibliographical references and index.
ISBN-13: 978-0-8147-4284-6 (cloth : alk. paper)
ISBN-10: 0-8147-4284-X (cloth : alk. paper)
ISBN-13: 978-0-8147-4285-3 (pbk. : alk. paper)
ISBN-10: 0-8147-4285-8 (pbk. : alk. paper)
1. Mass media--Audiences. 2. Mass media and culture. 3. Mass
media—Influence. I. Title.
P96.A83J46 2006
302.23—dc22   2006008890

New York University Press books are printed on acid-free paper,
and their binding materials are chosen for strength and durability.

Manufactured in the United States of America
c 10 9 8 7 6 5 4 3 2 1
p 10 9 8 7 6 5 4 3 2

Contents

Introduction

Confessions of an Aca/Fan

Hello. My name is Henry. I am a fan.

Somewhere in the late 1980s, I got tired of people telling me to get a life. I wrote a book instead. The result was *Textual Poachers: Television Fans and Participatory Culture* (1992).

This past year, I completed a new book, *Convergence Culture: Where Old and New Media Intersect* (2006), which is in some loose sense a sequel to *Textual Poachers*.

Poachers described a moment when fans were marginal to the operations of our culture, ridiculed in the media, shrouded with social stigma, pushed underground by legal threats, and often depicted as brainless and inarticulate. Inspired by work in the Birmingham cultural studies tradition, which helped reverse the public scorn directed at youth subcultures, I wanted to construct an alternative image of fan cultures, one that saw media consumers as active, critically engaged, and creative. *Poachers* defines fans as "rogue readers." When I was writing the book, a number of fans were nervous about what would happen if their underground culture was exposed to public scrutiny. They didn't love the media stereotypes of "Trekkies," but they weren't sure they wanted to open the closet doors either.

Convergence Culture describes a moment when fans are central to how culture operates. The concept of the active audience, so controversial two decades ago, is now taken for granted by everyone involved in and around the media industry. New technologies are enabling average consumers to archive, annotate, appropriate, and recirculate media content. Powerful institutions and practices (law, religion, education, advertising, and politics, among them) are being redefined by a growing recognition of what is to be gained through fostering—or at least tolerating—participatory cultures. Many had argued that *Textual Poachers* should have been informed by political economy perspectives, often with the false assumption that if I had done so, I would have seen that fandom was created entirely from the top down by the studio's marketing efforts. *Convergence Culture* is very engaged with media industries, providing a more nuanced picture of how they think about their consumers. The picture that emerges is more complex and contradictory than would have been envisioned by either audience ethnographers or political economists a decade ago. *Convergence Culture* documents the struggle to define the terms of our participation in contemporary popular culture.

This book contains selected essays written primarily in the years between *Textual Poachers* and *Convergence Culture*. These essays formulate and reformulate my understanding of the interplay between the media industries and their consumers; they map my progression from the theories of audience resistance and appropriation that shaped *Poachers* toward new theories of audience participation and collective intelligence that have influenced *Convergence Culture*; they represent different experiments in how I negotiate my multiple identities as fan and scholar; and they represent my efforts to push these ideas into new spaces beyond the university bookstore ghetto. Some of these essays first appeared in other people's anthologies, decontextualized from the larger body of my work. Others appeared in small-circulation publications or were addressed to publics far removed from the academic world. My hope is that people reading this book may see the connections between these various projects.

Participatory culture is anything but fringe or underground today. Fan fiction can be accessed in astonishing quantities and diversities by anyone who knows how to Google. Media producers monitor Web forums such as "Television without Pity," planting trial balloons to test viewer response, measuring reaction to controversial plot twists. Game companies give the public access to their design tools, publicize the best results, and hire the top amateur programmers. The amateur subtitling and circulation of anime arguably helped to open the market for Asian cultural imports. And meetup.com formed as a way for collectors to trade Beanie Babies; its impact was first demonstrated by X-Philes as they lobbied to keep their show on the air; but it became a central resource in the 2004 presidential campaign. News stories appear regularly about media companies suing their consumers, trying to beat them back into submission, and the blogging community continues to challenge the mainstream news media and shake up the political parties.

At the same time, academic research on fan creativity, online communities, and participatory culture has become central to a range of different disciplines. In education, James Paul Gee, David Buckingham, and their students are exploring fan and gaming communities as sites of informal instruction.[1] In legal studies, Rosemary J. Coombe has explored the challenges grassroots expression poses to our traditional understandings of intellectual property law.[2] Steve Duncombe has written about zines as forms of subcultural expression and grassroots activism.[3] Kurt Lancaster has explored the ways people "perform" their relationships to the television show *Babylon 5* through fan costuming or role-playing games.[4] Robert Kuzinets has pioneered an entire field of marketing research focused on the cultures of committed consumers, whether understood as brand cultures or fan cultures.[5] Anthropologist Geraldine Bloustein uses amateur video-making to study the ways adolescent girls experiment with their identities in both public and private.[6] In philosophy, Thomas McLaughlin sees fan communities as among the most active sites of vernacular theory-making.[7] David A. Brewer and Carolyn Sigler have explored the roots of fan fiction in the responses of eighteenth- and nineteenth-century readers to works now considered parts of the literary canon.[8] And the list goes on and on. Fandom has provided a powerful lens for understanding important intellectual questions.

I can take neither the credit nor the blame for this explosion of academic interest in fandom. *Textual Poachers* was itself inspired by the shift in Cultural Studies toward audience ethnography represented by such writers as Ien Ang, Janice Radway, John Tulloch, David Morley, and John Fiske, among so many others.[9] Camille Bacon-Smith's *Enterprising Women* came out a little over a month before *Poachers,* and Constance Penley was already touring the conference circuit talking about her close encounters with homoerotic "slash" fan fiction.[10] Something was in the air in the early 1990s that would have resulted, one way or another, in the academic "discovery" of fandom. After all, the two have shadowed each other from the start: media scholars have long sought to escape the stigma of fandom, often at the expense of masking or even killing what drew them to their topics in the first place; and fans have often been hypercritical of academics because of their sloppiness with the details that are so central to fan interpretation. These conflicts unfold in the customer reviews on Amazon.com anytime a fan reader responds to an academic account of popular culture. Yet, since the 1990s it has become increasingly possible for people to merge the roles of fan and academic, to be explicit about the sources of their knowledge and about the passion that drives their research, and to seek collaborations between two groups that both assert some degree of expertise over popular culture.

In those heady early days, we used to call ourselves Aca/Fen, a hybrid identity that straddled two very different ways of relating to media cultures. ("Fen" was widely accepted—among fans—as the plural of "fan.") Today, the two do not seem very far apart. When I present my work at "Console-ing Passions," an annual cultural studies conference that has become one of the key centers for feminist work on television and new media, many of the other speakers are open about their fannish pleasures. When I speak at "The Witching Hour," a leading gathering of *Harry Potter* fans, I find myself sharing crumpets with academics from a range of disciplines. And when I read online publications such as *Swoosh* (for *Xena: Warrior Princess* fans), *Slayage* (for *Buffy the Vampire Slayer* fans) or *Joystick 101* (for gamers), academics, media makers, and fans trade insights on a regular basis. In the early days, I remember the anxieties academics felt as fans invaded their discussion lists for media studies. Now, we couldn't keep fans at bay even if we wanted to, and the fans who have crossed over have proven their value many times over. Indeed, many of them have gone to graduate school and become important cultural critics.

Fans, Bloggers, and Gamers is divided into three parts. "Inside Fandom" includes those essays that deal most directly with the politics and poetics of fan cultural production. When I first began my career, it was taken for granted that audience ethnographers stood outside the communities they researched, neither touching nor being touched by what they saw. The language of audience research drew heavily on the traditions of sociology and sought to efface the experiences and emotions of the researchers themselves. Given this context, my decision to "out" myself as a fan in the introduction to *Textual Poachers* proved controversial. This insider approach to media ethnography was embraced by many as opening up a space for more engaged writing about fan communities, but it was criticized by others for pretending to "have it all" or "going native" or simply "slumming it," all terms suggesting that, by definition, academics cannot be fans. My writing was informed by new work in anthropology that sought to acknowledge more directly the researcher's stakes in encounters with other cultures, by work in gender

and sexuality studies that wrote about culture from specific epistemological standpoints, and, more generally, by a shift toward autobiographical perspectives in cultural studies and critical theory. Stylistically,
these essays were inspired by the "new journalists," writers like Hunter
S. Thompson and Tom Wolfe who used evocative language and provoc-
ative techniques to show us what it felt like to be a participant in significant cultural practices or a member of a subcultural community.[11]

Matt Hills has criticized the first generation of fan researchers, myself
included, for pulling back from the affective dimensions of fandom in
favor of a focus on the cognitive dimensions of meaning production.[12]
Meaning in that sense is divorced from the emotional investments fans
make in particular texts or in their own cultural practices. Fans would
reject such a clear separation between feelings and thoughts: their
favored texts are both tools for thought and spaces for emotional exploration. I see the essays in this section as struggling to find critical language and rhetorical forms that communicate those investments to
readers who are not part of the communities being described.

"Going Digital" includes essays about the impact of digital media on
our everyday lives. This section trace both my own tentative steps into
the digital realm and the process by which fans learned how to use new
media resources to increase their visibility and expand their influence
over popular culture. The fan culture I described in *Poachers* was pre-
digital. Most zines were reproduced by photocopying and distributed
through the mail or passed hand to hand at conventions, usually called
"cons" by fans. Over the past decade, fandom has both been reshaped
by and helped to reshape cyberculture. I wrote one of the first ethnogra-
phies of an online fan community, alt.tv.twinpeaks, and as the decade
continued, I became very interested in mapping what digital theory
could teach us about fandom, as well as what fandom could teach us
about the place of digital technologies in our everyday lives. In more
recent work, I have examined new sites of audience expression—game
modding, blogging, digital filmmaking—that have emerged as everyday
people have gotten their hands on the tools of media production and
distribution.

"Columbine and Beyond" explores the public policy debates that
emerged in the wake of the shootings in Littleton, Colorado, especially
those concerning the impact of popular culture on teens and the censorship of computer and video games. These essays illustrate a shift in my
focus away from writing intended primarily for circulation within the

scholarly community and more toward journalism addressing a larger public. John Hartley has coined the term "intervention analysis" to refer to a mode of scholarship that seeks to mobilize and amplify the perspectives of media consumers in order to ensure that they get a fair hearing by people in power. Many of these essays reflect an effort to intervene in public policy debates that have a significant impact on the communities I research. The essays here were published in *Harpers, Salon,* and *Technology Review* and in a range of publications aimed at teachers. They were intended as resources for parents, youth, and educators. These essays also reflect on my own public activities—testifying before the U.S. Senate Commerce Committee, defending *Grand Theft Auto 3* on *Donahue,* joining amicus briefs to challenge court decisions, designing educational games, and promoting media literacy education. If the first two parts of the book reflect my efforts to explore and redefine the line separating academics and fans, the third part reflects my efforts to break down the walls that prevent scholars from having a more direct role in shaping and guiding our media environment.

Each essay is prefaced by some personal reflections on how it came to be written. It is hard to imagine providing any kind of intellectual context for these essays that doesn't deal with my personal stakes in the content. What I write about is deeply personal. As you will see, several of these essays were created in collaboration with members of my family, and others reflect upon the role that media plays in the life of our family. A few are written as first-person narratives describing this strange character, "Professor Jenkins," and his misadventures in public life. Even where these essays are not explicitly personal, they deal with forms of culture that have captured my imagination and sparked my passion. To me the essence of being methodologically self-conscious is to be honest about how you know what you know. And most of what I am writing about here I know from the inside out.

PART I

Inside Fandom

1

Excerpts from "Matt Hills Interviews Henry Jenkins"

The following conversation was recorded one evening at the "Console-ing Passions" conference in 2001 at the University of Bristol. A much longer version appeared online in Intensities: The Journal of Cult Media *that same year.*

In many ways, this conversation reflects the explosion of fan scholarship since Textual Poachers first appeared. The fact that the interview appeared in an online journal devoted entirely to cult media and its audiences would have seemed inconceivable at the time I first began studying fans. Matt Hills, my partner for this conversation, is one of the founding editors of Intensities and the author of Fan Cultures, a book that includes a painfully close reading of Textual Poachers. Matt had the uncanny ability to locate those passages that left me most hesitant or those where I compromised on my original wording in order to appease some colleague or mentor. It was as if he broke into my house and found the rough draft, zeroing in on every marked out passage. A bit frightened at how deep this guy got inside my head, I was determined, following ancient advice, to keep him close by my side. This conversation was the first we'd had since Fan Cultures had appeared in print and some of it has the feel of settling scores or clarifying the relationship between our two perspectives.

It is telling that we recorded it at "Console-ing Passions." For most of my academic career, "Console-ing Passions," a conference on gender and television studies, has been one of my intellectual homes. I presented a version of the chapter on slash fiction from Textual Poachers at the very first "Console-ing Passions" and have not missed one since. What I love about the conference is the openness participants have about their own investments in popular culture. Matt and I recorded this session in an empty room with no audience.

Matt Hills: [Let's start with] a quote from *Perverse Spectators,* by Janet Staiger:

> While most studies of fans emphasize the positive features of exchange and empowerment deriving from interests in often marginal objects of pleasure, I would point out that scholars may need to shift their presumptions even here—although not back to the days when fans were considered pathological spectators. Without going that far, I would argue that some fans and fan communities might benefit from more critical social theory. . . . Fandom . . . cannot be easily bifurcated into good and bad; the historian's responsibility is adequate description and thoughtful evaluation.[1]

This is a quote that really struck me. I suppose it speaks to what I'm trying to do in *Fan Cultures.* I find Staiger's statement rather contradictory, but perhaps that's also why I find it so compelling: she seems to argue that fandom can't be divided up into the "good object" and the "bad object," into "good" fan appropriation and "bad" fan complicity, but at the same time as challenging this moral dualism, there is an investment in the "critical" which seems to be completely about reinstating the authority to divide fandom into aspects to be applauded and aspects to be criticized. Can we, or should we, be "critical"? And if so, what fan practices and fan communities are we going to be critical of?

Henry Jenkins: This is a tricky space that I think we're all struggling with right now. When I write—having come out of a certain generation of academics—I still feel an enormous pressure to someplace say, "Is this progressive or is this reactionary?" It's probably both progressive and reactionary in some ways, both good and bad, but the need to declare yourself definitively at some point in the text is something that you have in the back of your mind when you write within a discipline like cultural studies, which was born out of political resistance at a particular historical moment and which has been shaped by Marxist discourse, which is itself a moral discourse as much as a political and economic one. One always has a fear of not being sufficiently political when you operate within cultural studies. It defined itself as a field around a category of "the political." . . .

MH: But a highly moralized sense of "the political"; so to be "political" was inherently good, almost, whereas if something "lacked" politics . . . well, "apolitical" is always going to be an insult.

HJ: I think it was Lawrence Grossberg who said, "If writing about popular culture isn't political then what good is it?" My answer is that there are plenty of things you can say about popular culture that aren't motivated purely from a political or moralistic stance. . . .

MH: Even though you accept that you are not just celebrating fandom, especially in *Science Fiction Audiences,* but also in *Textual Poachers,* if you look at textbook coverage of your work, you are constantly being accused of being too celebratory.

HJ: Well, you know, it's because I don't call fans "twits" and "anoraks" that for some people—

MH: —you must be being too celebratory!

HJ: I think we need to consider different generations of scholars within fandom, and moments within which those scholars are working. I think there are at least three moments of fan studies that get conflated together as if they are a unified body of theory. There is a body of work that began to stress active audiences and the use of ethnographic methods, derived in part from sociological methods, and I would put early John Tulloch, John Fiske, and Janice Radway in this body of work— they come from different places and so I don't want to lump them together as representing one totally unified body of work.

But it was important for these writers to be outside what they were writing about, to be free of any direct implication in their subject matter. They begin to acknowledge that audiences have an active role, but their prose is very depersonalized; there's often no acknowledgement of any affection they feel for the objects of study, or if there is, it's a token gesture. And there's sometimes an attempt to pull back from the fan community at the end of such writing and say, right, now we can arrive at the truth that the fans don't yet recognize about their own political activity. I've taken Radway to task for the closing chapter of *Reading the Romance* for that kind of gesture.[2] That's the first generation.

I see myself and others writing at the same time, Camille [Bacon-Smith] to some degree,[3] as a second generation that comes to a discourse already formulated around these axes of active/passive, resistance/co-opted. We're trying to find a way to alter that perception based on insider knowledge of what it is to be a fan, and struggling to find a language to articulate a different perspective that comes out of lived experience and situated knowledge. And it proves very difficult—there's a lot of resistance because the first generation are the readers responding to our manuscripts, the editors deciding whether they get published or not, the faculty deciding whether we get hired. So you end up struggling to negotiate between what you want to say, and what it's possible to say at a particular point in time, in order to get your work out at all. And there is a level of defensiveness there. When I was writing *Poachers* I was so frustrated by how badly fans had been written about. As a fan I felt implicated in that writing and I wanted to challenge it; there are passages in the book that are just out-and-out defenses of fandom, and others that are trying to pull back and describe, analyze, critique. By the time of *Science Fiction Audiences* (1995) the need to defend is no longer present. At that point you can write securely and you can then begin to look at fandom in a different way.

Now, I think all of that work paved the way for a whole generation of aca-fen, as I like to call them; that is, people who are both academics and fans, for whom those identities are not problematic to mix and combine, and who are able then to write in a more open way about their experience of fandom without the "obligation of defensiveness," without the need to defend the community. Therefore they can take up things like contradictions within it, disputes within it, re-raise awkward subjects that we papered over in our earlier accounts, and now there's a freedom to have real debate among ourselves about some of these core issues.

And so something like *Intensities* to my mind represents the establishment of a generation that is now arriving—that I think you represent very well—that has taken for granted for your entire academic career that it's legitimate to write sympathetically about fans, and now can ask a different set of questions, including going back and batting us around a bit for the things we didn't say. But you've got to recognize that these things weren't said in a historical context, or rather there was a historical context that made it difficult to say certain things. As it was, *Lingua Franca* took Constance Penley and me to task for even saying that we were fans at all, and said we had to be lying, said that this was a typical example of academics slumming it and wanting to be "one of the people." Well, it wasn't slumming it; I'd lived my entire life as a fan. I could be accused of putting on airs by becoming an academic, but I scarcely could be accused of slumming it.

MH: Constance Penley is equally taken to task in a piece by Richard Burt that I cite in *Fan Cultures*.[4] Burt accuses her work of displaying a particular fantasy, the fantasy of being able to "have it all," which is that the academic-fan can somehow occupy, without tensions or power relations, the position of being their own object of study. That kind of critique still lingers in a particular way, and perhaps it still has some force too.

HJ: Your own focus on fans-as-intellectuals in *Fan Cultures* points to one way out of that problem, which is to recognize that a lot of fans carry a large amount of intellectual capital around with them. They are very good critics; they are very good theorists. Thomas McLaughlin's notion of "vernacular theory," which says theory production doesn't just reside in the academy, it takes place in all these other sites, is a helpful way into that, although it still tends to hold onto an "academic" versus "vernacular" theory separation, whereas I would say that academic theory production is simply one subcultural or institutional practice among many.[5] It doesn't need to be separated out from those other kinds of theory; it has its own language, its own goals, its own systems of circulation, and fans are inevitably locked out of that. But many of them are trained academics, librarians, or teachers, many of them decided consciously not to become academics, having had some exposure to academic knowledge, and many of them are professionals in other sectors. To say that they don't have intellectual capital is a bizarre statement. And I think your stuff talks really nicely about fans as critics or fans as intellectuals, and we need to pay more attention to that. . . .

That was something that I tried to get at in an essay that I did with Shoshanna Green and Cynthia Jenkins, "Normal Female Interest in Men Bonking" (see chapter 3 below). We tried to reproduce slash fans' theorizing of their own practice, which met with some resistance with the academic reviewers of the manuscript. They couldn't accept the idea that there was any legitimacy in seeing how fans actually theorize their own practice, even though we would take for granted the fact that an avant-garde artist's manifesto is a way of at least partially understanding the work that they produce. . . . "Normal Female Interest in Men

Bonking" was a model of a dialogic text, and yes, I do have a piece in there because I was part of the fan community that I was drawing on, but I don't label it as somehow distinct from the other fan voices there.

MH: I refer to that essay in *Fan Cultures,* and I think it's very strong. For me, it's one of the pieces that really starts to open up the question of "fan" versus "academic" knowledge.

HJ: It's not auto-ethnography; in a sense it's simply an outing, an exposure of myself in my normal fan activity, since I never wrote that piece with the intent of it seeing academic publication. It had existed in fandom as a part of my intervention in fan debates. The other two editors of the piece agreed that each of us should include passages of our own fan discourse, and I let them choose among the things I had written. So I gave up a certain degree of control over my own discourse in order for that to work out.

Now, that's not without problems. One of the responses to that piece in fandom was that fans wanted me to adjudicate disputes between fans, because I introduce a lot of fan disputes in the piece but I don't comment on them, and I don't take sides. And almost all the fans wanted me to side with them over the other side, and they assumed that if I had presented a more authoritative version of the debate, and it wasn't dialogic, then I would have sided with them! By being dialogic and open, then, somehow I was seen as giving too much space to the opposed view in the dispute. . . .

As an academic you speak with a certain degree of authority. I can't be a normal fan anymore, not because I've somehow distanced myself from fandom, but because I'll walk in the room and the response is different. When passages of your book are used as signature lines on people's emails, and when fan Web sites describe Henry Jenkins as "the guy who dignified fandom," then these sorts of statements make it very hard for me to speak without it in some sense carrying a level of authority that I'm uncomfortable with. It's not what I want the relationship to be between fans and academics, but because the press calls on me as a spokesman for the fan community week in, week out, my role gets communally reinscribed in journalistic practices, and because *Textual Poachers* has now been passed from generation to generation of fans, it's one of the things you read when you want to be integrated into the fan community. They say, "You want to be a fan? Read this." It's become a sort of "how-to" book.

MH: So now it has become part of the "initiation process" that you actually describe in *Textual Poachers*!

HJ: That's really tricky to know what to do with. There are T-shirts that have the cover of *Textual Poachers* on them which circulate in the fan economy, and the work of that artist, Jean Kluge, went up in value within the art hierarchy of fandom because it was associated with the book. She became a more valuable fan artist as a result of that. So you can't go in and totally shed academic authority, which is so ironic to me; I'd been involved in the fan community for a long time, and I was just leaving graduate school when I wrote *Textual Poachers*. In the academic world I was truly puny; I was not yet a heavyweight by any stretch of the imagination, so that this book carried the authority it did was a little disarming.

I saw myself as an agent of dialogue. But it's not just academics who police this dialogue. The fan community has an investment in academic authority on one level, and yet, as you suggest, other fans say, "Sod off, don't bring this language into our space, you're making too much of things that don't matter," and there's a resistance, an anti-intellectualism in some fan circles that equally makes it hard to create that kind of dialogue. We all bring our own baggage to that conversation, which is to say that the identities of the fan-academic or the academic-fan are always problematic ones that have to be sorted through, even though I think there's more freedom to shed that issue today.

MH: There's no utopian solution to that problem; there are still cultural contexts that work to constrain and enable dialogue and fan-academic hybridity, with "constrain" being a key part of that process.

HJ: For example, we're having this discussion at "Console-ing Passions," and I would say that two-thirds of the papers at the conference were delivered by fans of the medium they were discussing. Many of them were actively involved with fan communities, and very few of them felt the need to overtly declare that allegiance because it was taken for granted in the tone of the language, the types of information they mobilized, and the way they dressed and embodied themselves. . . . What our generation did was dismantle some of that to create a comfort zone between fan and academic. . . .

When I first starting saying at academics gatherings, "I'm a fan," I felt a bit like Davy Crockett waltzing into the U.S. senate dressed in buckskin [laughs]—"I'm a real frontiersman." There's a sense in which I'm embodying this community that I'm writing about, but it's nevertheless the case that it becomes a myth the minute you assert it in a particular space; it's a mythic identity as well as a lived identity, and its shock value comes from the assertion of something that was unspeakable at a certain point in time.

MH: So at a certain moment authenticity and scandal interlock, and that's a productive, tactical exercise?

HJ: Yes, and I think that *Textual Poachers* was written at a moment when those two things were interwoven. That is, to be true to my experience of the fans was to produce at least a small-scale scandal within academia.

The result was that most of the early reviews projected onto me whatever remaining stereotypes of fandom I'd not successfully dismantled. So I was described as "blowing it out of proportion," "not separating myth from reality," "being preoccupied with trivia." All of these things that are clichés about fans got projected onto the book. Having asserted that I was a fan, reviewers could either say that I was wrong about fans, or they could assert that I was exactly what they thought a fan was! . . .

MH: I've come armed with another quote that I use in *Fan Cultures*. I thought it might initiate discussion. It's from David Giles's *Illusions of Immortality*, which has a chapter on fans and stalkers; "Fans and Stalkers" as a chapter title, perhaps that's a problem in terms of fan stereotypes! Anyway, Giles says: "Henry Jenkins reports some research conducted by Jewett and Lawrence on what was then a recent emergence of *Star Trek* fans. The researchers concluded that this was 'a strange electronic religion in the making,' and that the publications of the group were 'written in the spirit . . . of religious devotion.' For Jenkins this is a typically 'pathologizing' and 'absurdly literal' account of fandom by academics, but . . . [t]here is nothing intrinsically pathologizing about comparing media fans to religious devotees, since in both instances the roots of devotion are remarkably similar, and the texts produced by *Star Trek* fans . . . are not unlike the religious texts of the Middle Ages, which had a similar degree of reinterpretation (of, say, the Gospels) and turned the authors and translators into famous figures."[6]

Giles basically revisits your critique of Jewett and Lawrence's American Monomyth piece and although his work seems to dehistoricize or ahistoricize fandom, he asks a useful question: how can we assume that it is intrinsically pathologizing to compare media fans to religious devotees?

HJ: We have somewhat different views about the value of the religion analogy . . . my reservations about it are, I guess, rooted in the word "fan" itself. It goes back to "fanaticus," that is, from the very beginning it referred to false and excessive worship. . . . I think the meaning of "fanaticus" surrounded fans as a scandalous category from the very beginning, so whether "fan" came from "fanaticus" or "fancy" doesn't really matter because the connotation of excessive worship is still stuck to "fan" in a certain way. It's very hard, as an academic, to make a religious analogy that doesn't invoke that notion of false worship. For me it's particularly troubling because to my mind the defining basis of religion is belief or faith. And to some degree that has to be grounded in some literalization, so for me the difference between a religion and a mythology is that a mythology can articulate a set of ethical or moral values through stories, and people are deeply invested in those stories. They retell them, they recirculate them, they see them as revealing some deeper truth about human experience. But they don't necessarily believe them to be true. They believe them to be fabricated as an encapsulation of certain sets of values. And I believe cult texts can function as a mythology in that sense. As a religion you bring back in this notion of literal belief, and it implies that fans are unable to separate fiction from reality, or that they supposedly act on the text as if it were literally true. That's what I find troubling in the use of the word "religion." I respect religions as exercises of faith and belief, and I wouldn't elevate fandom to the level of a religion. Nor would I denigrate fans for having false beliefs, because it's not about belief, it's about ethics and about narrative that encapsulates shared values.

MH: I absolutely see the distinction that you're making there. I have two initial responses to it. One would be that you talk about "faith" and "literal belief," but it's the "literal belief" that is actually the marker of difference between a religion and a mythology. Fans could still have some kind of faith in a particular version of the narrative universe that they're invested in, or the characters that they're invested in. There is still some kind of relationship there that implies a significant "faith." . . .

HJ: But to be part of a mythology you are expressing a faith that these values are good, these stories contain something of value, but that's different from saying these stories are true. That's the distinction I'm getting at. To some degree it depends on where your model of religion comes from. The fact that I was raised a Southern Baptist and so was brought up with fundamentalism leaves me with the sense that religion is about a literal truth. If I was born in a different faith that saw biblical stories as human attempts to grasp God and as always inadequate to the divine truth, say—a different theological model—then *Star Trek* might start to feel more like a religion to me, although I still don't think that fans elevate the truths there to that level. There is still not the notion of a hierarchy of the divine or the numinous that's part of religious practice.

MH: This leads into my second point. You're talking about a faith in values, and the values are in the stories. What's so important about fandom, surely, is that, yes, we can believe in certain values, but we could find those values in any number of different stories in our culture. What's important to fans, however, is that these values are found in a very specific set of texts, which implies in a sense that these texts are elevated, that they are numinous. These texts hold the fans' attention in a certain way; they compel fan attention, and therefore the faith that the fan would feel in a certain narrative universe is very much fixed on that universe.

HJ: Except that it's not an exclusive relationship. Insofar as fans are nomadic and can share multiple texts as deeply meaningful to them, there is a flexibility to mix and match those universes that religions don't enjoy. I can't be a Muslim and a Jew at the same time; there is an exclusiveness about the commitment of a religion. But I can be a *Blake's 7* fan and a *Babylon 5* fan and a *Buffy the Vampire Slayer* fan and a

Survivor fan all at the same moment. I'm not being disloyal to one in order to express a commitment to the others.

MH: Although we could both be fans of multiple texts, if you were pushed, would you not still say that one of those texts you would elevate above the others, or hold in higher esteem?

HJ: No; I'm a total media slut! [laughs] I'm absolutely promiscuous, and I don't rate my lays; I have passions and commitments to different works and they satisfy me deeply in the moment that I'm engaged with them, but I don't have any hierarchical or "monogamous" relationship to texts. I'm not ranking *Babylon 5* in relation to *Buffy*. At any given time I may feel slightly more passionate about one or the other—

MH: I'm not saying that you would rank them, I'm saying that you'd have a sense of one text being more significant to your fan identity, and mattering more to you, to use Grossberg's idea of a "mattering map."[7] . . .

HJ: Certainly I could map these texts mattering to me, in your terms, but it would not be an exclusive mapping, it would be a cluster of things that I really got deeply involved with, another that I watched regularly, another that I was curious about and watched when I thought of it. There would be layers like that, but there would not be, at the top, a single true faith in the sense that one would feel an allegiance to a religion. So there, again, I think the analogy breaks down.

The other problem is that people use religion as a metaphor to refer to the social practices of fandom; this is a community that people belong to and which articulates shared values and beliefs. In that sense I don't see why the metaphor should be a religion any more than it could be a union or a political party or a social club or a fraternity, any number of which serve that same social function of being a community that articulates values and shared affect. None of those are adequate to what fandom is, but fandom is simply one form of social affiliation alongside others. And in order to make the religion analogy you erase all those other kinds of social affiliations from the map and say, "Let's look at religion, let's look at fandom; they have this in common, that people meet their partners there, both are passed from generation to generation, there's an emotional bond there—"

MH: There are a number of overlaps then.

HJ: There are overlaps, but only when you render all these other potential categories invisible can you say, "Oh, that's an absolute fit." There are more differences between fandom and religion than there are similarities, and the similarities extend to any social organization that serves multiple functions in the lives of its members and becomes a site of meaning and emotion.

MH: It's worth pointing out that in my own work I don't use the term "religion"; I try to mark a distinction between "religion" as an organized social group and "religiosity" as an impulse toward meaning and affect. So yes, I do back off from making that absolutely literal connection between fandom and religion. One of the phrases that I seem to have arrived at is that fandom is about religiosity and not religion. There is some kind of impulse that might be about a kind of individualized search for meaning—which doesn't mean that we're taking the individual as a starting point or a final point in analysis, since we are individualized within culture in certain ways. I'm suggesting that there is a culturally contextualized individual search for some kind of authenticity, connection, and meaning beyond the purely semiotic. This shift to religiosity rather than religion is discussed in the sociology of religion, and this might allow us to think about the voluntaristic ways in which fandom emerges but then forms very tightly knit communities around something. It's only following on from that emergence that there are "initiation rites" or "scriptures," or whatever the metaphors would be.

So, there are two points here: do you see the same problems you've already carefully elaborated around "religion" still holding for "religiosity"? And what sense could you make of fans who themselves draw on religious discourses to try to make sense of the notion that fandom is about more than just words, and about more than the semiotic? Because if we're in such an affective space then perhaps we look around for discourses to try to validate that experience. Otherwise how do you communicate to somebody that you're not mad? Using discourses of religiosity within fandom might actually be part of a fan's performance of an appropriate fan identity that says, "I know you can't understand the intensity of my interest in this text, so think of it as this," assuming that religiosity and religion could be viewed as having some kind of cultural validity. How would you approach either fan religiosity or the fan appropriation of discourses of religiosity and religion?

HJ: I think the two questions are closely bound up with each other. I get your point about the distinction between religion and religiosity, and I like religiosity better, but I still fret over it because of its strong connections back to religion. I might hold onto it to make some distinctions within different kinds of fan relationships to texts. I think lots of times fans, you're right, use metaphors from religion, or sometimes from addiction, to refer to intense emotional experiences of texts that our culture doesn't give them an adequate vocabulary to talk about. And it is when our sense-making framings break down that we fall on other things that we do blindly, or that are about a loss of control or a respect for a higher authority, or a compulsion or so forth.

The language is there. The question is, How would we read it? I think it has to be situated; in many cases it's used with laughter following it, or with people consciously putting quotes around it; it's framed as hyperbole; it's framed as excess; it's framed as an inadequate way of describing what's going on, but the best available word at the time.

Other times there is some level at which the fan feels like it bleeds over; that there is a spiritual relationship to a text or a spiritual relationship to a character, and there are spiritual truths revealed to them. And I take that very seriously as a description of what that person is experiencing. Now what happens when ethnographers who are not in fandom discuss this language is that they just collapse together those two very different uses of religious language, and it becomes a very literalizing interpretation. . . .

Whereas I would want a nuanced account that saw a continuum between playful, self-conscious invoking of those categories and those moments which I would then hold onto religiosity to describe, when the fan is saying, "I was moved spiritually by, say, an episode of *Beauty and the Beast,* and out of that I became a better person, a more charitable person." At that point they are describing something that's closer to an experience of religion, in which a religious conversion changes one's ethical or moral behaviors. That's a useful connection to make, but in a very, very narrow sense, and only applied to very specific kinds of fan experiences that I think are not the majority of what people talk about when they are talking about a religious analogy.

MH: In what you've just said you link the experience of religiosity to behavior and ethics, and you place "religiosity" as a very specific experience. But this makes me think of fans' "becoming-a-fan" stories, where fans use the languages and discourses of religious conversion, and where in a sense they are talking about something that really moved them that they can't quite explain; now this would be quite a common experience for a lot of fans rather than a highly narrow or specific experience. And it doesn't imply your ethical dimension—

HJ: No, but it does—

MH: Well it doesn't say "I became a better person"; it says "I became a fan."

HJ: But for many fans those things are not easily separable. The conversion metaphor also works for political radicalization, right? These people tell the same "coming out" stories about signing up as a Marxist, or about coming out as gay, or whatever: there's a variety of conversion narratives within our culture that could act as middle terms and separate fandom from religion. So to link those two terms together is still a problem because it neglects the whole continuity of a level of emotional experiences that we have and that we can't really articulate. And these experiences change how we see ourselves or how we see the world, or the values we operate on; these things are woven together when we use the language of conversion. Religious conversion, to my mind, is only a subset of a whole range of conversion experiences in culture.

MH: In *Fan Cultures* I focus on two languages that are available to fans to rationalize or defend their sense of fan experience; religiosity is one, and the other is aesthetics—being transformed by one's experience of an art form. Now it might take more empirical work to develop this, but it's interesting to me that discourses of religious transformation and discourses of aesthetic transformation seem to be quite prevalent within fandom, whereas some of the other possible languages you've mentioned—the social club, the union, or politics—don't seem to be drawn on as widely.

HJ: Actually, female fans often talk about fandom as a sorority if they're talking in a predominantly female space. To some degree fans jokingly call themselves a "consumer advocate" group, which is another way of framing what it is that they're involved with, and which pulls you toward union or political party; but there's often resistance to political labels altogether within fandom, and I think it's legitimate to say that fans themselves are more likely to use, you're right, aesthetic or religious analogies rather than political analogies.

MH: And that's about a subcultural context in which certain terms just seem too loaded.

HJ: Exactly. And I think they are still drawing on the reservoir of meanings that surround the term "fan" from its very inception. What's interesting about the language of aesthetics that you're talking about is that it is exactly those moments where the language of aesthetics allows fans to talk about feeling or emotion or the personal that breaks down [Pierre] Bourdieu's notion of aesthetic distance as being bound up in high art. That is, when you see that look of sublime pleasure on the face of someone listening to classical music, which is not about holding it at a distance, it's about being awash in it, being affected by it, that's when that classical music consumption is connected to fandom in a very real way. Fandom is not about Bourdieu's notion of holding art at a distance, it's not that high art discourse at all; it's about having control and mastery over art by pulling it close and integrating it into your sense of self.[8] And that is an aesthetic transformation, but it's not the way that discourses of high art usually operate, although it is a way individuals talk about their relationship to high art. But you never really see an art critic talk about that moment of passionate transcendence in which they couldn't articulate why they were responding to the music or the painting. . . .

MH: I wonder if, in certain fandoms, moments of affective transformation are written out as well. I'm thinking of horror fandom, where there's a sense in which it's the (imagined) non-fans who are affected or scared or shocked, whereas the fans are all stoically and heroically able to endure horror films as well as displaying their fan cultural capital— maybe to an extent this is about gendered reading positions. . . .

HJ: It could also be about a language of aesthetic appreciation, with fans saying, "Man, that was beautiful" about a gore scene, or drawing on Clive Barker's notion of "glistening, blood-covered bodies" as aesthetic artifacts—that language of aesthetic appreciation becomes a way of holding the emotion at a distance whilst still acknowledging that you were touched or moved by the text, but not in a pathologizing[9] way. . . . Which is to say that different kinds of fandom create different notions about what is the right way to explain that moment of transcendence. When I talked about religiosity I used the example of *Beauty and the Beast*—that was a fandom that was built around notions of romance but also around a sort of spiritual, New Age community. So the language of that fan community was much more a language of religiosity than, say, *Star Trek* fandom, which often embraces a political category of celebrating "difference." . . .

Part of what we're talking about here is a difference I've noticed in our work about affect and meaning. You talk a lot in *Fan Cultures* about what you call a cognitive or cognitivist preoccupation with fan interpretation and meaning at the expense of discussing affect. And that seems to me a very odd way of understanding what I mean by "meaning," which is that meaning is always bound up with affect on multiple levels: meaning is not data, trivia, or information. Meaning is contextualized. It grows out of an affective set of experiences, and is the vehicle for creating social connections with other people. So it's not purely an intellectual or abstract, cognitive category for me: it's embedded and embodied in all kinds of affect. When I talk about meaning and investment, those are both words that, to my mind, are already talking about affect.

MH: "Investment" is certainly a term that's important to writers who directly talk about affect, and so it's central to Lawrence Grossberg's work, for example. "Meaning," I think, is again a matter of how words are "loaded" and a matter of what connotations they carry. Even if you mean "meaning" to mean this particular thing, the term is so loaded—in terms of a bias around the cognitive, or around matters of interpretation, or as being about disembodied thought—that it plays out within a kind of modernist mind/body dualism in popular culture and in much academic writing. These connotations and their links to "meaning" are tested in some academic spaces—I'm thinking of certain feminist writing—but this struggle against how "meaning" is thought about culturally is still a battle that needs to be fought.

HJ: I guess we come back to where we were on religion, but I'm on the opposite side here! To me, words like "knowledge" and "meaning" are words worth fighting for. And yes, we need to enlarge what they mean. I've been driven by that feminist critique of "knowledge" and "meaning" because I think fandom itself understands "meaning" in that affective, saturated way. So when you say, "That was a very meaningful experience for me," for example, you're using the word "meaning" to refer to an emotional experience that had consequences in the way in which you thought about the world.

MH: I agree with you that a certain discourse of "meaning" would be used in fandom to say, "I had some transformative experience." But I suppose the problem for me is that "meaning" has also been used academically within certain forms of cultural theory in a way that does not speak to "the meaningful." In forms of work indebted to semiotics— I'm thinking of the work of John Fiske, Stuart Hall, and David Morley —the term "meaning" has been restricted to matters of cognitive interpretation and "decoding," so to say that was "meaningful" in the sense of "I was emotionally invested in that" wouldn't actually make sense in terms of the model of audience activity and interpretation that these writers put forward. You struggle with this kind of model in *Poachers,* but I think it structures what you're able to say to an extent even while, at the same time, you are trying to rework it.

HJ: There's an argument in semiotics that seems to imply that meaning can be derived from a text and then you throw the text away. The difference is that fans don't throw the text away, that there's an emotional connection to the text that survives any generation of meaning from it.

Now, we get back to what I was struggling with at the moment when I was writing *Poachers,* which was negotiating the transition from one generation of fan studies to another. *Poachers* contains a long chapter on fan criticism that explicitly invokes the feminist model of subjective investment as a way of understanding how fan critics derive meaning from a text, while struggling to bring that feminist critique of "knowledge-as-abstracted" in line with the old cultural studies notion of meaning production, via semiotics, that belonged to the previous generation. I saw the work as creating an affective semiotics that focused on how meaning was derived, but it was also written in a language saturated with emotion which tried to evoke the fans' quality of feeling through description and prose style rather than using the objectifying, distanced prose of that earlier generation of cultural scholars. Insofar as my writing and John Tulloch's feel very different, I would say mine pulled toward the affective and the ways in which I see meaning as tied to emotion, including my own. Whereas I think there is always an objectification or a distancing rhetoric in Tulloch's work so that he ends up struggling with his own fandom, and has to bury it or kill it in order to put the words on the page—

MH: I think he kills his fandom rather less in *Watching Television Audiences* (2000).[10]

HJ: He's getting closer to capturing his fandom there. But there's a generational struggle that I see in his writing that comes out of his prose style as much as what he says about fans. I think that I had a different struggle, which was that as a transitional figure I had to use a language that connected to that generation but which I also thought was pulling in a very different direction. So I would say that my entire work has been about intensity and emotional engagement, but what I lack, and still do—I haven't seen anyone later introduce one—is an adequate language to describe emotion or affect in theoretical terms that would be acceptable within academic discourse. . . .

MH: You're discussing a tension that runs through *Textual Poachers,* which for me is a very powerful tension between using the generational theoretical frameworks that were available to you, and trying to bring in a sense of fan affect. Given that tension, you could argue that there is a movement toward a kind of affective semiotics in *Poachers.* But something that we could call a developed "affective semiotics" would require such a vast theoretical and conceptual armory. . . .

HJ: I don't think I adequately achieved what I set out to do, but to expect a newly minted Ph.D. to quite pull it off, in the absence of other discursive resources, is probably a bit unfair! [laughs]

MH: We can set high standards! [laughing]

HJ: I set high standards for myself, and I still look with pride at a lot of what *Textual Poachers* pulled off, but it was an immature work in the fullest sense of the word. I'm still not sure I'm adequate to dealing with what it set out to do—it is still a really difficult problem to address.

MH: I'm not sure that anyone has fully "dealt" with the problem of an affective semiotics. It's something that I suppose my work continues to focus on, and it's something that I will probably also fail to achieve, although hopefully I'll fail in an interesting way.

HJ: It's a worthy goal. I think we've all got to struggle toward it, and we may be closer to it now insofar as there are more people in the academy who share that structure of feeling and know what an affective semiotics would be even if they can't articulate it yet. There's a potential for communication that we're gesturing toward, even if we can't bring it out in the full light of day. It seems to me that the very structures of academia make it hard to express, while the structures of fandom make this same thing ridiculously easy to express. And it's those of us who straddle those two categories who are very aware of those differences. It's probably the most profound difference between being a fan and being an academic, how to bring the affective in. We used to be taught about the affective fallacy as one of a couple of fallacies. Fans commit all of the fallacies that we were taught to avoid in literature classes.

MH: On a regular basis.

HJ: But the affective fallacy may be one of their greatest heresies from the point of view of traditional literature teaching.

MH: When I first started thinking about affect, and having partially come out of an English lit. background, the affective fallacy was one of the first things that sprang to mind. One of the problems is that we're talking about "affect" and not "love" or "emotion" or a more colloquial term, which as Rebecca Farley has pointed out to me is rather ironic. If I want to argue that academics should focus more on emotion —their own and others' emotions—then why do I have to call this "a theory of affect"? . . . Otherwise perhaps you've lost the battle already, and you're doing a Vulcan version of philosophies of emotion. That's one of the more pressing problems with an "affective semiotics," that the very tension between fan and academic situations is already overwritten by this as a concept. It speaks too singularly to an academic way of doing things. But if that's what we have to do to get the subject onto the agenda then I suppose we're back to the idea of tactical interventions.

HJ: I wonder if fan studies should learn from, say, a pro-sex politics. Both in- and outside the academy, there are people who have had to own up to their own sexuality and their own erotic feelings and experiences in order to break down hierarchies and categories for thinking about good and bad sex. Pat Califia would be an interesting role model for the fan-academic to think about what it is to articulate pleasure or desire or emotion in terms of fandom because she doesn't cut herself off from the implications of her own writing about sex and sexuality. She incorporates her own sexual experience and her own knowledge of the body into a larger theoretical project that gets articulated both in an academic language and in a vernacular language and everything in between. Pat Califia moves between writing an advice column for *The Advocate,* telling people how to do sex and how to have pleasurable sex, to presenting as an academic theorist at an academic conference. So the language of sex may in fact, ironically, be more developed around this than the language of fan culture, which is potentially less scandalous ultimately.

MH: The problem I can see there is to do with intersubjectivity. You can perhaps try to communicate to another how to do sex in a certain way—there is some kind of assumption that sex can be done in the same or similar ways by other people, and with the same or similar pleasures being involved. But I don't know how, in the same way intersubjectively, you could explain to somebody how to "do" fandom, because there isn't automatically that same space for assumed intersubjectivity.

HJ: When Califia moves into talking about S & M, for example, and the ways in which pleasure and pain relate to each other within the particular structure of feeling around sadomasochism, that is not something that is automatically going to be read intersubjectively by everyone who reads that essay. There's a shock, a discomfort, a resistance, an anxiety, or whatever, that circulates around that part of her argument, but I think she's very effective at conveying, inside-out, what the pleasures of S & M feel like, even to readers who may never directly experience those sets of sexual practices. And that's not unlike the challenge confronting the fan-academic. But I don't want to push fandom and sex too far as an analogy—we'll get into the whole fandom and religion problem again. It's inadequate. But what I'm getting at is, where else in the academy are we articulating emotion and our own direct personal experience of emotion through theoretical language? And it seems to me that the area of studying sex is one of those areas where there's starting to be a way of working through those problems, and it's a way that may be more advanced than where fan studies has got to at the moment. . . .

MH: OK, another point that I'd like to raise concerns ethnography and the doing of empirical research. A criticism of *Fan Cultures* that you've raised is that it never quite gets to the fan cultures; in other words, there isn't really much in the way of what we'd call "empirical" work in the book. And I suppose that comes out a sense of hesitancy on my part about doing empirical work. I'm concerned with the intensely problematic nature of doing that kind of work.

I know that ethnography is typically discussed in terms of academic power, and who has the right to speak for whom, but my particular concern is with what counts as "the real" in the doing of empirical research. And that's why I've been holding back. If you're going to go out "into the field" to "talk to real people"—so that there's a moral language about an encounter with the real—then what is going to be counted as the real? There seems to have been a curious splitting in cultural studies between theory, which has been viewed as a set of abstractions, and empirical work, which has been viewed as getting access to the real. I've examined this split in a piece for *Diegesis* on the "common sense" of cultural studies.[11] And I think that one symptom of this split is Paul Willis's emphasis on "surprise" as part of the value of ethnography, although actually he's talking about participant-observation; so there's a famous quote from Willis that Dave Morley has used, that Shaun Moores has used, that Ien Ang has used . . .

HJ: I've used it on occasions, although I'm not sure I buy it anymore.

MH: So this quote's been used endlessly to justify ethnography as the method in cultural studies, but what Willis effectively goes on to say is that he's a Marxist, and so nothing he finds in the field will persuade him that he shouldn't be a Marxist. So he says, "It's important to be surprised, but I'm a Marxist and so I'm going to interpret in this way," and the second part of his statement tends to disappear in the cultural studies celebration of surprise. Don't get me wrong, this emphasis has certainly allowed good work to be done, and people like Morley and Ang have done some of that excellent work, but what tends to drop out of the picture is the extent to which their empirical surprises hinge on a theorized version of what counts as the real. Their surprises depend on a certain version of Marxism, or on a certain version of sociology, or on a certain version of feminism, all of which precede and structure what they are able to account for, describe, and analyze.

My basic point is that if you use different theoretical frameworks— say, certain kinds of psychoanalysis—in empirical work, then what counts as the real will be different. What counts as the real for Sherry Turkle is different to what counts as the real for Dave Morley. Hypothetically they could go and talk to the same respondents, and have the same conversations, but then they'd go away and write these interviews up using different discourses. And they would see different things: that person twitched then, or they held their body in that way, or they spoke in that way, they were excited about this, anxious about that, they got that word muddled up . . . these things might matter to a psychoanalytic empiricist but not to a certain type of empirical sociologist.

HJ: Let me give you a practical illustration of this. In the research methods class that I teach, I play this videotape of an interview I did while researching *Textual Poachers* with a particular fan music video producer. I asked how she had begun as a fan writer and her first response was, "It had to do with the death of my father." As I play the tape I see Camille Bacon-Smith's analysis grabbing that and talking about her using fan fiction to work through the death of her father and the emotions that were bound up with it. As the interview goes on, she talks in a very analytic and crafts-oriented way about how she writes in different ways for different audiences, and about how she sees herself as responding to the community's traditions and genres; there's a whole analytical level. What I used in *Poachers* was that second piece of the interview, and the problem I present to my students is how do you decide which part of that interview you use to explain what's going on. In some sense you need both—

MH: That would be my point.

HJ: —and so to some degree the blindness of both of those earlier accounts was that they only mobilized one part of a problematic and overstated it in a way because of the different traditions that Camille and I came out of. And it's precisely what you're saying: different interpretive grids map onto bits of the real—and that's not a word that I use very much—in different ways and produce very different interpretations, which is why that notion of a surprise or discovery seems less and less valid to me.

To my mind the value of ethnography is not ultimately that it allows you to talk to the real but that it introduces notions of dialogue and accountability. And different ethnographic methods arrive at dialogue and accountability in different ways. So you could look at, say, David Morley's *Family Television* as a work that is very invested in the real; it strips out psychoanalysis altogether and it produces transcripts and data points and so on, but it's never clear what accountability he had to the research subjects he talks about.[12] Did they read a draft of the book? Were they allowed to comment on his interpretation and theorizing? To what degree did their own analysis of their experience impinge on his account? None of that is addressed in Morley's work.

I saw *Poachers* as responding to that, and building a different relationship between theory and the real by introducing a kind of dialogic element, by allowing fans to comment on the manuscript and to have this woven back into the work—

MH: Although as you've said, it is perhaps a shame that that process isn't more clearly highlighted in the work.

HJ: But the goal was there to do that, and there was an actual accountability, which meant that I changed things that the community critiqued or commented on. It wasn't just pure theory that was removed from anyone's life experience; it was written as a dialogue with something that's out there. The type of ethnography that I do is responsive to the researched community, and therefore there's a check on its assertions.

MH: There's a sense of "checks and balances" in how you're presenting the process. Was there ever an occasion where you had a criticism from the fan community, but you thought, "Well, no, I'm going to stick with my original assertion"? In other words, yes, it's important to have that sense of obligation to respondents, but some reviewers have accused you of "going native" or selling academia down the river in some way; I'm thinking of John Hartley's comments in *Popular Reality* (1996).[13] How far does your obligation to respondents stretch?

HJ: There is a divided loyalty between fandom and the academy that you're always negotiating. I would say that the *Beauty and the Beast* chapter in *Textual Poachers,* which almost no one looks at—probably because the series itself didn't resonate within an academic community —is where that crisis came to bear for me. I was writing about how fans fell out of love with the text and developed their own alternative to the direction the program had taken. But clearly not all fans fell out of love with the text, and so there was a violent backlash when I circulated that chapter from fans who said, "No, we love those new developments." Ironically, I loved those new developments too on a certain level; they actually resembled my fan pleasures more than the resistant reading that I was mapping, so there was a different thing that I papered over.

But what I acknowledged was a divergence between the story I wanted to tell and the response from the community to certain aspects of the story, with the result that I indicated that this was a partial truth, it was not a whole account. It was part of an account, and it dealt with certain issues that were academically important to the argument I wanted to make and were true and valid as part of a situated intervention, or "intervention analysis," to use Hartley's term, which I guess I understand differently than John does. So I saw that work as an intervention analysis for some segments of the fan community, while I had to acknowledge that I was not responding to claims made by another section. That's where the text becomes most blurred, around those divided loyalties, and I could have written a whole book on issues around that chapter.

There are arguments in the fan community that you just won't agree with, so you have to say, "Look, this is a section of the community that will fundamentally disagree with what I am saying, and this is their rationale and why, but this is why I'm still saying what I'm saying." The choice that I made was not to bow to the fan community's critique, but still to foreground it as a dispute that put into brackets, to some degree, the truth claims being made in that particular chapter.

Getting back to the notion of intervention analysis, I took that category from Hartley when he said that academics needed, at certain points, to take the side of the audience in their disputes with producers, because we had access to discourses of power and authority which enabled our voices to be heard more loudly. Intervention analysis, as I see Hartley spelling it out, means that we act as an amplifier for an existing community's dispute, and as an intermediary between that community and other powerful institutions. So it's ironic to me that several of my essays—particularly the one on the Gaylaxians—address John Hartley's idea of intervention analysis, and yet he wrote that passage where he seemed to think I'd gone native. I'm not sure how he would then understand what he means by intervention analysis.

MH: He presumably means intervening on behalf of an audience in such a way as to ultimately conserve academic authority and expertise. When he makes the accusation that you've gone native he's talking about how we can find a balance between listening to the audience but still recognizing our own academic expertise. You could call it a matter of balance or you could describe it as contradictory, since the argument ends up saying that academics . . .

HJ: . . . have more knowledge and authority! He's responding to moments where I turn the lens of fandom not on industry but on academia, and that's what makes him uncomfortable, the degree to which I'm saying that maybe there are things that academics could learn from fan interpretive practices.

MH: But that's exactly the rhetoric he uses as well, which is what's so curious about his reading of your work. He says we need to learn from fans and audiences.

HJ: Including thinking about our own interpretive practices and thinking critically about the way knowledge is produced in the academy, from the point of view of the fan. You realize that there are interpretive moves or theoretical terms that fans have developed that might enlarge or enrich the academy's vocabulary for talking about popular culture.

MH: There's a question of whether the academic self is either recentered or decentered at the end of this intervention. Part of what you're arguing for, and it's absolutely what I would argue for too, is that the intervention has to turn back on the academic subculture—which itself is another subculture—so that there is some kind of decentering there, some kind of challenge to our own sense of expertise. Whereas perhaps for John Hartley, the issue is to intervene as an academic expert, with that expertise remaining securely in place before and after any intervention. . . .

HJ: Surely the academy does have valuable kinds of expertise that are needed in a variety of conversations at the present moment, but in order for that expertise to be mobilized it has to adopt a language which doesn't just play to other academics, it has to play to a wider public. This means rethinking academic rhetoric. And it means recognizing that there are other kinds of expertise that also bring something to the table in that conversation. . . . The problem is that the academy has cut itself off from dialogues that it should be part of.

So it's not that I totally devalue academic knowledge; when I turn to fans and say that we could learn something from them, I'm not saying that we know nothing. Somehow people see this as a zero-sum either/or game where either we as academics have all the power or we have no power.

MH: I've mentioned Ian Craib's work before, and there's a hilarious chapter in the book *Experiencing Identity*—I really love this book—where he talks about the "psychodynamics of theory."[14] And he analyzes theoretical maneuvers that are supposedly about logic, but he says that actually they're not about rationality at all, they're about affect and emotional attachments. He talks about "logical hatchet work," which is the need to get rid of a threatening argument or position that is too complex, that doesn't fit into the cultural categories that people are comfortable with. These complex conjunctions have to be done away with, and how this happens is that you find one logical flaw or one problem and you then through that you dismiss the entire thing.

And this seems to be something that happens when you try to move beyond a position where fans are powerless and academics are powerful; if you transgress these comfortable associations, and suggest that fans aren't entirely powerless and academics aren't entirely powerful, then this position has to be expelled as too threatening. When you challenge fan stereotypes in *Textual Poachers* then you are also challenging a sense of the academic self that defines itself against that stereotype, and the same thing happens if you suggest that academics should give up some of their expertise; again, this is a threat to how we imagine ourselves versus the other who doesn't have our expertise.

HJ: I think that some of the changes that I'm advocating are not about giving up power, they are about accepting power and responsibility and enlarging the sphere of action by getting rid of those negative traits in the academy that block us from actually exercising power that legitimately should be ours. . . .

When I began my career I had enormous ambivalence about being an academic, because I felt this enormous tension between the academic world and the fan world, and I felt uncomfortable with speaking from the position of an academic because it was such an antagonistic space. As the academy has made its peace with fandom, to some degree, and as we've closed the gap between those identities, then I've come to feel much more settled in what I think an academic is, as well as beginning to redefine what the role of the academic is in response to other sectors of knowledge production.

MH: Your work has enabled later writers to "come out" as fans and to work on things that they are passionate about. The work that you've done has certainly been part of a shift within sections of the academy, so people now probably don't feel the same tension that you would have felt around the question, What does it mean to be a fan and an academic?

HJ: . . . In 1991 when *Poachers* came out I never imagined that it would still be in print a decade later, let alone still being actively taught. That's not something as junior faculty that you can see for yourself or imagine. I saw *Poachers* as provisional work, as tentative work. But as we said earlier, there's a scriptural economy that we get pulled into, and now I get people quoting my words as if they were biblical and as if they had this enormous authority and certainty behind them, as if things that I tentatively put forward were well-established and proved once and for all: all you have to do is turn to Jenkins and quote it, and that's the end of the story. I'm horrified by that; I want to shake those people when I hear it. This was the work of some guy one year out of grad school; yeah, it opened up the field and asked some important questions, but it wasn't set in stone.

I've written tons about audiences since then, but people almost always go back to the moment of *Poachers,* which is historically specific in the development of the field, the history of fandom, and it's on the eve of the Internet explosion in fandom which changed almost everything I talk about, one way or another. To go back to that work, as if that was the right tool to unlock the present moment without regard to the fan community, the text, the historical moment, the medium of expression . . . that's my worst nightmare. Save me from my friends as much as my enemies! Ask some new questions, push in new directions, challenge what I said, as you do in your book. Don't just accept it at face value, because it's not a biblical text. . . . In other words, folks, get a life! [laughs]

2

Star Trek Rerun,
Reread, Rewritten
Fan Writing as Textual Poaching

One of my first and most often reproduced essays, "Star Trek Rerun, Reread, Rewritten," was the rough draft for Textual Poachers. *The idea of writing about fan cultures can be traced back to the culture shock I experienced upon entering graduate school at what can now be seen as a moment of transition within American media studies. When I arrived, the University of Iowa's communication studies program was dominated by the language of subject positioning and ideological manipulation associated with the British film journal* Screen; *by the time I left two years later, the program was still absorbing the impact of a visit by John Fiske, who had introduced my cohort to Birmingham School perspectives and ethnographic audience research. My arrival compelled me to write the essay because my previous experiences as a fan were so at odds with what I was being taught; Fiske's visit enabled me to write it because his mentorship provided a context in which what I wanted to say might get a sympathetic hearing.*

Rereading the essay today, it strikes me how late the concept of "poaching" entered my thinking: this was my third attempt at a theoretical framing, and many of the paragraphs are holdovers from previous drafts. The passages most often quoted were among the very last I wrote. Like all metaphors, "poaching" enabled us to see certain things about fandom, offering a powerful counterimage to prevailing stereotypes of fans as passive consumers and cultural dupes; yet it also masked or distorted some significant aspects of the phenomenon, focusing on the frustration more than the fascination, encouraging academics to read fan fiction primarily in political terms, and constructing a world in which producers and consumers remain locked in permanent opposition. My more recent work has been more focused on negotiations or collaboration as media industries embrace some still ill-formulated and often contradictory notion of audience participation.

Today, I find myself returning to the concept of "moral economy" that runs through the closing sections of this essay, but which disappeared from Textual Poachers *itself. In some cases, the moral economy of fandom justifies fans' active appropriation of media content; in others, it sets limits on what they can do with those contents. The moral economy balances between the community's own desires and its respect for creators' rights. At the present moment, that moral economy is frayed because of the hostile rhetoric and practices of media companies eager to regulate peer-to-peer culture. The companies might productively rethink their relations to their consumers based on principles of legitimacy and reciprocity rather than legality. I am sometimes shocked to see people write about this essay as if it were still an accurate description of* Star Trek *fandom. How could it be? It was written before the impact of the Internet was felt on the fan community, before the death of Gene Roddenberry, and before* Star Trek: The Next Generation, *let alone the three subsequent television series. Over the past decade and a half, everything I described here has changed. The nature of these changes can be glimpsed through subsequent essays in this collection.*

"Star Trek *Rerun, Reread, Rewritten" first appeared in* Critical Studies in Mass Communications *in June 1988.*

Suppose we were to ask the question: what became of the Sphinx after the encounter with Oedipus on his way to Thebes? Or, how did Medusa feel seeing herself in Perseus' mirror just before being slain?

—Teresa de Lauretis, *Alice Doesn't* (1982)

How does Uhura feel about her lack of promotion, what does she try to do about it, how would she handle an emergency, or a case of sexual harassment? What were Chapel's experiences in medical school, what is her job at Starfleet headquarters, what is her relationship with Sarek and Amanda now . . . ?

—E. Osbourne, *Star Trek* fan (1987)

In late December 1986, *Newsweek* marked the twentieth anniversary of *Star Trek* with a cover story on the program's fans, "the Trekkies, who love nothing more than to watch the same 79 episodes over and over."[1]

The *Newsweek* article, with its relentless focus on conspicuous consumption and "infantile" behavior and its patronizing language and smug superiority to all fan activity, is a textbook example of the stereotyped representation of fandom found in both popular writing and academic criticism: "Hang on: You are being beamed to one of those *Star Trek* conventions, where grownups greet each other with the Vulcan salute and offer in reverent tones to pay $100 for the autobiography of Leonard Nimoy" (p. 66). Illustrated with photographs of a sixty-six-year-old bookstore worker who goes by the name of "Grandma Trek" and who loves to play with toy spaceships, of a balding and paunchy man in a snug Federation uniform, and of an overweight, middle-aged woman with heavy eyeshadow and rubber "Spock ears," the article offers a lurid account of the program's loyal followers. Fans are characterized as "kooks" (p. 68) obsessed with trivia, celebrity, and collectibles; as social inepts, cultural misfits, and crazies; as "a lot of overweight women, a lot of divorced and single women" (p. 68). . . .

The fan constitutes a scandalous category in contemporary American culture, one that calls into question the logic by which others order their aesthetic experiences, one that provokes an excessive response from those committed to the interests of textual producers. Fans appear to be frighteningly "out of control," undisciplined and unrepentant, rogue readers. Rejecting "aesthetic distance," fans passionately embrace favored texts and attempt to integrate media representations within their own social experience. Like cultural scavengers, fans reclaim works that others regard as "worthless" trash, finding them a source of popular capital. Like rebellious children, fans refuse to read by the rules imposed upon them by the schoolmasters. For the fan, reading becomes a kind of play, responsive only to its own loosely structured rules and generating its own kinds of pleasure.

Michel de Certeau has characterized this type of reading as "poaching," an impertinent "raid" on the literary "preserve" that takes away only those things that seem useful or pleasurable to the reader: "Far from being writers . . . readers are travelers; they move across lands belonging to someone else, like nomads poaching their way across fields they did not write, despoiling the wealth of Egypt to enjoy it themselves."[2] De Certeau perceives popular reading as a series of "advances and retreats, tactics and games played with the text" (p. 175), as a kind of cultural bricolage through which readers fragment texts and reassemble the broken shards according to their own blueprint, salvaging bits and pieces of found material in making sense of their own social experience. Far from viewing consumption as imposing meanings upon the public, de Certeau suggests, consumption involves reclaiming textual material, "making it one's own, appropriating or reappropriating it" (p. 166).

But such conduct cannot be sanctioned; it must be contained, through ridicule if necessary, since it challenges the very notion of literature as a kind of private property to be controlled by textual producers and their academic interpreters. Public attacks on media fans keep other viewers in line, making it uncomfortable for readers to adapt such "inappropriate" strategies of making sense of popular texts. . . . Such representations isolate potential fans from others who share common interests and reading practices, marginalize fan-related activities as outside the mainstream and beneath dignity. These same stereotypes reassure academic writers of the validity of their own interpretations of the program content, readings made in conformity with established critical protocols, and free them of any need to come into direct contact with the program's "crazed" followers.[3]

In this essay, I propose an alternative approach to fandom, one that perceives "Trekkers" (as they prefer to be called) not as cultural dupes, social misfits, or mindless consumers, but rather as, in de Certeau's terms, "poachers" of textual meanings. Behind the exotic stereotypes fostered by the media lies a largely unexplored terrain of cultural activity, a subterranean network of readers and writers who remake programs in their own image. Fandom is a vehicle for marginalized subcultural groups (women, the young, gays, and so on) to pry open space for their cultural concerns within dominant representations; fandom is a way of appropriating media texts and rereading them in a fashion that serves different interests, a way of transforming mass culture into popular culture. . . . For these fans, *Star Trek* is not simply something that can be reread; it is something that can and must be rewritten to make it more responsive to their needs, to make it a better producer of personal meanings and pleasures.

No legalistic notion of literary property can adequately constrain the rapid proliferation of meanings surrounding a popular text. But there are other constraints, ethical constraints and self-imposed rules, enacted by the fans, either individually or as part of a larger community, in response to their felt need to legitimate their unorthodox appropriation of mass media texts. E. P. Thompson has suggested that eighteenth- and nineteenth-century peasant leaders, the historical poachers behind de Certeau's apt metaphor, responded to a kind of "moral economy," an informal set of consensual norms, that justified their uprising against the landowners and tax collectors in terms of a restoration of a preexisting order being corrupted by those who were supposed to protect it.[4] Similarly, the fans often cast themselves not as poachers but as loyalists, rescuing essential elements of the primary text "misused" by those who maintain copyright control over the program materials. Respecting literary property even as they seek to appropriate it for their own uses, these fans become reluctant poachers, hesitant about their relationship to the program text, uneasy about the degree of manipulation they can "legitimately" perform on its materials, policing each other for "abuses" of their interpretive license, as they wander across a terrain pockmarked with confusions and contradictions. . . .

Fan Readers / Fan Writers

The popularity of *Star Trek* has motivated a wide range of cultural productions, creative reworkings of program materials from children's backyard play to adult interaction games, from needlework to elaborate costumes, from private fantasies to computer programming and home video production. This ability to transform personal reaction into social interaction, spectatorial culture into participatory culture, is one of the central characteristics of fandom. One becomes a "fan" not by being a regular viewer of a particular program but by translating that viewing into some kind of cultural activity, by sharing feelings and thoughts about the program content with friends, by joining a "community" of other fans who share common interests. For fans, consumption naturally sparks production, reading generates writing, until the terms seem logically inseparable. . . .

Many fans characterize their entry into fandom in terms of a movement from the social and cultural isolation doubly imposed upon them as women within a patriarchal society and as seekers after alternative pleasures within dominant media representations, toward more and more active participation in a "community" receptive to their cultural productions, a "community" within which they may feel a sense of "belonging." . . . Some fans are drawn gradually from intimate interactions with others who live near them toward participation in a broader network of fans who attend regional, national, and even international science fiction conventions. . . .

For some women, trapped in low-paying jobs or within the socially isolated sphere of the housewife, participation within an (inter)national network of fans grants a degree of dignity and respect otherwise lacking. For others, fandom offers a training ground for the development of professional skills and an outlet for creative impulses constrained by their workday lives. Fan slang draws a sharp contrast between the "mundane"—the realm of everyday experience and/or those who dwell exclusively within that space—and fandom, an alternative sphere of cultural experience that restores the excitement and freedom that must be repressed to function in ordinary life. One fan writes, "Not only does 'mundane' mean 'everyday life,' it is also a term used to describe narrow-minded, pettiness, judgmental, conformity, and a shallow and silly nature. It is used by people who feel very alienated from society."[5] To enter fandom is to "escape" from the "mundane" into the marvelous. . . .

Over the twenty years since *Star Trek* was first aired, fan writing has achieved a semi-institutional status. Fan magazines, sometimes hand-typed, photocopied, and stapled, other times offset printed and commercially bound, are distributed through the mail and sold at conventions, frequently reaching an international readership. . . . *Datazine,* one of several magazines that serve as central clearinghouses for information about fanzines, lists some 120 different *Star Trek*–centered publications currently in distribution. Although fan publications may take a variety of forms, fans generally divide them into two major categories: "letterzines," which publish short articles and letters from fans on issues surrounding their favorite shows, and "fictionzines," which publish short stories, poems, and novels concerning the program characters and concepts.[6] . . .

It is important to distinguish between these fan-generated materials and commercially produced works, such as the series of *Star Trek* novels released by Pocket Books under the official supervision of Paramount, the studio that owns the rights to the *Star Trek* characters. Fanzines are totally unauthorized by the program producers and indeed face the constant threat of legal action for their open violation of the producer's copyright authority over the show's characters and concepts. Paramount has tended to treat fan magazines with benign neglect so long as they are handled on an exclusively nonprofit basis. Producer Gene Roddenberry and many of the cast members have been known to contribute to such magazines. Bantam Books even released several anthologies showcasing the work of fan writers.[7] . . .

Gendered Readers / Gendered Writers

Media fan writing is an almost exclusively feminine response to mass media texts.[8] Men actively participate in a wide range of fan-related activities, notably interactive games and conference-planning committees, roles consistent with patriarchal norms that typically relegate combat— even combat fantasies—and organizational authority to the "masculine" sphere. Media fan writers and fanzine readers, however, are almost always female. Camille Bacon-Smith has estimated that more than 90 percent of all media fan writers are female.[9] The greatest percentage of male participation is found in the "letterzines," like *Comlink* and *Treklink,* and in "nonfiction" magazines, like *Trek,* that publish speculative essays on aspects of the program's "universe"; men may feel comfortable joining discussions of future technologies or military lifestyle, but not in pondering Vulcan sexuality, McCoy's childhood, or Kirk's love life.

Why this predominance of women within the media fan-writing community? Research suggests that men and women have been socialized to read for different purposes and in different ways. David Bleich asked a mixed group of college students to comment, in free-association fashion, on a body of canonized literary works. His analysis of their responses suggested that men focused primarily on narrative organization and authorial intent, while women devoted more energy to reconstructing the textual world and understanding the characters. He writes, "Women enter the world of the novel, take it as something 'there' for that purpose; men see the novel as a result of someone's action and construe its meaning or logic in those terms."[10] In a related study, Bleich asked some 120 University of Indiana freshmen to "retell as fully and as accurately as you can [William] Faulkner's 'Barn Burning,'" and again, noted substantial differences between men and women:

> The men retold the story as if the purpose was to deliver a clear simple structure or chain of information: these are the main characters, this is the main action, this is how it turned out. . . . The women present the narrative as if it were an atmosphere or an experience. (p. 256)

Bleich also found that women were more willing to enjoy free play with the story content, making inferences about character relationships that took them well beyond the information explicitly contained within the text. Such data strongly suggest that the practice of fan writing, the compulsion to expand speculations about characters and story events beyond textual boundaries, draws more heavily upon the types of interpretive strategies common to the "feminine" than to the "masculine."

Bleich's observations provide only a partial explanation as they do not fully account for why many women find it necessary to go beyond the narrative information while most men do not. . . . Texts written by and for men yield easy pleasures to their male readers yet may resist feminine pleasure. To fully enjoy the text, women are often forced to perform a kind of intellectual transvestism—identifying with male characters in opposition to their own cultural experiences, or constructing unwritten countertexts through their daydreams or through their oral interaction with other women—that allows them to explore their own narrative concerns. This need to reclaim feminine interests from the margins of "masculine" texts produces endless speculation that draws the reader well beyond textual boundaries into the domain of the intertextual. Mary Ellen Brown and Linda Barwick have shown how women's gossip about soap opera inserts program content into an existing feminine oral culture.[11] Fan writing represents the logical next step in this cultural process: the transformation of oral countertexts into a more tangible form, the translation of verbal speculations into written works that can be shared with a broader circle of women. To do so, their status must change; no longer simply spectators, these women become textual producers.

Just as women's gossip about soap operas assumes a place within a preexisting feminine oral culture, fan writing adopts forms and functions traditional to women's literary culture. Cheris Kramarae has traced the history of women's efforts to "find ways to express themselves outside the dominant modes of expression used by men," to circumvent the ideologically constructed interpretive strategies of masculine literary genres. Kramarae concludes that women have found the greatest room to explore their feelings and ideas within privately circulated letters and diaries and through collective writing projects.[12] Similarly, Carroll Smith-Rosenberg has discussed the ways in which the exchange of letters allowed nineteenth-century women to maintain close ties with other women, even when separated by great geographic distances and isolated within the narrow confines of Victorian marriage. Such letters provided a covert vehicle by which women could explore common concerns and even ridicule the men in their lives.[13] ...

Fan writing—with its circulation conducted largely through the mail, with its marketing mostly a matter of word of mouth, with the often collective construction of fantasy "universes," and with its highly confessional tone—clearly follows within that same tradition and serves some of the same functions. The ready-made characters of popular culture provide these women with a set of common references that can help to facilitate discussions of their similar experiences and feelings with others with whom they may never have enjoyed face-to-face contact. They draw upon these shared points of reference to confront many of the same issues that concerned nineteenth-century women: religion, gender roles, sexuality, family, and professional ambition.

Why Star Trek?

While most texts within a male-dominated culture potentially spark some sort of feminine countertext, only certain programs have generated the kind of extended written responses characteristic of media fandom. Why, then, has the bulk of fan writing centered on science fiction, which Judith Spector has characterized as a "genre which ... [has been until recently] hostile toward women," a genre "by, for and about men of action"?[14] Or around others like it (the cop show, the detective drama, or the western) that have represented the traditional domain of male readers? Why do these women struggle to reclaim such seemingly unfertile soil when there are so many other texts that more traditionally reflect "feminine" interests, and which feminist media critics are now trying to reclaim for their cause? In short, why *Star Trek*?

Obviously, no single factor can adequately account for all fanzines, a literary form that necessarily involves the translation of homogeneous media texts into a plurality of personal and subcultural responses. One partial explanation, however, might be that traditionally "feminine" texts—the soap opera, the popular romance, the "woman's picture"— do not need as much reworking as science fiction and westerns do in order to accommodate the social experience of women. The resistance of such texts to feminist reconstruction may require a greater expenditure of creative effort and therefore may push women toward a more thorough reworking of program materials than so-called feminine texts that can be more easily assimilated or negated.

Another explanation would be that these "feminine" texts satisfy, at least partially, the desires of traditional women yet fail to meet the needs of more professionally oriented women. Indeed, a particular fascination of *Star Trek* for these women appears to be rooted in the way that the program seems to hold out a suggestion of nontraditional feminine pleasures, of greater and more active involvement for women within the adventure of professional space travel, while finally reneging on those promises. Sexual equality was an essential component of producer Gene Roddenberry's optimistic vision of the future. A woman, Number One (Majel Barrett), was originally slated to be the *Enterprise*'s second-in-command. Network executives, however, consistently fought efforts to break with traditional "feminine" stereotypes, fearing the alienation of more conservative audience members.[15] "Number One" was scratched after the program pilot, but throughout the run of the series, women were often cast in nontraditional jobs, everything from Romulan commanders to weapons specialists. The networks, however reluctantly, were offering women a future, a "final frontier," that included them.

Fan writers, though, frequently express dissatisfaction with these women's characterizations within the episodes. In the words of fan writer Pamela Rose (1977), "When a woman is a guest star on *Star Trek*, nine out of ten times there is something wrong with her."[16] Rose notes that these female characters have been granted positions of power within the program only to demonstrate through their erratic, emotion-driven conduct that women are unfit to fill such roles. Another fan writer, Toni Lay, expressed her mixed feelings about *Star Trek*'s social vision:

> It was ahead of its time in some ways, like showing that a Caucasian, all-American, all-male crew was not the only possibility for space travel. Still, the show was sadly deficient in other ways, in particular, its treatment of women. Most of the time, women were referred to as "girls." And women were never shown in a position of authority unless they were aliens, i.e., Deela, T'Pau, Natira, Sylvia, etc. It was like the show was saying "Equal opportunity is OK for their women but not for our girls."[17]

Lay states that she felt "devastated" over the repeated failure of the series and the later feature films to give Lieutenant Penda Uhura command duties commensurate with her rank: "When the going gets tough, the tough leave the womenfolk behind" (p. 15). She contends that Uhura and the other women characters should have been given a chance to demonstrate what they could do confronted by the same kinds of problems that their male counterparts so heroically overcome. The constant availability of the original episodes through reruns and shifts in the status of women within American society throughout the past two decades have only made these unfulfilled promises more difficult to accept, requiring progressively greater efforts to restructure the program in order to allow it to produce pleasures appropriate to the current reception context.

Indeed, many fan writers characterize themselves as "repairing the damage" caused by the program's inconsistent and often demeaning treatment of its female characters. Jane Land, for instance, characterizes her fan novel *Kista* as "an attempt to rescue one of *Star Trek*'s female characters [Christine Chapel] from an artificially imposed case of foolishness."[18] Promising to show "the way the future never was," *The Woman's List*, a recently established fanzine with an explicitly feminist orientation, has called for "material dealing with all range of possibilities for women, including: women of color, lesbians, women of alien cultures and women of all ages and backgrounds." Its editors acknowledge that their publication's project necessarily involves telling the kinds of stories that network policy blocked from airing when the series was originally produced. A recent flier for that publication explains:

> We hope to raise and explore those questions which the network censors, the television genre and the prevailing norms of the time made it difficult to address. We believe that both the nature of human interaction and sexual mores and the structure of both families and relationships will have changed by the twenty-third century and we are interested in exploring those changes.

Telling such stories requires the stripping away of stereotypically feminine traits. The series characters must be reconceptualized in ways that suggest hidden motivations and interests heretofore unsuspected. They must be reshaped into full-blooded feminist role models. While in the series Chapel is defined almost exclusively in terms of her unrequited passion for Spock and her professional subservience to Dr. McCoy, Jane Land represents her as a fiercely independent woman, capable of accepting love only on her own terms, prepared to pursue her own ambitions wherever they take her, outspoken in response to the patronizing attitudes of the command crew. C. A. Siebert has performed a similar operation on the character of Lieutenant Uhura, as maybe suggested by this passage from one of her stories:

> There were too few men like Spock who saw her as a person. Even Captain Kirk, she smiled, especially Captain Kirk, saw her as a woman first. He let her do certain things but only because military discipline required it. Whenever there was any danger, he tried to protect her. . . . Uhura smiled sadly, she would go on as she had been, outwardly a feminine toy, inwardly a woman who was capable and human.[19]

Here, Siebert attempts to resolve the apparent contradiction created within the series text by Uhura's official status as a command officer and her constant displays of "feminine frailty." Uhura's situation, Siebert suggests, is characteristic of the way that women must mask their actual competency behind traditionally "feminine" mannerisms within a world dominated by patriarchal assumptions and masculine authority. By rehabilitating Uhura's character in this fashion, Siebert has constructed a vehicle through which she can document the overt and subtle forms of sexual discrimination that an ambitious and determined woman faces as she struggles for a command post in Star Fleet (or for that matter, within a twentieth-century corporate boardroom).

Fan writers like Siebert, Land, and Karen Bates (whose novels explore the progression of a Chapel–Spock marriage through many of the problems encountered by contemporary couples trying to juggle the conflicting demands of career and family)[20] speak directly to the concerns of professional women in a way that more traditionally "feminine" works fail to do.[21] These writers create situations in which Chapel and Uhura must heroically overcome the same kinds of obstacles that challenged their male counterparts within the primary texts and often discuss directly the types of personal and professional problems particular to working women. Land's fan novel, *Demeter,* is exemplary in its treatment of the professional life of its central character, Nurse Chapel.[22] Land deftly melds action sequences with debates about gender relations and professional discrimination, images of command decisions with intimate glimpses of a Spock–Chapel marriage. An all-woman crew, headed by Uhura and Chapel, is dispatched on a mission to a feminist separatist space colony under siege from a pack of inter-galactic drug smugglers who regard rape as a "manly" sport. In helping the colonists to overpower their would-be assailants, the women are at last given a chance to demonstrate their professional competence under fire, forcing Captain Kirk to reevaluate some of his command policies. *Demeter* raises significant questions about the possibilities of male–female interaction outside of patriarchal dominance. The meeting of a variety of different planetary cultures that represent alternative so-cial philosophies and organizations, alternative ways of coping with the same essential debates surrounding sexual difference, allows for a far-reaching exploration of contemporary gender relations.

Genre Switching: From "Space Opera" to "Soap Opera"

If works like *Demeter* constitute intriguing prototypes for a new breed of feminist popular literature, they frequently do so within conventions borrowed as much from more traditionally "feminine" forms of mass culture as from *Star Trek* itself. For one thing, the female fans perceive the individual episodes as contributing to one great program text. As a result, fan stories often follow the format of a continuous serial rather than operating as a series of self-enclosed works. Tania Modleski has demonstrated the ways that the serial format of much women's fiction, particularly of soap opera, responds to the rhythms of women's social experience.[23] The shaky financing characteristic of the fanzine mode of production, the writers' predilections to engage in endless specula-tions about the program content and to continually revise their under-standing of the textual world, amplifies the tendency of women's fiction to postpone resolution, transforming *Star Trek* into a "never-ending story." Fan fiction marches forward through a series of digressions as new speculations cause the writers to halt the advance of their chroni-cles to introduce events that "must have occurred" prior to the start of their stories or to introduce secondary plotlines that pull them from the main movement of the event chain. . . .

Moreover, this type of reading and writing strategy focuses greater attention on ongoing character relationships than on more temporally

concentrated plot elements. Long-time fan writer Jacqueline Lichtenberg has summarized the difference: "Men want a physical problem
with physical action leading to a physical resolution. Women want a
psychological problem with psychological action leading to a psychological resolution."[24] These women express a desire for narratives that
concentrate on the character relationships and explore them in a "realistic" or "mature" fashion rather than in purely formulaic terms, stories
that are "true" and "believable" not "syrupy" or "sweet." Fan writers
seek to satisfy these demands through their own *Star Trek* fiction, to
write the kind of stories that they and other fans desire to read.

The result is a kind of genre switching, the rereading/rewriting of
"space opera" as an exotic type of romance (and, often, the reconceptualization of romance itself as feminist fiction). Fanzines rarely publish
exclusively action-oriented stories glorifying the *Enterprise*'s victories
over the Klingon–Romulan Alliance, their conquest of alien creatures,
their restructuring of planetary governments, or their repair of potential flaws in new technologies, despite the prevalence of such plots in
the original episodes. When such elements do appear, they are usually
evoked as a background against which the more typical romance or
relationship-centered stories are played or as a test through which female protagonists can demonstrate their professional skills. In doing so,
these fan writers draw inspiration from feminist science fiction writers,
including Joanna Russ, Marion Zimmer Bradley, Zenna Henderson,
Marge Piercy, Andre Norton, and Ursula Le Guin, whose entry into the
genre helped to redefine reader expectations about what constituted science fiction, pushing the genre toward greater and greater interest in
"soft" science and sociological concerns and increased attention on
interpersonal relationships and gender roles.[25] *Star Trek*, produced in a
period when "masculine" concerns still dominated science fiction, is re-
considered in light of the newer, more feminist orientation of the genre,
becoming less a program about the *Enterprise*'s struggles against the
Klingon–Romulan Alliance and more an examination of characters' efforts to come to grips with conflicting emotional needs and professional
responsibilities.

Women, confronting a traditionally "masculine" "space opera,"
choose to read it instead as a type of women's fiction. In constructing
their own stories about the series' characters, they turn frequently to the
more familiar and comfortable formulas of the soap, the romance, and
the feminist coming-of-age novel for models of storytelling technique.

While the fans themselves often dismiss such genres as too focused on "mundane" concerns to be of great interest, the influence of such materials may be harder to escape. . . . As fans attempt to reconstruct the feminine "countertexts" that exist on the margins of the original series episodes, they have, in the process, refocused the series around traditional "feminine" and contemporary feminist concerns, around sexuality and gender politics, around religion, family, marriage, and romance.

Many fans' first stories take the form of romantic fantasies about the series' characters and frequently involve inserting glorified versions of themselves into the world of Star Fleet. A story by Bethann, "The Measure of Love," for instance, deals with a young woman, recently transferred to the *Enterprise,* who has a love affair with Kirk:

> We went to dinner that evening. Till that time, I was sure he'd never really noticed me. Sitting across the table from him, I realized just what a vital alive person this man was. I had dreamed of him, but never imagined my hopes might become a reality. But, this was real—not a dream. His eyes were intense, yet they twinkled in an amused sort of way. "Captain . . ."
> "Call me Jim."[26]

Her romance with Kirk comes to an abrupt end when the young woman transfers to another ship without telling the Captain that she carries his child because she does not want her love to interfere with his career.

Fans are often harshly critical of these so-called "Lieutenant Mary Sue" stories, which one writer labeled "groupie fantasies"[27] because of their self-indulgence, their often hackneyed writing styles, their formulaic plots, and their violations of the established characterizations. In reconstituting *Star Trek* as a popular romance, these young women have reshaped the series characters into traditional romantic heroes, into "someone who is intensely and exclusively interested in her and in her needs."[28] But many fan writers are more interested in what happens when this romantic ideal confronts a world that places professional duty over personal needs, when men and women must somehow reconcile careers and marriage in a confusing period of shifting gender relationships. Veteran fan writer Kendra Hunter writes, "Kirk is not going to go off into the sunset with anyone because he is owned body and soul by the Enterprise."[29] *Treklink* editor Joan Verba comments: "No believable character is gushed over by so many normally levelheaded characters such as Kirk and Spock as a typical Mary Sue."[30] Nor are the women of tomorrow apt to place any man, even Jim Kirk, totally above all other concerns.

Some, though by no means all, of the most sophisticated fan fiction also takes the form of the romance. Both Radway and Modleski note popular romances' obsession with a semiotics of masculinity, with the need to read men's often repressed emotional states from the subtle signs of outward gesture and expression. The cold logic of Vulcan, the desire to suppress all signs of emotion, make Spock and his father, Sarek, especially rich for such interpretations. Consider this passage from Jean Lorrah's *Full Moon Rising*:

> The intense sensuality she saw in him [Sarek] in other ways suggested a hidden sexuality. She [Amanda] had noticed everything from the way he appreciated the beauty of a moonlit night or a finely-cut sapphire to the way his strongly-molded hands caressed the mellowed leather binding of the book she had given him. . . . That incredible control which she could not penetrate. Sometimes he deliberately let her see beyond it, as he had done earlier this evening, but if she succeeded in making him lose control he would never be able to forgive her.[31]

In Lorrah's writings, the alienness of Vulcan culture becomes a meta-phor for the many things that separate men and women, for the factors that block total intimacy within marriage. She describes her fiction as the story of "two people who are different physically, mentally, and emotionally, but who nonetheless manage to make a pretty good mar-riage" (p. 2). While Vulcan restraint suggests the emotional sterility of traditional masculinity, their alien sexuality allows Lorrah to propose alternatives. Her Vulcans find sexual inequality to be "illogical," allow-ing very little difference in the treatment of men and women, an as-sumption shared by many fan writers. Moreover, the Vulcan mind-meld grants a degree of sexual and emotional intimacy unknown on earth; Vulcan men even employ this power to relieve women of labor pains and to share the experience of childbirth. Her lengthy writings on the decades-long romance between Spock's parents, Amanda and Sarek, represent a painstaking effort to construct a feminist utopia, to propose how traditional marriage might be reworked to allow it to satisfy the personal and professional needs of both men and women.

Frequently, the fictional formulas of popular romance are tempered by women's common social experiences as lovers, wives, and mothers under patriarchy. In Karen Bates's novels, Nurse Chapel must confront and overcome her feelings of abandonment and jealousy during those long periods of time when her husband, Spock, is totally absorbed in his work. Consider this passage from *Starweaver Two*:

> The pattern had been repeated so often, it was ingrained. . . . Days would pass without a word between them because of the hours he labored and poured over his computers. Their shifts rarely matched and the few hours they could be together disappeared for one reason or another. (p. lo)

Far from an idyllic romance, Bates's characters struggle to make their marriage work in a world where professionalism is everything and the personal counts for relatively little. Jane Land's version of a Chapel–Spock marriage is complicated by the existence of children who must remain at home under the care of Sarek and Amanda while their parents pursue their space adventures. In one scene, Chapel confesses her confused feelings about this situation to a young Andorian friend: "I spend my life weighing the children's needs against my needs against Spock's needs, and at any given time I know I'm shortchanging someone" (p. 27).

While some male fans denigrate these kinds of fan fiction as "soap operas with Kirk and Spock,"[32] these women see themselves as constructing "soap operas" with a difference—"soap operas" that reflect a feminist vision. In C. A. Siebert's words, "I write erotic stories for myself and for other women who will not settle for being less than human."[33] Siebert suggests that her stories about Lieutenant Uhura and her struggle for recognition and romance in a male-dominated Star Fleet have helped her to resolve her own conflicting feelings within a world of changing gender relations and to explore hidden aspects of her own sexuality. Through her erotica, she hopes to increase other women's awareness of the need to struggle against entrenched patriarchal norms. Unlike their counterparts in Harlequin romances, these women refuse to accept marriage and the love of a man as their primary goal; rather, these stories push toward resolutions that allow Chapel or Uhura to achieve both professional advancement and personal satisfaction. Unlike almost every other form of popular fiction, fanzine stories frequently explore the maturing of relationships beyond the nuptial vows, seeing marriage as continually open to new adventures, new conflicts, and new discoveries. . . .

Fan writing is a literature of reform, not of revolt. The women still acknowledge their need for the companionship of men, for men who care for them and make them feel special, even as they are asking for those relationships to be conducted in different terms. Jane Land's Nurse Chapel, who in *Demeter* is both fascinated and repelled by the feminist separatist colony, reflects these women's ambiguous and sometimes contradictory responses toward more radical forms of feminism. In the end, Chapel recognizes the potential need for such a place, for a "room of one's own," but sees greater potential in achieving a more liberated relationship between men and women. She learns to develop self-sufficiency, yet chooses to share her life with her husband, Spock, and to achieve a deeper understanding of their differing expectations about their relationship. Each writer grapples with these concerns in her own terms, but most achieve some compromise between the needs of women for independence and self-sufficiency on the one hand, and their needs for romance and companionship on the other. If this does not constitute a radical break with the romance formula, it does represent a progressive reformulation of that formula that pushes toward a gradual redefinition of existing gender roles within marriage and the workplace.

"The Right Way": The "Moral Economy" of Fan Fiction

Their underground status allows fan writers the creative freedom to promote a range of different interpretations of the basic program material and a variety of reconstructions of marginalized characters and interests, to explore a diversity of different solutions to the dilemma of contemporary gender relations. Fandom's IDIC philosophy ("Infinite Diversity in Infinite Combinations," a cornerstone of Vulcan thought) actively encourages its participants to explore and find pleasure within their different and often contradictory responses to the program text. It should not be forgotten, however, that fan writing involves a translation of personal response into a social expression and that fans, like any other interpretive community, generate their own norms, which work to ensure a reasonable degree of conformity among readings of the primary text. The economic risk of fanzine publishing and the desire for personal popularity ensure some responsiveness to audience demand, discouraging totally idiosyncratic versions of the program content. Fans try to write stories to please other fans; lines of development that do not find popular support usually cannot achieve financial viability.

Moreover, the strange mixture of fascination and frustration characteristic of fannish response means that fans continue to respect the creators of the original series, even as they wish to rework some program materials to better satisfy their personal interests. Their desire to revise the program material is often counterbalanced by their desire to remain faithful to those aspects of the show that first captured their interests. E. P. Thompson has employed the term "moral economy" to describe the way that eighteenth-century peasant leaders and street rioters legitimized their revolts through an appeal to "traditional rights and customs" and "the wider consensus of the community," asserting that their actions worked to protect existing property rights against those who sought to abuse them for their own gain.[34] The peasants' conception of a "moral economy" allowed them to claim for themselves the right to judge the legitimacy both of their own actions and those of the landowners and property holders: "Consensus was so strong that it overrode motives of fear or deference" (pp. 78–79).

An analogous situation exists in fandom: the fans respect the original texts yet fear that their conceptions of the characters and concepts may be jeopardized by those who wish to exploit them for easy profits, a category that typically includes Paramount and the network but excludes Roddenberry and many of the show's writers. The ideology of fandom involves both a commitment to some degree of conformity to the original program materials, as well as a perceived right to evaluate the legitimacy of any use of those materials, either by textual producers or by textual consumers. The fans perceive themselves as rescuing the show from its producers, who have manhandled its characters and then allowed it to die. In one fan's words, "I think we have made *ST* uniquely our own, so we do have all the right in the world (universe) to try to change it for the better when the gang at Paramount start worshipping the almighty dollar, as they are wont to do."[35] Rather than rewriting the series content, the fans claim to be keeping *Star Trek* "alive" in the face of network indifference and studio incompetence, of remaining "true" to the text that first captured their interest some twenty years before: "This relationship came into being because the fan writers loved the characters and cared about the ideas that are *Star Trek* and they refused to let it fade away into oblivion."[36] Such a relationship obliges fans to preserve a certain degree of "fidelity" to program materials, even as they seek to rework them toward their own ends. *Trek* magazine contributor Kendra Hunter writes, "*Trek* is a format for expressing rights, opinions, and ideals. Most every imaginable idea can be expressed through *Trek*. . . . But there is a right way."[37] Gross "infidelity" to the series' concepts constitutes what fans call "character rape" and falls outside of the community's norms. In Hunter's words:

> A writer, either professional or amateur, must realize that she . . . is not omnipotent. She cannot force her characters to do as she pleases. . . . The writer must have respect for her characters or those created by others that she is using, and have a full working knowledge of each before committing her words to paper. (p. 75)

Hunter's conception of "character rape," one widely shared within the fan community, rejects abuses by the original series writers as well as by the most novice fan and implies that the fans themselves, not program producers, are best qualified to arbitrate conflicting claims about character psychology because they care about the characters in a way that more commercially motivated parties frequently do not. In practice, the concept of "character rape" frees fans to reject large chunks of the aired material, including entire episodes, and even to radically restructure the concerns of the show in the name of defending the purity of the original series concept. What determines the range of permissible fan narratives is finally not fidelity to the original texts but consensus within the fan community itself. The text they so lovingly preserve is the *Star Trek* they created through their own speculations, not the one that Gene Roddenberry produced for network airplay.

Consequently, the fan community continually debates what constitutes a legitimate reworking of program materials and what represents a violation of the special reader–text relationship that the fans hope to foster. The earliest *Trek* fan writers were careful to work within the framework of the information explicitly included within the broadcast episodes and to minimize their breaks with series conventions. In fan writer Jean Lorrah's words, "Anyone creating a *Star Trek* universe is bound by what was seen in the aired episodes; however, he is free to extrapolate from those episodes to explain what was seen in them."[38]

Leslie Thompson explains, "If the reasoning [of fan speculations] doesn't fit into the framework of the events as given [on the program], then it cannot apply no matter how logical or detailed it may be."[39] As *Star Trek* fan writing has come to assume an institutional status in its own right and therefore to require less legitimization through appeals to textual "fidelity," a new conception of fan fiction has emerged, one that perceives the stories not as a necessary expansion of the original series text but rather as chronicles of "alternate universes," similar to the program world in some ways and different in others. . . .

Such an approach frees the writers to engage in much broader play with the program concepts and characterizations, to produce stories that reflect more diverse visions of human interrelationships and future worlds, to overwrite elements within the primary texts that hinder fan interests. But even "alternate universe" stories struggle to maintain some consistency with the original broadcast material and to establish some point of contact with existing fan interests, just as more "faithful" fan writers feel compelled to rewrite and revise the program material in order to keep it alive in a new cultural context.

Borrowed Terms: Kirk/Spock Stories

The debate in fan circles surrounding Kirk/Spock (K/S) fiction, stories that posit a homoerotic relationship between the show's two primary characters and frequently offer detailed accounts of their sexual couplings, illustrates these differing conceptions of the relationship between fan fiction and the primary series text.[40] Over the past decade, K/S stories have emerged from the margins of fandom toward numerical dominance over *Star Trek* fan fiction, a movement that has been met with considerable opposition from more traditional fans. For many, such stories constitute the worst form of character rape, a total violation of the established characterizations. Kendra Hunter argues that "it is out of character for both men, and as such, comes across in the stories as bad writing. . . . A relationship as complex and deep as Kirk/Spock does not climax with a sexual relationship" (p. 81). . . . Others struggle to reconcile the information provided on the show with their own assumptions about the nature of human sexuality: "It is just as possible for their friendship to progress into a love affair, for that is what it is, than to remain status quo. . . . Most of us see Kirk and Spock simply as two people who love each other and just happen to be of the same gender."[41]

Some K/S fans frankly acknowledge the gap between the series characterizations and their own representations but refuse to allow their fantasy life to be governed by the limitations of what was actually aired. One fan writes, "While I read K/S and enjoy it, when you stop to review the two main characters of *Star Trek* as extrapolated from the TV series, a sexual relationship between them is absurd."[42] Another argues somewhat differently:

> We actually saw a very small portion of the lives of the Enterprise crew through 79 episodes and some six hours of movies. . . . How can we possibly define the entire personalities of Kirk, Spock, etc., if we only go by what we've seen on screen? Surely there is more to them than that! . . . Since I doubt any two of us would agree on a definition of what is "in character," I leave it to the skill of the writer to make the reader believe in the story she is trying to tell. There isn't any limit to what could be depicted as accurate behavior for our heroes.[43]

Many fans find this bold rejection of program limitations on creative activity, this open appropriation of characters, to be unacceptable since it violates the moral economy of fan writing and threatens fan fiction's privileged relationship to the primary text:

> [If] "there isn't any limit to what could be depicted as accurate behavior of our heroes," we might well have been treated to the sight of Spock shooting up heroin or Kirk raping a yeoman on the bridge (or vice-versa). . . . The writer whose characters don't have clearly defined personalities, thus limits and idiosyncrasies and definite characteristics, is the writer who is either very inexperienced or who doesn't have any respect for his characters, not to mention his audience.[44]

But as I have shown, all fan writing necessarily involves an appropriation of series characters and a reworking of program concepts as the text is forced to respond to the fan's own social agenda and interpretive strategies. What K/S does openly, all fans do covertly. In constructing the feminine countertext that lurks in the margins of the primary text, these readers necessarily redefine the text in the process of rereading and rewriting it. As one fan acknowledges, "All writers alter and transform the basic *Trek* universe to some extent, choosing some things to emphasize and others to play down, filtering the characters and concepts through their own perceptions."[45] If these fans have rewritten *Star Trek* in their own terms, however, many of them are reluctant to break all ties to the primary text that sparked their creative activity and, hence, feel the necessity to legitimate their activity through appeals to textual fidelity. The fans are uncertain how far they can push against the limitations of the original material without violating and finally destroying a relationship that has given them great pleasure. Some feel stifled by those constraints; others find comfort within them. . . .

What should be remembered is that whether they cast themselves as rebels or loyalists, it is the fans themselves who are determining what aspects of the original series concept are binding on their play with the program material and to what degree. The fans have embraced *Star Trek* because they found its vision somehow compatible with their own, and they have assimilated only those textual materials that feel comfortable to them. Whenever a choice must be made between fidelity to their program and fidelity to their own social norms, it is almost inevitably made in favor of lived experience. The women's conception of the *Star Trek* realm as inhabited by psychologically rounded and realistic characters ensures that no characterization that violated their own social perceptions could be satisfactory. The reason some fans reject K/S fiction has, in the end, less to do with the stated reason that it violates established characterization than with unstated beliefs about the nature of human sexuality that determine what kinds of character conduct can be viewed as plausible. . . .

Conclusion

The fans are reluctant poachers who steal only those things that they truly love, who seize televisual property only to protect it against abuse from those who created it and who have claimed ownership over it. In embracing popular texts, the fans claim those works as their own, remaking them in their own image, forcing them to respond to their needs and to gratify their desires. Female fans transform *Star Trek* into women's culture, shifting it from space opera into feminist romance, bringing to the surface the unwritten feminine countertext that hides in the margins of the written masculine text. Kirk's story becomes Uhura's story and Chapel's and Amanda's as well as the story of the women who weave their own personal experiences into the lives of the characters.

Consumption becomes production; reading becomes writing; spectator culture becomes participatory culture.

Neither the popular stereotype of the crazed Trekkie nor academic notions of commodity fetishism or repetition compulsion are adequate to explain the complexity of fan culture. Rather, fan writers suggest the need to redefine the politics of reading, to view textual property not as the exclusive domain of textual producers but as open to repossession by textual consumers. Fans continuously debate the etiquette of this relationship, yet all take for granted the fact that they are finally free to do with the text as they please. The world of *Star Trek* is what they choose to make it. . . . The one text shatters and becomes many texts as it is fit into the lives of the people who use it, each in her or his own way, each for her or his own purposes. . . .

Like de Certeau's poachers, the fans harvest fields that they did not cultivate and draw upon materials not of their making, materials already at hand in their cultural environment, but they make those raw materials work for them. They employ images and concepts drawn from mass culture texts to explore their subordinate status, to envision alternatives, to voice their frustrations and anger, and to share their new understandings with others. Resistance comes from the uses they make of these popular texts, from what they add to them and what they do with them, not from subversive meanings that are somehow embedded within them. . . .

Alert to the challenge such uses pose to their cultural hegemony, textual producers openly protest this uncontrollable proliferation of meanings from their texts, this popular rewriting of their stories, this trespass upon their literary properties. Actor William Shatner (Kirk), for instance, has said of *Star Trek* fan fiction: "People read into it things that were not intended. In *Star Trek*'s case, in many instances, things were done just for entertainment purposes."[46] Producers insist upon their right to regulate what their texts may mean and what kinds of pleasure they can produce. But such remarks carry little weight. Undaunted by the barking dogs, the "no trespassing" signs, and the threats of prosecution, the fans have already poached those texts from under the proprietors' noses.

3

"Normal Female Interest in Men Bonking"

Selections from the Terra Nostra Underground and Strange Bedfellows

Shoshanna Green, Cynthia Jenkins, and Henry Jenkins

From the start, I had been uncomfortable with the imbalance of power between scholars and the audiences they wrote about. Historically, academics had abused that power, constructing exotic and self-serving representations of fans. Even many of the most sympathetic audience ethnographers signaled their distance from the communities they described. I did not have the option of distancing myself from the fan community. What I knew about fandom I knew from the inside out. My early work still shows an uncertainty about how to integrate my direct personal experience into my academic writing. One way I dealt with this dilemma was to create a dialogue through the writing process with the fan community itself, circulating drafts for feedback and incorporating that feedback directly into the finished content.

"Normal Female Interest in Men Bonking" grew out of my desire to create an even richer dialogue with the fan community. By the time we embarked on this particular project, Textual Poachers, Enterprising Women, *and Constance Penley's essays on slash fans had seen print. Many academics who had little or no direct exposure to the fan community itself were writing increasingly inaccurate depictions of fan practices and perspectives. Even at its best, the academic theorizing seemed to be reproducing concepts that the fans had themselves generated to explain their activities, placing them into more academically respectable language. Later I would discover Thomas McLaughlin's useful defense*

of vernacular theory in his book Street Smarts and Critical Theory. *But at the time, all I had was the impulse that fans were important theorists of their own practices.*

I worked with two fellow fans (one of them my wife) to edit together excerpts from one of the most theoretically oriented of the existing fan discussion forums about slash. My goal was to move as far as possible away from any magisterial perspective on the material. This project inspired me to include a range of essays by female gamers in From Barbie to Mortal Kombat: Gender and Computer Games *(1998). Those interested in the discussion here of female-female slash might want to check out my contextualization of a* Thelma and Louise *fan story in my essay "Reception Theory and Audience Research: The Mystery of the Vampire's Kiss," in Christine Gledhill and Linda Williams, eds.,* Reinventing Film Studies *(2000).*

For the three editors, one of the essay's most important contributions was the acknowledgment that many slash writers and readers identified themselves as queer. Much of the early writing on slash had been preoccupied by the shocking discovery that straight women composed and consumed erotic fantasies about same-sex relations between men. What got lost was the kind of dialogue that was emerging within slash fandom among women (and some men) of various sexualities. In some ways, having a shared set of bodies onto which to map erotic fantasies created a common ground where queers and straights could talk about their desires outside the polarization occurring in the identity politics of the era.

"Normal Female Interest in Men Bonking" first appeared in Cheryl Harris and Alison Alexander, eds., Theorizing Fandom: Fans, Subculture, and Identity *(1998).*

Yes, fans analyze because they're fans. Or are we fans because we analyze?
—B.T., "Strange Tongues," *Strange Bedfellows* 3, November 1993

[Is slash] anything other than normal female interest in men bonking?
—M. Fae Glasgow, "Two Heads Are Better Than One,"
Strange Bedfellows 2, August 1993

Slash is one of the most pervasive and distinctive genres of fan writing. Most fans would agree that slash posits a romantic and sexual relationship between same-sex characters drawn from film, television, comic books, or popular fiction. Most often, slash focuses on male characters, such as *Star Trek*'s Kirk and Spock or *The Professionals*' Bodie and Doyle. However, the parameters of slash are under constant debate and negotiation within media fandom. Many fans would point out that the relationships are not always romantic, that the characters are not always drawn from other media, and that the central characters are not always male. Slash stories circulate within the private realm of fandom, published in zines, distributed through the mail, through email, or passed hand to hand among enthusiasts. The noncommercial nature of slash publishing has been necessitated by the fact that these stories make unauthorized use of media characters.

Although a private, subcultural practice, slash has, over the past five years, increasingly become the focus of academic and journalistic scrutiny. . . . If the initial academic interest in slash came from people who were themselves tied to the fan community, attentive to its traditions and familiar with its own theoretical and critical categories, slash has quickly become a point of reference for writers who know of it only secondhand and who seem to have no clear grasp of the concept. (More than one writer refers to "slasher" fan fiction, for example, while literary critic Mark Dery uses the term "slash" to refer to all forms of "textual poaching," as if it encompassed the full range of fan production.) The differences in the ways academics and fans talk about slash are striking:

1. Most academic accounts center almost exclusively upon Kirk/Spock stories, primarily because academic writers and readers are most familiar with *Star Trek* references. In fact, slash is written about a broad range of fictional characters, and some slash fans speak of being fans of slash itself, rather than, or in addition to, being fans of a particular show or set of characters. Many fanzines, both slash and nonslash, publish stories based on a variety of sources; fans call such collections "multi-media" rather than "single-fandom" zines.

2. Academic accounts of slash tend to deal with it in isolation from the larger framework of genres within fan fiction. Fans, on the other hand, understand slash in relation to many other re-readings and rewritings of program material, such as hurt/comfort (which focuses on nurturing, but not necessarily sexual, relations between characters) and heterosexual romance.

3. Academic accounts of slash seem preoccupied with the question of why straight women write stories about gay male characters, seeing slash as a heterosexual appropriation of queerness. In fact, lesbian and bisexual women have always participated alongside straight women in slash fandom, and people of all sexual orientations have found slash a place for exploring their differences and commonalities.

4. Academic accounts tend to focus on slash's uniqueness, its difference from other forms of popular culture. Fan critics are interested in exploring slash's relationship to other forms of commercial fiction (ranging from gay erotica to popular romances, from Dorothy Sayers to Mary Renault) and to traditions of retelling and rewriting within folk culture.

5. Academic accounts often consider slash to be a static genre, making generalizations that assume a consistent subject matter and thematics over time and across all slash stories. Slash fans, on the other hand, see the genre as always in flux and are interested in tracing shifts in its construction of sexuality, its story structures, character relationships, and degrees of explicitness.

6. Academic accounts have tended to be univocal in their explanations of why fans read and write slash, looking for a theory that can account for the phenomenon as a whole. Slash fans, on the other hand, are interested in exploring the multiple and differing motivations that led them to this genre.

Almost all of the theoretical explanations of slash that academics have proposed are refinements of theories that have long circulated within the fan community. This article presents some fannish discussion of slash over the past five years, selecting excerpts from two apas: the *Terra Nostra Underground* and *Strange Bedfellows*.

The word *apa* originated in science fiction fandom as an acronym for "amateur press association." It describes a sort of group letter, regularly circulated to its members. Each member writes a contribution, called an apazine, and makes a number of copies of it, one for each member. She or he then sends them to the apa's editor, who collates all the contributions together and sends a complete set to each member. Apas can serve as forums for discussion, as a way of circulating fiction and other writing by their members, as regular business conferences, and the like.

The Terra Nostra Underground (TNU) was founded in the fall of

1989 as a quarterly apa for discussion among slash fans; it began with eight members, and its membership had reached twenty-three when it folded three and a half years later. Shoshanna Green founded Strange Bedfellows (SBF) as a successor to the TNU, and its current membership is thirty-seven, including Cynthia Jenkins and Henry Jenkins. Members are mostly female, but three men regularly participate at present and others have in the past. The group includes bisexual, gay, and straight people. About half of the members have written fan fiction and/or published fanzines, and that proportion is not, we think, too far above that in media fandom as a whole; the fan community tends to assume that everyone can write and that some people simply haven't done so (yet). There is no sharp distinction between readers and writers in most of the discussion that follows. Both are considered creative. Apa members come from various educational and class backgrounds, although most are middle class and tend to have at least a college degree; most are American, but there are eight European members (including one living in the United States) and one Western woman living in Japan. As far as we know, all the members are white, but since the apa is conducted through the mail rather than in person, we are not certain.

Discussions vary widely. In addition to the kinds of analysis excerpted here, members talk about everything from the NAMES Project quilt to their summer vacations, from Tailhook to ice-skating and the exigencies of apartment living. Apa writing can be personal and confessional or more abstract and speculative. Often, arguments are made through collaboration and brainstorming among group members and are understood in relation to previous discussions both within the apa and elsewhere in fandom.

In any one issue of the apa, then, there are up to three dozen apazines written by as many members, ranging from three to thirty pages long, each adding to ongoing conversations and introducing potential new topics for discussion. It's rather like a party with many conversations going on at once, and people moving from group to group, or like a printed version of an electronic bulletin board.

This article excerpts some of the discussions undertaken in these two apas over the last five years. We have chosen these particular apas as sources, rather than any of the many other apas, letterzines, and the like that we might have used, simply because we are members of them. This meant, first of all, that we had easy access to the five years' history of these discussions; but it also meant that we compiled this essay as fans as well as academics. We participated in many of the conversations we are reproducing. . . .

As we circulated drafts of this essay among the fans we are quoting, some argued strongly that certain themes we were pursuing were secondary and misrepresentative of overall fannish concerns; often these same themes were ones that other members felt were central. What is central often depends on where you are standing. We drew on discussions that seemed important and that could be clearly and interestingly presented here. Some complex and important discussions could not be included, exactly because they were so involved; they were too long to be summarized, too complex to be excerpted, and so embedded in media fan culture that nonfans would require long explanatory prefaces. These included such things as: fine-grained analysis of particular slash stories; meditations on subgenres within slash and the attitudes of fans and academics toward them; arguments about the mechanics and ethics of fan publishing; and much more. . . .

Watching Television, Creating Slash

Where does slash come from? Does it originate in the series text or in the fan's reading of it? These questions have occupied fans much as they have interested academics. Cat, a French fan, has offered one explanation for why female viewers construct homoerotic fantasies. Her account focuses on narrative conventions and female identifications in television:

> Why are so many women interested in slash in the context of media related material? TV is a convenient source for fictional material that can be shared with a great number of people and benefits from the structure of general fandom. [. . .] This explains why slash is media-related and why I have never heard of any mainstream Fag-Hag APA to this date. [. . .] To enjoy television that way, empathy with the fictional characters will have to be strong and rewarding. The woman (me, you, whoever) views the fictional piece from the character's point of view, and her emotions parallel his: anguish when he is hurt, triumph when he wins, etc. . . . (One identifies with more than one character, usually, and can easily switch from one to the other according to need, but let us say that the "hero" is the main reference.) So in this society, someone

enriching/feeding their fantasy life with TV fare will come across variations of the traditional pattern: the hero (dashing); the buddy (his confidant and accomplice); the screaming ninny (his romantic interest).

In this threesome, there are reasons to identify with the hero:

1. He is usually the main character (the heroine being seen less often, usually a supporting character).

2. He does all the exciting things and seems to enjoy them. He is the one to whom the adventure happens and the one who makes it happen. He must pit his wit and resources against danger and foes. (If the woman has spunk, it is not a value in itself but a source of excitement or annoyance for the hero. At worst, it is considered as cute.)

There are reasons not to identify with the heroine:

1. A woman, having internalized the values of our culture, might feel that women are devalued per se, regardless of script, thus the woman-heroine becomes a worthless object of identification.

2. When female characters are shown to be effective and powerful, it is often through their "feminine wiles" (unless they are ugly frustrated lesbians. Who wants to identify with a loser, the Russian general played by Lotte Lenya in *From Russia with Love*?) As to women powerful through the use of their beauty and seduction (i.e. their power to manipulate men to further their schemes), they could easily become alien, incomprehensible creatures for "average" women full of self-doubt or teenage angst, since they represent values that are not only difficult to achieve, but also considered obsolete. [. . .]

So you don't want to be her, you don't want to enjoy the emotions she feels. The male hero is easier to "feel" the adventure with: what he is made to feel you enjoy. And if you are of the daydreaming kind, you will "borrow" him, to make him feel some more interesting things.

If you do not want sex or romance to be absent from your daydreamings and you are identifying with the male hero, seeing the adventure from his viewpoint, who the heck are you going to use as a romantic interest? Not him, because since you are living the adventure through him, the point is to make him feel the feelings of sex and romance, and then identify with it. So he has to have a relationship with someone other than himself, with someone who produces emotional reactions in him that you find interesting. And that person is unlikely to be the screaming ninny (because, if you liked her, you would have identified with her and "tinkered" with her to start with). Of course, you can daydream a female character you'd enjoy identifying with or fancying, but to create from scratch an original, interesting character is hard work, and she might not feel as real as the faces on the screen. Also, by that time, you could have internalized enough of our society's values to make the prospect unexciting. Or you can daydream yourself into the script. (Hi there, Mary Sue.) [. . .]

This is where the male buddy comes in, since he is the only one (with the screaming ninny and the enemy) who shows a sustained interest in the hero. The woman who has empathy for the hero will enjoy the emotions produced in the hero by the buddy. (She does not have to find the buddy breathtakingly attractive herself [some are willing to overlook Napoleon's chin for Illya's sake, for instance], but it helps.) And what type of relationship do buddy and hero have? One version could be that on the screen, there is a caring relationship. It is not tainted with sexism, with expectations of a given role, because the one is female and the other male. It is equality. Not in practical terms: the buddy can be less or more strong or skillful than the hero. But his weakness is not perceived as something that makes him in essence inferior or different. It has a different cultural meaning. They are attracted to each other's personalities, not because they're made blind by their gonads or "devalued" prettiness. [. . .]

[. . .] Identification with the other gender means liberation from one's own gender-related taboos. However, we have no personal, direct, experience of the cultural constraints the other gender has to submit to, so these constraints, although known to us, are not felt as being as binding as our own. This I would call the "tourist approach." One feels freer to behave differently in a place that is not directly relevant to everyday life, and where the landmarks, although not very different, have shifted enough to create new perceptions: you are free of the rules of your country of origin, but not bound by the rules of the holiday country because you don't know them, or if you do, they don't mean the same things to you as to the natives.

—Cat Anestopoulo, "Darkling Zine," *TNU* 3, August 1990

B.T. offered a different explanation for the slash potential of a program; she stresses that the ways women watch television shape their responses to the conventional representation of male sexuality:

One explanation I've heard about why slash seems so natural to fans has to do with how fans perceive TV characters. Instead of taking emotions and speech as directed at the audience, the fan game is to see everything in context of the show itself. If an actor, or a pair of them, are busy projecting rampant sexuality, the fan mindset is to look within the program for the object. In a cop-partner show (for instance), there are typically two men projecting subliminal sex appeal for all they're worth, and nobody else on screen with any regularity. Certainly, no female characters. Strictly within the show framework, there's nobody but the two men themselves to justify the sexual display, so the concept of slash (instead of the fan just thinking what a sexy, appealing show it is to her, herself) arises.

—B.T., "Strange Tongues," *TNU* 6, May 1991

M. Fae Glasgow, among others, rejects the idea that her interest in slash involves identification with the characters, asserting a pleasure in exerting her own authorial control over sexy male bodies:

Oh, such delight! Someone else who doesn't think that the slash writer necessarily inserts herself into one of the personae! Isn't manipulation and watching so much fun? That's what I do; I never, ever, insert myself (perhaps because I lack the necessary plumbing? Sorry. Facetiousness is a hobby of mine . . .) into the character or the story. I may be present in the form of a narrative voice, but that's more because of my heritage of storytelling and the typical Scottish style of writing which almost invariably has a very strong "voice" or lyricism to it. To be honest, I don't even identify with any of the characters. I'm just fascinated by them. Plus, I'm prurient and salacious and simply adore to watch.

—M. Fae Glasgow, "Two Heads Are Better Than One,"
TNU 8, November 1991

Sandy and Agnes contributed observations about why slash's focus on male protagonists may facilitate identification more easily than stories focusing on female characters would:

As an experiment last week, I gathered all of the female slash I had into one pile (largely *Blake's 7*, since it has more strong females than the rest of slash fandom's favorite shows put together . . .) and read it all one after another. I realized that my distance from the material is different in female slash. I have all of that equipment, I have sex with women—I wasn't able to go with the flow so much. There was an intermediate level doing the rather stupid job of checking each piece of action and thinking, "would I like this," "have I done this," "would I do this with Jenna (Y), Beverly (Maybe), Gina (Y), Trudy (Y), Cally (Y), Dayna (YES, YES, YES), Servalan (not unless I had someone holding a gun on her at the same time). I don't know what this means, but I'd love to hear from other women about it—queer and straight.

—Sandy Hereld, "T-shirt Slogans Are Intellectual Discourse,"
TNU 12, November 1992

Your comments to Barbara about female slash, about familiarity (with the equipment, the activities, etc.) making it more difficult to "go with the flow," reminded me of the discussion of "PC slash" on the email list, when a few folks complained about the tendency of some slash to be too "realistic" or concerned with accuracy to the real world as we know it, which they felt interfered with the fantasy. I've been trying to figure out ever since discovering slash just why it might be that two guys getting it on would be exciting to women, and especially to lesbians, and I think this may have something to do with it. Writing (and reading) about things we can't experience directly, we can fantasize that these relations can be far beyond the best sex WE may have ever had, not limited by or interpreted through our own direct experience. I'm reminded of a passage from Henry Miller (in one of the Tropics, I think—it's been a while) comparing the size of his childhood universe (a few blocks in reality, but limitless in imagination) with that of his adult world (far more extensive in reality, having traveled widely and seen many parts of the world, but as a consequence proportionately limited in imagination, because once he knew what some place was really like, he could no longer imagine it any way he wanted)—so that, in a curious way, the more he experienced in his life, the smaller were the possibilities of his imagination.

—Agnes Tomorrow, "Notes from Tomorrow," *SBF* 1, May 1993

The question of the role that identification plays in reading and writing slash is frequently raised in the context of why straight women would be interested in the intimate relations between two members of the same sex or why lesbians would be interested in the sex lives of men:

> By now it must be obvious that slash readers include women of all gender preferences. A more universal form of your question about why lesbians would want to read about men is, why should anyone want to read about characters who aren't anything they could ever be, and would actively dislike in life? Why do we read (with relish) about space pirates, neurotic rock stars, or melancholy Danish princes? Fiction isn't about reasonable wish-fulfillment or simple identity matches. Why should any of us watch *Professionals,* starring as it does two macho-prick studs?
>
> —B.T., "Strange Tongues," *TNU* 9, Winter/Spring 1992

Rewriting Masculinity

As both fans and academics agree, slash represents a way of rethinking and rewriting traditional masculinity. Sarah argued that slash's appeal lies in its placing "emotional responsibility" on men for sustaining relationships while in reality men frequently dodge such responsibility:

> In a letter I just wrote to Jane Carnall, I talked about it in terms of seeing men take on emotional responsibility for, and interest in, relationships. . . . It explains why we already see, or read, sex into TV shows whose male characters have a supposedly platonic, yet intimate relationship on screen. We see that intimacy and experience sexuality. [. . .][1] I think part of what slash is about is reading intimacy between peers as itself erotic. They don't just happen to have sex, their sexuality is a natural product of their mutual feelings of closeness. [. . .] We need our pornography to be about people we know and we are interested in exploring as many different scenarios as we can imagine. [. . .] In a way, just as the characters' sexual relationship is an expression of their intimacy, we as slash readers also need that intimacy with the characters we write about. That's where the sexual excitement for us comes from; or at least that's one source of it."[2]
>
> —Sarah Katherine, "Writing from the Margins," [1] *TNU* 12, November 1992; [2] *TNU* 13, February 1993

Henry suggested that slash addresses some of the social forces that block intimacy between men:

> When I try to explain slash to non-fans, I often reference that moment in *Star Trek: The Wrath of Khan* where Spock is dying and Kirk stands there, a wall of glass separating the two longtime buddies. Both of them are reaching out towards each other, their hands pressed hard against the glass, trying to establish physical contact. They both have so much they want to say and so little time to say it. Spock calls Kirk his friend, the fullest expression of their feelings anywhere in the series. Almost everyone who watches that scene feels the passion the two men share, the hunger for something more than what they are allowed. And, I tell my nonfan listeners, slash is what happens when you take away the glass. The glass, for me, is often more social than physical; the glass represents those aspects of traditional masculinity which prevent emotional expressiveness or physical intimacy between men, which block the possibility of true male friendship. Slash is what happens when you take away those barriers and imagine what a new kind of male friendship might look like. One of the most exciting things about slash is that it teaches us how to recognize the signs of emotional caring beneath all the masks by which traditional male culture seeks to repress or hide those feelings."
>
> —Henry Jenkins, "Confessions of a Male Slash Fan,"
> *SBF* 1, May 1993

Misogyny

The female slash writers have struggled, however, with the genre's primary, if not exclusive, focus on male characters. Should they be writing stories about women? Should slash deal with lesbianism as well as male homosexuality? Is slash's frequent exclusion of female characters misogynist?

> My only problem with slash is that I miss women. Sometimes reading about male bodies feels foreign, and I find myself wishing for the familiarity of a woman's body, or even just a significant, three-dimensional, female character.
>
> —Sarah Katherine, "Writing from the Margins,"
> *TNU* 13, February 1993

Male buddy-shows are attractive to us because they show something that's rare in men. One point is that it's not rare in women. [. . .] It's the cold-loner depiction of a woman that stands out in the media; and by their nature, cold loners don't run in pairs. In one sense, slash shows men as honorary women: doing what women-as-we-perceive-them do normally. It's extraordinary and sexy because the men don't (usually) lose the strengths of men-as-we-perceive them; the slash character is a hermaphroditic combination of the best of both types

—B.T., "Strange Tongues," *TNU 11*, August 1992

The writers of the series [*Blake's 7*] showed much more imagination when pitting the male characters against each other, in complex multi-layered interrelationships which continue to stimulate discussion, while the female characters were primarily pawns and patsies, taking little active part in the working out of their destinies [. . .]. I think it's commendable that there have been so many fan stories involving the female characters, given the material as presented in the series, and that this demonstrates the determination of writers to expand on potential barely hinted at.

—Agnes Tomorrow, "Notes from Tomorrow,"
TNU 3, August 1990

I still think that misogyny plays a significant part in some segments of slash writing and reading. Some stories leave women characters completely out. For instance, even though *The Professionals* routinely depicts women as full members of CI5, many B/D slash stories posit CI5 as an all-male force. Other stories will "feminize" a male character (Doyle, Vila, Illya, sometimes Avon) and then pile explicit sexual humiliations on him with the overt or covert implication that he "really wants it"; this shows a certain amount of homophobia as well, i.e. bash the "pansy." Some stories portray strong women characters in a show as jealously shrewish, completely evil bitches; some of the depictions of Ann Holly or Dr. Kate Ross (both from *Pros*) or T'Pring (*Trek*) immediately come to mind. A few slash readers, writers and/or editors have expressed overt distaste or disgust at the idea of Lesbian sexuality, all while extolling the glories of male/male relationships.

But I'm now sure that misogyny is not the only reason for the vast overabundance of men. [. . .] As women, reading and writing about men in a mostly women's "space" may be a way for women to deal with their feelings about men in our male supremacist society. Even Lesbians have to learn about how to deal with men (most of us can't go off into a "womyn's paradise"). Lesbians don't usually engage in sexual relationships with men, but we see men in their positions of power. Straight and bisexual women usually have to deal with men in a more intimate way.

—Nina Boal, "Lavender Lilies, addendum" *TNU* 6, May 1991

I'm still bloody insulted by people in general insisting that I need "strong female role models." Some of us already have one. It's called a mirror.

—M. Fae Glasgow, "Two Heads are Better Than One,"
SBF 1, May 1993

Nina, who has written slash stories involving female characters, commented on some of the difficulties she has encountered:

Actually, I've found it MUCH more of a challenge to write about female/female sexuality. First, I find I have to wean the women from the feeling that they MUST center their lives around men. Then I have to convince these characters that they DON'T have to then "retreat" to a lesbian separatist commune. It's not rejection of men, it's affirmation of women. Once that is done, men can become human rather than be gods whom women are supposed to worship. It definitely goes against the grain of societal conditioning to make the women the center of the story rather than adjuncts to the male characters.

—Nina Boal, "Lavender Lilies," *TNU* 4, November 1990

Homophobia and Gay Identity

Making the characters in a slash story lovers leads to the question of whether they are gay. Some slash stories explicitly situate the characters as gay or bisexual people facing a homophobic society; others briefly raise the problem of homophobia only to dismiss it; and some deny that the lovers are "gay" at all. Some stories relocate the characters into science fictional or fantasy contexts, putting them in cultures that are not homophobic or in which "sexual orientation" itself may be a meaningless concept. For some fans, a queer awareness is a crucial part of slash;

for others, it is irrelevant or intrusive. The question of whether slash is or should be about gay and bisexual men, the existence of homophobia both in slash writing and among slash fans, and the relationship between gay male and female sexualities have been topics of conversation and debate in the apas since the founding of the *TNU*. In the first few issues of the apa, several fans explicitly connected their own sexual and political orientations with their enjoyment of slash.

> I am a lesbian, so some of my approach to slash is political—I want to see how a gay couple (of any gender) reacts to and is reacted to by their society. The stories that assume society accepts such couples without question are a lovely relief and often fun to read, since they can concentrate on the individuals and their relationship. Stories which try to face a here-and-now reaction to homosexuality are more, well, contemporary and realistic (though I admit they're more fun to write than to read . . . usually). [. . .] I firmly agree that much attraction in slash is the concentration on what is common to all humans, since sexual differentiation has been bypassed. The characters have to relate as different individuals, not as members of different sexes.
>
> —B.T., "Strange Tongues," *TNU* 2, May 1990

Fans who see queer identity as part of slash are distressed by what they see as evidence of homophobia in the slash community. Nina's and Shoshanna's comments, below, sparked continuing discussion.

> Most people who are involved in slash fandom are hetero women. Some of these women bring their own homophobic baggage into slash fandom. They thrill at the idea of two men doing it, and they see themselves as INCREDIBLY open-minded. But this sort of fan would be repulsed by the idea of two women doing it. [. . .] Homophobic slash fans also tend to say things such as "(the partners) aren't Gay, they're heterosexual men who just HAPPEN to fall in love with each other." I've even read a letter in a Kirk/Spock letterzine where a fan said that K & S aren't "limp-wristed faggots; they're MEN!"
>
> Fortunately, I've met many slash fans who aren't homophobic. They speak out for Gay rights, and sometimes do such things as volunteer for AIDS organizations. And they'll speak out for Lesbian as well as Gay male rights. When I show them my Uhura/Saavik story, they read it with interest and curiosity. [. . .] I have a feeling that Lesbian slash

makes some women uncomfortable because they fear exploring the varied aspects of their own sexuality.

—Nina Boal, "Lavender Lilies," *TNU* 2, May 1990

Having recently read a huge stack of Bodie/Doyle and Napoleon/Illya slash, I'm on a slow burn about homophobia in the genre. [. . .] Many writers generally accept without thought, as something natural and inevitable, the marginalization of gay people, pairings and love which straight society tries to impose, and participate in it, continue it, in their stories. Sometimes it's the "they're not gay, they just love each other" excuse (which I paraphrase as "we're not gay, we just fuck each other.") Often the authors seem to think that it wouldn't bother the characters to have to hide (which N/I would have worse than B/D, since they're ten years earlier), that they wouldn't get frustrated and humiliated and angry. *Blake's 7* slash is generally not so bad at this, but often only because they haven't got a conveniently handy tawdry gay underculture to denigrate. ("Have you ever—done this with a man before, Napoleon?" "Y-yes . . . but they were only one night stands; it's never been like this before.") The "it's never been like this before" can be another form of marginalization by putting the love affair on a pedestal —it's so wonderful nothing else could ever compare, therefore it is entirely different from everything else and has no relation with anything else. (It can also easily slip into really dreadful misogyny—"no woman could ever understand / be so good a lover / make him feel so secure.") Without denying the existence of homophobia, both in their settings and quite possibly in the characters themselves [. . .] it is still possible to create a story in which the men are gay and human both.

—Shoshanna Green, "For the World Is Hollow and
I Fell off the Edge," *TNU* 2, May 1990

"They're Not Really Gay, But . . . " usually goads me too! Often though, it's a matter of whether that opinion is that of the author or of the characters. Denial is part of coming out, and a couple of old closet cases like Illya and Napoleon really would have a hard time with that. I can believe they'd deny it to themselves even while they were doing it— but a good writer will make it clear that's a symptom of their times, their agency, their lifestyles and NOT something the reader is expected to agree with. [. . .] I'm not defending homophobic slash with these comments. They only touch on a couple of borderline cases to try to clearly see that line and fine-tune the definition. There is homophobic slash. It's ugly. Most of the time it's repulsively blatant. Liked your point about "It's So Wonderful Nothing Else Could Ever Compare." What I find ironic is that both excuses are things I've heard often from people in the process of coming out. At the point where they haven't come out to themselves and they're scared to death. These ideas can be gut-real and gritty if the writer knows what comes next in the process and makes some progress towards getting there—or points up the tragedy of it if the characters don't grow. [. . .] Is it possible that this type of homophobic story is the same process for the writer? That slash writers who aren't gay still have to go through a process of coming out to themselves about their own stories and accepting that they like them?

—Adrian Morgan, "Criminal Love," *TNU* 3, August 1990

Nice to know I'm not the only one who gets annoyed with slash fiction where the characters never have to worry about being openly gay, and other unrealistic depictions of gay/lesbian/bi life. Another thing that boggles my mind to no end is the type of slash story where *A* is desperately in love with *B* and the fan author decides to solve it by simply having character *A* blurt out his undying love to *B* without ever having given a thought to *B*'s reaction to the news that *A* is gay in addition to his being in love with *B*. Super-unrealistic happy ending! I'm not against happy endings but such hastily written stories leave out the weeks or months of soul-searching it takes to work up the courage to approach that other person who is of your own gender because you don't know whether or not she is straight. Sometimes, I've had a crush on another woman and I've never told her my true feelings for her because I was so in love that I was afraid of losing a friendship . . . forever.

—Nola Frame-Gray, "Wonderframe," *TNU* 5, February 1991

I have heard the statement a lot that many female writers, particularly the early ones, are not interested in writing about gay men. I have heard and read the rationales behind this many times. I'm still baffled by the whole issue. For me, it is vitally important that slash is about gay men (and/or lesbians). Slash doesn't work for me unless the characters are clearly gay (even if they are in various stages of denial about it). The vibrant fantasy here for me is that the flaming hets I see on TV come out of the closet and turn out actually to be GAY!!!!

—Nina Boal, "Lavender Lilies," *TNU* 7, August 1991

But, for other fans, slash is not a gay genre and should not be evaluated by political criteria.

> Homosexuality has as much to do with Slash as Civil War history did with *Gone with the Wind*. Burning Atlanta gave Scarlet something to deal with and homosexuality has given Bodie and Doyle something to deal with—sodomy. But *GWTW* wasn't about the causes of the Civil War, the plantation economy, battle strategy and slavery, just as slash isn't about gay rights, creating positive gay identities for Bodie and Doyle, or exploring the gay male sex scene.
>
> Two heterosexual males becoming involved in a sexual relationship is my standard definition of slash. Why specifically "heterosexual" males? Because I view slash as a product of female sexuality, and I'll be frank here [. . .] slash is an intricate part of MY sexuality and a sexual outlet. Bodie and Doyle are both men, so homosexual is technically accurate, but hardcore porn is technically heterosexual but I don't see my sexuality in that, either. What I want as a woman, how I view sex and intimacy is not reflected in male homosexuality.
>
> My attraction to a fandom starts with the televised character. If I am attracted physically to at least one guy and the character lends itself to being slash (this isn't a given with me), then I'm hooked. I am not physically attracted to homosexual men. Portraying Bodie and Doyle in a "realistic" gay milieu is taking them from the realm of my sexuality.
>
> Two heterosexual males becoming involved in a sexual relationship. [. . .] To me slash is the process of getting these characters into bed. [. . .] This process can be Pon Farr, a knock on the head, the gradual dawning of whatever lust/love, the point is that beginning with the aired characterizations gives us a common starting point. And like the Math test where the teacher wants to "see the work" seeing the author's process *X* let's us recognize the guys who end up snuggling in bed together.
>
> Two heterosexual males becoming involved in a sexual relationship. To say that there is no relationship between homosexuality and slash is absurd. To say that slash is just another name for homosexuality is equally absurd. We have appropriated men's bodies and sexual activities for our own gratification. Sounds a lot like complaints about male porn made by women, doesn't it? I'm waiting for a demonstration by gay men where they carry placards complaining that we are using them as "relationship objects." [. . .]

Three years ago I wouldn't have made a distinction between sexual and homosexual. Since the beginning, slash writers have appropriated what we want from the physical side, adapted it to fit female hot buttons, and pretty much kept the relationship female oriented in terms of "true love," virginity, h/c, monogamy, etc. Now the situation has changed.

Somewhere along the line, our appropriation of the physical act of homosexual sodomy [. . .] has been coupled with the obligation to portray these acts realistically and to also give the characters the emotional make-up of homosexual men. The failure to do this is taken as evidence of the writers 1)naivete; 2)homophobia; 3)social irresponsibility; 4) all of the above.

My question, selfish and self-serving, is where do I fit into this? Something that was an extension of me is now being reality checked to fit the sexuality of a group of people who don't even READ slash because —like Wilford Brimley and oatmeal—it is the right thing to do. [. . .]

Why is it our duty to accurately reflect the gay male experience? Is it the duty of gay male writers to accurately portray the lives of spinster librarians? How they interpret my life will be done through the filter of their own sexuality?

What is the difference between the slash and gay characters? "Slash" characters excite by being extensions of female sexuality while the "gay" characters excite by being a window into an alien sexuality, that of homosexual men. It is internal vs. external in a way. The writers who prefer their characters gay can find more conformity because they are reworking a culture that actually exists—that of homosexual men. There is no island of slash men with sociological texts detailing their behavior. To find where slash comes from we must look inside ourselves. [. . .] My "sick" stories (the ones I'll never write) are the dark places in my sexuality. The issues I will write about, power and trust, concern me as a woman, not Bodie and Doyle as gay men. I am fulfilling my kink, not accurately portraying the kink of gay men.

That said, if YOUR kink is gay men, then state it as a kink, not as the realistic way to write slash or the morally responsible way or the two-letter designation that also abbreviates Personal Computers.

—Lezlie Shell, "W.H.I.P.S., Women of Houston in Pornography,"
SBF 5, May 1994

B.T. offers an alternative account of the relationship between women and gay men.

As long as you ask, I'll be happy to ramble on about how and why slash stories are written about gay men, yet are not "about" gay men. (This is normally so obscure a point that I see no reason to bore people with my fine gradations of meaning.) Slash stories are, typically, narratives featuring two male characters from a TV show who fall in love. And have sex, usually. This defines them as carrying on a homosexual affair, and characterizes them as gay or bi within the meaning our society understands. [. . .] At the same time, the writers are (with few exceptions) middle-class British and American women, expressing their concerns to an audience of peers through story-writing. Their reasons for writing are not gay-male reasons, but female-middle-class-sexual-orientation-unspecified reasons. The stories are written to address, not gay men, but the author's own feelings and sometimes those of her friends and fan audience. The male leads become metaphorical representations of the writer and, if she communicates well enough, the story's readers.

On the level of writing that creates plot, surface detail, and setting, a slash story about male TV characters is about gay men, and should plausibly include gay male styles of action. (Bodie should wear leather and not lace in public; government employees in Britain fear losing their jobs; Starsky finds that being fucked anally feels good [or bad].) The less immediately obvious aspects of a story, such as theme and moral stance, are very much governed, in slash, by the female writers' perceptions of the world and their ideas of what is good and bad. Much slash is primarily about love or lust—which are shown as positive in general, and as the catalysts for a permanent relationship. This is an expectation trained into our culture's women. The emphasis on partnership and cooperation (even in stories that don't postulate the characters as lovers) is also something women are taught is important, while men more often focus on competition. The sexual descriptions often reflect what women know about their own erotic feelings, and omit what they don't know about men's; extensive foreplay, for instance, and extragenital erogenous zones are common in slash sex scenes, but not in men's descriptions of their own sexuality.

In good writing, these two sets of meanings work together to reinforce the overall message. Slash is so evocative and important to its fans because the position of gay men in society and the position of women correspond in many ways: excluded from the entrenched power structure, emblematic of sexuality, having an often-clandestine network (or

a need for it) with other gays or women, able to communicate nonver-
bally with other gays or women to a degree, suspected of even greater
communication and collaboration with other gays/women than is true,
seen by straight men as "artistic" and "emotional," and so on and so
on. A story about men in a tight relationship, as a metaphor for how
women see love, can illustrate that both sexes need affection and support, that the need is simply human. [. . .] The cross-gender metaphor
carries much of the bite of slash: men and male couples as symbols (not
really stand-ins) for women suggest what we feel we are, as opposed to
how we're seen, how women are forced to think of themselves, in our
culture.

—B.T., "Strange Tongues," *TNU* 9, Winter/Spring 1992

. . .

I don't like stories in which the author, usually through Bodie and
Doyle's mouths, maintains vehemently that they're "not gay." [. . .] I
believe that this vehement protest often indicates an underlying belief
on the part of the author as well as the characters that, first, there are
two alternatives, gay and straight; second, that being gay is distasteful
or unpleasant; third, that B & D's involvement is qualitatively different
from that of any two given men, because "any two given men" would
be gay and B & D aren't. Their sexual love is something else, something
above, and hence not gay and distasteful.
A: Gays are icky.
B: Bodie and Doyle are not icky.
C: Therefore, Bodie and Doyle are not gay.
[. . .] This is homophobia. It's also a form of biphobia, if only in the
absolute invisibility of bisexuality. [. . .] Of course, it's possible for the
characters to think being gay is icky, while the author does not. It's also
possible for a story to be good—well written, well paced, good characterizations—while still displaying political views which I dislike.

—Shoshanna Green, "For the World Is Hollow and
I Fell off the Edge" *TNU* 8, November 1991

. . .

I have never seen slash writing as being gay writing. Rather, it has always struck me as being what Joanna Russ called "the first truly female
writing"—by women for women without any political agenda or being
filtered through the censorship of commercial publishing. Sure, there

are fannish conventions and taboos, but these have been broken since day one. There's always howls of outrage, but that's the point—if we aren't free to write what we like in fandom, where are we? This doubtlessly accounts for [another member's] perception of a lot of fannish writing as two heterosexuals transposed on same-sex couples. A lot of the early readers of slash seemed to me (sweeping generalization here!) straight middleclass women from the Midwest/East. But there's always been a much higher gay component of slash writers and readers than what I'd observed in media fandom in general, which has brought in a genuinely gay perspective as well.

—Kathleen Resch, "I Used to be Trek Monogamous, but Now I'm a Media Slut!," *TNU* 12, November 1992

Inappropriate Fantasies

The push toward realism or explicitness in slash writing has provoked some uncomfortable responses within the fan community. M. Fae, one of the more "adventurous" slash writers, discussed the relationship between her highly psychological stories to the larger slash tradition.

Well, as a NEW fan, people would ask me what I liked most about slash, why I had got involved in it, etc. And then would appear shocked when I said, "Oh, that's easy. It's the sex!" The standard answer was still the "love, romance, caring," etc., and the majority were very taken aback when I said that I was open to any fandom, as long as it was slash and as long as we had at least two men buggering each other into next week. Now, no-one bats an eye at that. [. . .]

By the way, I think there is some room for the argument that I often don't write slash. I don't follow many of the rhythms of slash stories, I frequently approach the same topic from a diametrically opposite point of view from fan canon, I often discount such supposed cornerstones of slash as love, romance, friendship, equality, trust and of course, happily ever after. I rarely write my stories from the traditional skew of "how do we get them to love each other forever and/or commit to each other?": I almost invariably write them from the point of view of "what makes people tick? What would motivate a man like this, if we were to focus on this aspect of his personality?" Apart from that, it's usually for the sex itself, or to explore some interesting question that's come up either in the programme/book or in society in general or in slashdom [. . .] I rarely feel the need to write the nicer stories, simply because there are so many good ones already being done. [. . .]

I'm very well aware of my own world view colouring certain things I do—but equally, the characters very frequently express things that are purely them, and opposite to me. I really don't write slash as any kind of allegory for women's issues: they are simply allegories for human issues, which I consider transcends the limits of gender. They are also, to get to the core of it for me, stories of sexual and/or emotional satisfaction, attractive fictional men manipulated as much as possible to give as much pleasure as possible.

—M. Fae Glasgow, "Two Heads Are Better Than One,"
TNU 10, May 1992

Have fans increasingly broken from the conventions of the traditional romance in more recent stories? Fans have debated what to make of a growing number of stories that incorporate less overtly "romantic" sexual content.

"Your Porn Is OK, My Porn Is OK"

I agree with you that romantic slash is more tolerated because the fantasies are "acceptably feminine" whereas rape, hurt/comfort etc. are not. Looking at larger societal debates over pornography, the anti-porn movement, when they admit to positive sexuality at all, seems to want to distinguish between good sex (feminine sex that is relationship oriented, caring, tender, and based in mutual love) and bad sex (typified by the bulk of mainstream pornography, which is alienated, emotionless, sometimes not sweet and frequently does not occur within a secure relationship). [. . .] The dominant streams of thought within this movement do not allow much room for fantasy. Somehow all fantasy and representation are seen as leading towards actualization of the ideas or images. [. . .] The assumption seems to be that our fantasies control us, not that we control our fantasies. [. . .]

In many ways slash can be seen as the ideal "feminine erotica." It is relationship oriented as hell, oh so caring and tender, and all about love. The hiccup comes in with some of the harder edged slash that has started to surface more recently. There is a temptation to see romantic slash as good porn, which is to say as reflecting a feminine sensibility, as erotica v. harder edged slash as bad porn, which is to say reflecting a more masculine sensibility, to see it as pornography in the negative-value-laden sense of the word. [. . .]

The types of fiction that provoke virulent response are precisely those that draw on the tropes of male erotica. Those slash stories mess up all those nice neat categories people are used to thinking in. Rape? Tying up your partner and flogging him? Esoteric practices like pissing into his bladder? Long tender descriptions of mutilated bodies? These are tender scenes of love?

The damnedest part of it is, that for the most part, they are.

When slash develops s&m or b&d it usually does so in the context of the same relationship that structures more vanilla stories about sex and love. The relationship is consensual and the sex is the expression of a very mutual, caring and usually permanent bond. Part of what is curious is that the anti-porn argument suggesting that inherent power inequalities make it impossible for women to give real consent to participate in sexual games involving power (like s&m scenes) falls to pieces if both characters are acknowledged as masculine. [. . .] But slash stories assume that games can be just that: games. Or they assume that role-playing can serve some therapeutic purpose. But they virtually always see the people as controlling the games, not the other way around. They actively construct an argument against anti-porn fears that power differential is fixed, that it is invariably harmful, and that pain- or power-centered imagination and bedroom practice will corrupt the way we interact outside the bedroom. The point of the stories is to situate these practices in the context of a relationship and examine how they function as a part of that relationship. [. . .]

Rape stories, though they may start out with male porn clichés about desire overwhelming control, or some such, usually go on to deal with the ramifications of the act. The point of the story isn't the rape; it's how the characters deal with the rape. Can they salvage anything from the wreckage created by the violence? Do they want to? Alternatively, if the rape is rewritten (either within the course of the narrative, or within sequels) so that it isn't really a rape (he really liked it) the narratives still focus on the dynamics of the relationship.

Hurt/comfort stories often contain enough gore to send shivers down the back of activists concerned with the conflation of sex and violence. [. . .] How can anyone get off on seeing a character suffer from gunshot wounds or auto accidents? Why does this so often lead to sex, and so often to highly improbable sex, at that, while the wounded partner is still suffering to a degree that renders erotic response improbable? It is as if the vulnerability of the physical body is being used symbolically to illustrate the vulnerability of the emotional makeup of men. The breakdown of the physical body leads to a breakdown of personal barriers, of emotional defenses. And this (in slash) leads to a breakdown of physical barriers and to sex. Yes, there is lots of pain and suffering, sometimes very precise descriptions of which bones are broken or which internal organs are bruised, or how bloody the wound is, or how labored the breathing patterns are. But once again, unlike the material I suspect h/c is implicitly being analogized to, the hurt is not so much directly erotic as it is the means by which a sufficient degree of vulnerability and openness is achieved that an intimate relationship can develop.

So the sub-genres of slash that all too often provoke wondering looks, or less polite queries as to how the fan could like that, strike me as curious hybrids of romantic feminine-style sex and elements of masculine porn that are central to debates concerning the availability and impact of sexually explicit material. Those elements of the pornographic imagination that are least accessible to many women are co-opted and explored within the context of the familiar romantic relationship. True, romantic stories are seen as acceptably feminine, but I would argue that slash stories about beating your partner until his backside glows in the dark are also "feminine" by the same criteria.

Thoughts? Does this make any sense?

—Cynthia Jenkins, "Menage a Deux," *SBF* 3, November 1993

A Universe of One's Own

Many fans feel freer in fandom than outside of it to express themselves, ask questions, and discuss alternative viewpoints. Teresa commented on what have been for her the benefits of participation in the slash community:

> I still find it incredible writing to people and being able to talk about "slash" and use all those words that polite Catholic girls are not supposed to know (you know the ones—penis, cock, fucking)—as a Catholic, I knew Sodom existed as a town, but didn't dare ask what Sodomy was. [. . .] I think the reason I like slash fiction has more to do with the emotion in the story than the act itself. Our house was emotionally very

cold. Any emotion had to be hidden—I grew up feeling embarrassed if I looked happy in public let alone if I cried in public. I like the emotional romances that just don't seem to exist outside of slash fiction. Mind you, I like the pure sex ones as well.[1] [. . .] People like Leslie Fish and M. Fae have taught me so much about the human body and also about the human mind. The ideas bound up in some of these stories about what constitutes male/female good/bad acceptable/unacceptable sex have opened my eyes to the way society forces its ideas on us.[2]

—Teresa Hehir, "To Be Announced," [1] *TNU* 9, Winter/Spring 1992; [2] *SBF* 2, August 1993

What many slash fans enjoy is the sense of creating their own culture, of participating in the emergence of a new genre that more perfectly expresses their own social visions and fantasies:

What I love about fandom is the freedom we have allowed ourselves to create and recreate our characters over and over again. Fanfic rarely sits still. It's like a living, evolving thing, taking on its own life, one story building on another, each writer's reality bouncing off another's and maybe even melding together to form a whole new creation. A lot of people would argue that we're not creative because we build on someone else's universe rather than coming up with our own. However, I find that fandom can be extremely creative because we have the ability to keep changing our characters and giving them new life over and over. We can kill and resurrect them as often as we like. We can change their personalities and how they react to situations. We can take a character and make him charming and sweet or cold-blooded and cruel. We can give them an infinite, always-changing life rather than the single life of their original creation. We have given ourselves license to do whatever we want and it's very liberating.

— Kim Bannister, (untitled), *SBF* 1, May 1993

The multiple perspectives of fandom on the same set of characters allow us to do one thing better than virtually any other form of contemporary literature; they allow us to know one set of characters with tremendous depth. People are not as simple as even the most complex literary character in a single presentation. Any breathing human being is really many people, many of whom are contradictory. Reading overlapping versions of Ray Doyle, for example, leads to an understanding

that is in many ways more real for its breadth and depth, detail and yes, even its contradictions. I do not think it is coincidental that so many fans have been or are drawn to mainstream literary universes consisting of multiple retellings of the same sets of stories by different authors— Arthurian myths and the Robin Hood legends spring immediately to mind as two other "evolving" universes. How is what we do different?
—Cynthia Jenkins, "Menage a Deux," *SBF* 2, August 1993

I think part of what makes slash so alluring is not so much that it's taboo, although that does give it an extra edge, but that we create it, our community, unhindered by all the rules of creative writing professors, of publishers and of marketers. We create the fiction we want to read and, more importantly, we allow ourselves to react to it. If a story moves or amuses us, we share it; if it bothers us, we write a sequel; if it disturbs us, we may even re-write it! We also continually recreate the characters to fit our images of them or to explore a new idea. We have the power and that's a very strong siren. If we want to explore an issue or see a particular scenario, all we have to do is sit down and write it. It gets read and instantly reacted upon in a continuing dialogue among fans. You can't do that very often in the "real" world. For me, that's one of the strongest callings of slash in particular and fandom in general.
—Kim Bannister, "Desert Blooms," *SBF* 2, August 1993

Summing Up

What has sustained this discussion for more than five years is the complex set of questions that slash poses and the absence of easy, satisfying answers. Morgan and B.T. examine what they see as the power and the "paradox" of slash.

Slash makes you think. It presents you with scenarios and situations that confront and transgress our nicely constructed ideas of the "norm." It flat refuses to swallow the party line about who has what emotions in what circumstances. It is produced, mainly by women, in an effort to search through questions and answers about ourselves and our constructed sexuality/identity. In slash, we do what is unthinkable, we put the "wrong" people in bed, in the "wrong" situations. In a world that creates the individual's identity in terms of sexuality, we respond by challenging, rearranging, that sexuality, that identity.

—Morgan, "A Different Eye," *SBF* 3, November 1993

Paradoxes surround slash literature. Slash has been confusing everyone including its creators for years. But isn't this because it's an expression of the hopelessly confusing and contradictory world women live in, and the confused and contradictory view society has of sex? [. . .] Slash is defined and shaped by women, and if it seems contradictory, or seems to tell more than one kind of story at times, maybe there's a reason. The writers aren't following anyone else's guidelines; they're writing, as best they can, what they feel.

—B.T., "Strange Tongues," *TNU* 4, November 1990

4

"Out of the Closet and into the Universe"

Queers and Star Trek

Henry Jenkins with John Campbell

Janice Radway was one of the first academics to embrace my work on fan communities, in part because it paralleled her own observations of and experiences with romance readers. She had been one of the peer reviewers for "Star Trek Rerun, Reread, Rewritten." She had told me that the original draft spent too much time trying to prove that audiences were active, when what the field then needed were ever more detailed descriptions of how different groups made sense of popular culture. "Out of the Closet and into the Universe," along with "Do You Enjoy Making the Rest of Us Feel Stupid" (also in this volume) and "It's Not a Fairy Tale Anymore," responded to that challenge. This essay represented my first attempt at what John Hartley calls "intervention analysis" and in that sense help to pave the way for some of the popular writings I have done on Columbine and the debates about game violence.

In American Cultural Studies, John Hartley and Roberta Pearson argue that the so-called new journalists, writers like Tom Wolfe and Hunter S. Thompson, were important popular predecessors of and influences on the American cultural studies tradition. At its best, their work was deeply ethnographic, taking us inside unfamiliar communities or cultural sites and expressing the way participants understood themselves and their own practices, while being honest about their own subjective stakes in the process and remaining accessible to the broadest possible readership. "Out of the Closet and into the Universe" was self-consciously influenced by Tom Wolfe's efforts to capture the "voice" of different communities. In this condensed version, I strip away much of the academic baggage allowing the more journalistic dimensions to surface.

I should note that my key informant and research assistant on this project was John Campbell, who was then a member of the Gaylaxians but who subsequently decided to go on to graduate school in media studies. He has written a remarkable first book, Getting It On Online: Cyberspace, Gay Male Sexuality, and Embodied Identity *(2004), which emerges from his own participation-observation within various gay sex chatrooms.*

"Out of the Closet" first appeared in Science Fiction Audiences: Watching Doctor Who and Star Trek *(London: Routledge, 1995), which I co-authored with John Tulloch.*

> *Star Trek* celebrates its 25th anniversary in 1991. In that quarter century, one of the most important aspects of the series . . . has been the vision that humanity will one day put aside its differences to work and live in peace together. *Star Trek,* in its various television and motion picture forms, has presented us with Africans, Asians, Americans and Andorians, Russians and Romulans, French and Ferengi, Hispanics and Hortas, human and non-human men and women. In 25 years, it has also never shown an openly gay character.
> —Franklin Hummel, *Gaylactic Gazette*[1]

> Perhaps someday our ability to love won't be so limited.
> —Dr. Beverley Crusher, "The Host," *Star Trek: The Next Generation*

"Two, four, six, eight, how do you know Kirk is straight?" the Gaylaxians chanted as they marched down the streets of Boston on Gay Pride day. "Three, five, seven, nine, he and Spock have a real fine time!" The chant encapsulates central issues of concern to the group: How do texts determine the sexual orientation of their characters, and how might queer spectators gain a foothold for self-representation within dominant media narratives? How has *Star Trek* written gays and lesbians out of its future, and why do the characters and their fans so steadfastly refuse to stay in the closet? . . .

The Boston Area Gaylaxians is a local chapter of the international Gaylactic Network Inc., an organization for gay, lesbian, and bisexual science fiction fans and their friends.[2] Founded in 1987, the group has chapters in many cities in the United States and Canada. Adopting the slogan "Out of the closet and into the universe," the group has sought to increase gay visibility within the science fiction fan community and "to help gay fans contact and develop friendships with each other."[3] The group hosts a national convention, Gaylaxicon, which brings together fans and writers interested in sexuality and science fiction. Although only recently given official recognition from the network, group members have organized a national letter-writing campaign to urge Paramount to acknowledge a queer presence in the twenty-fourth-century future represented on *Star Trek: The Next Generation.* Their efforts have so far attracted national attention from both the gay and mainstream press and have provoked responses from production spokespeople and several cast members. Gene Roddenberry publicly committed himself to incorporating gay characters into the series in the final months before his death, but the producers never delivered on that promise. The series *has* featured two episodes that can loosely be read as presenting images of alternative sexuality, "The Host" and "The Outcast." Although the producers have promoted these stories as responsive to the gay and lesbian community's concerns, both treat queer lifestyles as alien rather than familiar aspects of the Federation culture and have sparked further controversy and dissatisfaction among the Gaylaxians.

The fans' requests are relatively straightforward—perhaps showing two male crew members holding hands in the ship's bar, perhaps a passing reference to a lesbian lover, some evidence that gays, bisexuals, and lesbians exist in the twenty-fourth century represented on the program. Others want more—an explicitly gay or lesbian character, a regular presence on the series, even if in a relatively minor capacity. As far as the producers are concerned, homosexuality and homophobia are so tightly interwoven that there is no way to represent the first without simultaneously reintroducing the second, while for the fans, what is desired is precisely a future that offers homosexuality without homophobia.

Intervention Analysis and Fan Culture

This chapter documents the Gaylaxians' struggles with Paramount over the issue of queer visibility on *Star Trek,* their efforts to gain a public acknowledgment that gay, lesbian, and bisexual people belong within the program's utopian community. I write from a partisan position within this debate as a *Star Trek* fan and a member of the Gaylaxians. John Hartley has called upon media scholars to engage in what he calls intervention analysis: "Intervention analysis seeks not only to describe and explain existing dispositions of knowledge, but also to change them."[4] Hartley advocates that media scholars write from the position(s) of media audiences, recognizing and articulating the interpretive work that viewers perform, documenting their creative engagement with the media content. Hartley continues:

> Intervention analysis certainly needs to take popular television more or less as it finds it, without high-culture fastidiousness or right-on political squeamishness, but it needs to intervene *in* the media and in the production of popular knowledge *about* them.[5]

Intervention analysis, Hartley argues, speaks from, about, and for the margins of popular culture.

My goal is thus to intervene in the debates about queer visibility on *Star Trek,* to trace the discursive logic by which producers have sought to exclude and fans have sought to include queer characters, to situate this issue within a larger social and cultural context of queer reception of science fiction and network representation of alternative sexuality. My goal is not to instruct or politicize audience response, since I believe that fans already exercise a form of grassroots cultural politics that powerfully reflects their interests in the media and their own ideological stakes. We need to create a context where fan politics may be acknowledged and accepted as a valid contribution to the debates about mass culture.

Children of Uranus

> During the course of our production, there have been many special interest groups who have lobbied for their particular cause. It is Gene Roddenberry's policy to present *Star Trek* as he sees it and not to be governed by outside influences.
>
> —Susan Sackett, executive assistant to Gene Roddenberry[6]

We had been the target of a concerted, organized movement by gay activists to put a gay character on the show.

—Michael Piller, *Star Trek* writing staff supervisor[7]

In the late 1960's, a "special interest group" lobbied a national television network to renew a series for a third season. If those networks had not listened to those with a special interest, *Star Trek* would not have returned and today *Star Trek* might very likely not be all of what it has become. You, Mr. Roddenberry, and *Star Trek* owe much to a special interest group: *Star Trek* fans. Perhaps you should consider listening to some of those same fans who are speaking to you now.

—Franklin Hummel[8]

The people who organized the national letter-writing campaign to get a queer character included on *Star Trek: The Next Generation* were not "outside influences," "special interest groups," or "gay activists."[9] They saw themselves as vitally involved with the life of the series and firmly committed to its survival. As Franklin Hummel, director of the Gaylaxian Network, asserts, "we are *part* of *Star Trek*." They saw their goals not as antagonistic to Roddenberry's artistic vision but rather as logically consistent with the utopian politics he had articulated in *The Making of Star Trek* and elsewhere. . . .

The fans reminded Roddenberry that he had said:

To be different is not necessarily to be ugly; to have a different idea is not necessarily wrong. The worst possible thing that can happen to humanity is for all of us to begin to look and act and think alike.[10]

When, they asked, was *Star Trek* going to acknowledge and accept sexual "difference" as part of the pluralistic vision it had so consistently evoked? They cited his successful fight to get a black woman on the *Enterprise* bridge and his unsuccessful one to have a female second-in-command, and wondered aloud "why can't *Star Trek* be as controversial in educating people about our movement as they were for the black civil rights movement?" (James).[11]

The people who organized the letter-writing campaign were *Star Trek* fans, and as such they claimed a special relationship to the series, at once protective and possessive, celebratory and critical. . . .

The producers' refusal to represent gay and lesbian characters cut deeply:

Frank: They betrayed everything *Star Trek* was—the vision of humanity I have held for over 25 years. They betrayed Gene Roddenberry and his vision and all the fans. They didn't have the guts to live up to what *Star Trek* was for.

. . .

To understand the intensity of the Gaylaxians' responses, we need to consider more closely what science fiction as a genre has offered these gay, lesbian, and bisexual fans. David, a member of the Boston group, described his early experiences with the genre:

I wasn't very happy with my world as it was and found that by reading science fiction or fantasy, it took me to places where things were possible, things that couldn't happen in my normal, everyday life. It would make it possible to go out and change things that I hated about my life, the world in general, into something that was more comfortable for me, something that would allow me to become what I really wanted to be. . . . Being able to work out prejudices in different ways. Dealing with man's inhumanity to man. To have a vision for a future or to escape and revel in glory and deeds that have no real mundane purpose. To be what you are and greater than the world around you lets you be.

Lynne, another Gaylaxian, tells a similar story:

I wasn't very happy with my life as a kid and I liked the idea that there might be someplace else where things were different. I didn't look for it on this planet. I figured it was elsewhere. I used to sit there in the Bronx, looking up at the stars, hoping that a UFO would come and get me. Of course, it would never land in the Bronx but I still had my hopes.

What these fans describe is something more than an abstract notion of escapism—the persistent queer fantasy of a space beyond the closet doorway. Such utopian fantasies can provide an important first step toward political awareness, since utopianism allows us to envision an alternative social order that we must work to realize ("something positive to look forward to") and to recognize the limitations of our current situation (the dystopian present against which the utopian alternative can be read). . . .

Nobody had expected the original *Star Trek* series, released in a pre-Stonewall society, to address directly the concerns of gay, lesbian, and bisexual fans. They had taken it on faith that its vision of a United Federation of Planets, of intergalactic cooperation and acceptance, included them as vital partners. Yet, when *Star Trek: The Next Generation* appeared, at a time when queer characters had been included on many American series, they hoped for something more, to be there on the screen, an explicit presence in its twenty-fourth century.

Where No (Gay) Man Has Gone Before

Mr. Roddenberry has always stated that he would be happy to include a character of *any* special interest group if such a character is relevant to the story.

—Susan Sackett[12]

Were Uhura and LeForge included because the fact they were black was relevant to a story? Was Sulu included because the fact he was Asian was important to the plot? Were Crusher and Troi and Yar included because the fact they were female was relevant to an episode? I do not think so. These characters were included because they were important to the *spirit* of *Star Trek*.

—Franklin Hummel[13]

"We expected *Star Trek* to do it because we expected more of *Star Trek* than other series," one fan explained. They looked around them and saw other series—*LA Law, Heartbeat, Thirtysomething, Quantum Leap, Northern Exposure, Days of Our Lives, Roseanne*—opening up new possibilities for queer characters on network television, while their program could only hint around the possibility that there might be some form of sexuality out there, somewhere beyond the known universe, that did not look like heterosexuality. *Star Trek* was no longer setting the standards for other programs.

"Sooner or later, we'll have to address the issue," Roddenberry had told a group of Boston fans in November 1986, while *Star Trek: The*

Next Generation was still on the drawing boards: "We should probably have a gay character on *Star Trek*."[14] "For your information, the possibility that several members of the *Enterprise* crew might be gay has been discussed in a very positive light. It is very much an area that a show like *Star Trek* should address," acknowledged David Gerrold, the man assigned to prepare the program bible for *Star Trek: The Next Generation*.[15]

What were the Gaylaxians to make of the absence of gays and lesbians in the program universe, of Roddenberry's silence on the subject, as season after season came and went? Steve K., writing in *The Lavender Dragon*, a fan newsletter, saw only two possibilities consistent with the fan community's realist reading of the series:

> As a U.S. Navy veteran, I have had firsthand experience with the military's discrimination against gays and lesbians. It could be that the United Federation of Planets also bans homosexuals from serving in Starfleet. . . . That would explain the large number of never-married officers on board the Enterprise. Except for Dr. Crusher, none of the regular officers have been married (chiefs, e.g. Chief O'Brian, are non-commissioned officers like sergeants). Does Starfleet have a huge closet? Still, this does leave the problem of civilian homosexuals. Since many of the episodes involve interaction with non-Starfleet characters, you would think that occasionally a gay or lesbian character would be somewhere in the 24th century. Has the Federation found a "cure" for homosexuality?[16]

Invisibility meant either that gays were closeted or that they had ceased to exist. Neither was an attractive alternative to a group, whose motto, after all, is "Out of the closet and into the universe."

If they had listened more carefully, the fans might have recognized the slippage in Roddenberry's original comments, from including gay people as *characters* to dealing with homosexuality as an *issue*. What the Gaylaxians wanted was to be visible without being an "issue" or a "problem" that the scriptwriters needed to confront and resolve. . . . As Theresa M. wrote:

> I want to see men holding hands and kissing in Ten-Forward. I want to see a smile of joy on Picard's face as he, as captain, joins two women

together in a holy union, or pain across his face when he tells a man
that his same-sex mate has been killed in battle. I want to hear Troi
assure a crew member, questioning their mixed emotions, that bisexuality is a way to enjoy the best of what both sexes have to offer. I want to
see crew members going about their business and acting appropriately
no matter what their sexual orientation in every situation.[17]

Such moments of public affection, community ritual, or psychological
therapy were common aspects of the program text; the only difference
would be that in this case, the characters involved would be recogniz-
ably queer. The fans wanted to be visible participants within a future
that had long since resolved the problem of homophobia. They felt this
utopian acceptance to be more consistent with the program's ideology
than a more dystopian representation of the social problems they confronted as gays, lesbians, and bisexuals living in a still largely homophobic society.

The program's producers would seem to agree, since their public responses to the letter-writing campaign often presuppose that queers
would have gained tolerance and acceptance within *Star Trek*'s future,
yet they evaded attempts to make this commitment visible on the screen.
. . . One can identify a series of basic assumptions about the representation of gay identities that underlie the producers' responses to the letter-
writing campaign:

1. The explicit representation of homosexuality within the program
text would require some form of labeling, whereas a general climate of
tolerance would have made the entire issue disappear. As Roddenberry
explained in a statement released to the gay newspaper *The Advocate*,
"I've never found it necessary to do a special homosexual-theme story
because people in the time line of *The Next Generation*, the 24th century, will not be labeled."[18]

2. The representation of homosexuality on *Star Trek* would necessarily become the site of some form of dramatic conflict. As Richard Arnold, the man appointed to serve as *Star Trek*'s liaison with the fan
community, explained:

In Gene Roddenberry's 24th century *Star Trek* universe, homosexuality
will not be an issue as it is today. How do you, then, address a non-
issue? No one aboard the starship could care less what anyone else's

sexual preference would be. . . . Do not ask us to show conflict aboard the Enterprise when it comes to people's choices over their sex, politics or religion. By that time, all choices will be respected equally.[19]

The producers, in a curious bit of circular logic, were insisting that the absence of gays and lesbians in the *Star Trek* universe was evidence of their acceptance within the Federation, while their visibility could only be read as signs of conflict, a renewed eruption of homophobia.

3. Representation of homosexuality on *Star Trek* would make the characters' sexuality obvious and therefore risk offense. As Arnold explained,

> Although we have no problem with any of our characters being gay, it would not be appropriate to portray them as such. A person's (or being's) sexual preference should not be obvious, just as we can't tell anyone's religious or political affiliations by looking at them.[20]

The signs of homosexuality, if they are there to be seen at all, automatically become too "obvious" in a homophobic society while the marks of heterosexuality are naturalized, rendered invisible, because they are too pervasive to even be noticed.

4. Representation could only occur through reliance on easily recognizable stereotypes of contemporary gay identities. With a twist, the group the producers didn't dare to offend turns out to be not the religious right (which has often put pressure on producers to exclude gay or lesbian characters) but the gay fans who are demanding representation within the program: "Do you expect us to show stereotypical behavior that would be more insulting to the gay community than supportive?"[21] Arnold asked a room of 1,200 *Star Trek* fans at Boston's Sheraton Hotel: "What would you have us do, put pink triangles on them? Have them sashay down the corridors?"[22]

5. Representation of gay characters would require the explicit representation of their sexual practice. Arnold asked, "Would you have us show two men in bed together?"[23] Since a heterosexist society has reduced homosexuals to their sexuality, then the only way to represent them would be to show them engaged in sexual activity.

6. Representation of gay characters and their relationships would be a violation of genre expectations. Adopting a suggestively feminine metaphor, Arnold asked, "Would you have us turn this [*Star Trek*] into

a soap opera?" To deal with homosexuality as part of the character's lifestyle would be to transform (and perhaps, emasculate) *Star Trek*, while to deal with heterosexuality as part of the character's lifestyle would be to leave its status as a male-targeted action-adventure program unchanged. Any sort of concerted effort to respond to this logic requires an attempt to make heterosexuality rather than homosexuality visible, to show how its marks can be seen on the characters, the plots, and the entire environment:

> *Frank*: How do we know any of the characters are heterosexual? How do you know? Because you see them interact with other people, especially in their intimate relations. *Star Trek* has done that over and over and over again. You know Picard is heterosexual. You know Riker is heterosexual. Why? Because they've had constant relationships with people of the opposite sex. This has been done systematically as character development. Why not this same development of a gay character?

7. As a last resort, having failed to convince the Gaylaxians with their other arguments, the producers sought to deny their own agency in the production of the program and their own control over its ideological vision, saying, "Should a *good* script come along that allows us to address the problems that the gay and lesbian community face on the planet today, then it will very likely be produced."[24] But, in fact, there had been a script, called "Blood and Fire," written by David Gerrold, in the very first season of *Star Trek: The Next Generation*, at a time when producers were desperately looking for material to keep the fledgling series on the air. Gerrold's script used Regalian Blood Worms as a metaphor to deal with the issue of AIDS and included a gay couple as secondary characters. . . .

Gerrold's script went through multiple revisions before being scuttled. The producers have consistently insisted that their decision not to produce "Blood and Fire" was based on its merits, not its inclusion of gay themes and characters. Gerrold, who parted company with Roddenberry shortly after this incident, has repeatedly challenged this account, charging that the episode was never filmed because the producers were uncomfortable with his attempts to introduce the issue of homosexuality into the *Star Trek* universe: "People complained the script had blatantly homosexual characters. Rick Berman said we can't do this in an afternoon market in some places. We'll have parents writing letters."[25]

Gerrold told his story at science fiction conventions, on the computer nets, and to lots and lots of reporters. Copies of the script have circulated informally among Gaylaxians and other fans. "Blood and Fire" became part of the fan community's understanding of the program history and was a key factor in motivating the Gaylaxians to adopt more aggressive strategies in lobbying for their cause. "Good scripts are accepted, and this script was deemed not to be a good script," said Ernest Over, an assistant to the executive producer.[26]

The producers had said, repeatedly, in so many different ways, that the only ways that queers could become visible within *Star Trek* was by becoming a problem, and so, gay, lesbian, and bisexual *Star Trek* fans became a problem for the producers. They organized a national letter-writing campaign; they posted notices on the computer nets; they went to the queer press and made their dissatisfaction with the producers' responses a public issue. Ernest Over, himself a gay community activist, told *The Advocate* that the *Star Trek* office had received "more letters on this than we'd had on anything else."[27]

In the midst of the publicity, just a few months before his death, Gene Roddenberry issued a statement: "In the fifth season of *Star Trek: The Next Generation,* viewers will see more of shipboard life in some episodes, which will, among other things, include gay crewmembers in day-to-day circumstances."[28] An editorialist in the *Los Angeles Times* reported:

> This season, gays and lesbians will appear unobtrusively aboard the Enterprise. . . . They weren't "outed" and they won't be outcasts; apparently they'll be neither objects of pity nor melodramatic attention. Their sexual orientation will be a matter of indifference to the rest of the crew.[29]

. . .

When the Gaylaxians sought confirmation of Roddenberry's statements, they received no response. When reporters from the *Washington Blade* called, they received only a tape-recorded message from executive producer Rick Berman: "The writers and producers of *Star Trek: The Next Generation* are actively exploring a number of possible approaches that would address the issue of sexual orientation."[30] Once again, "the issue of sexual orientation" had substituted for the promise of queer characters. And, as the new season premiered, queer fans learned that they would become "outcasts," after all.

A Human Failing

[Roddenberry] had discussed with us before his death the possibility of having two men hold hands in some scene, which was totally irrelevant to the issue of homosexuality. . . . So we decided to tell a story that was about sexual intolerance.

—Star Trek writing staff supervisor Michael Piller[31]

There is a curious footnote in Gene Roddenberry's novelization of Star Trek: The Motion Picture, one that members of the female fan writing community have long read as the producer's wink toward Kirk/Spock fiction. "Because t'hy'la [a term Spock used to refer to Kirk] can be used to mean lover, and since Kirk's and Spock's friendship was unusually close, this has led some to speculate over whether they had actually indeed become lovers," Roddenberry explained, acknowledging for the first and only time within a canonical Star Trek story that the concept, at least, of homosexuality still existed within his twenty-fourth-century universe.[32] Homosexuality is still the subject of "speculations," "rumors," perhaps of blackmail. Yet, Roddenberry allows Kirk to set the record "straight":

I was never aware of this lovers rumor, although I have been told that Spock encountered it several times. Apparently he had always dismissed it with his characteristic lifting of his right eyebrow which usually connoted some combination of surprise, disbelief, and/or annoyance. As for myself, although I have no moral or other objections to physical love in any of its many Earthly, alien and mixed forms, I have always found my best gratification in that creature woman. Also, I would dislike being thought of as so foolish that I would select a love partner who came into sexual heat only once every seven years.[33]

So, just as quickly as he makes it appear, Roddenberry begins to make homosexuality disappear again. Yet Roddenberry doesn't totally close the door here. With an extra bit of effort, we can peek into Kirk's closet and find hints of something perverse. What exactly does Kirk, this man of multiple worlds, mean when he says that his "best gratification" came through heterosexuality? How has he come to be in a position to make such an evaluation? He doesn't, after all, say that it was his only gratification. What experiences had Kirk had with "physical love in any of its many Earthly, alien and mixed forms"? And, so, Roddenberry, at one and the same time, authorizes a space for fan speculation and explicitly, directly, denies the possibility that homosexual desire might run between Kirk and Spock.

In an important contribution to queer media theory, D. A. Miller has traced the ways that Alfred Hitchcock's *Rope* makes its characters' homosexuality a matter of connotation rather than denotation, something that is suggested but never said. "Connotation will always manifest a certain semiotic insufficiency," Miller notes, allowing "homosexual meaning to be elided even as it is also being elaborated."[34] While the homosexuality of *Rope*'s major characters has been taken for granted by almost all critics writing about the film, their sexual preference is never explicitly stated and thus remains a matter of interpretation. The truth of denotation (i.e., the explicit representation or statement of homosexuality) is self-evident while the truth of connotation (i.e., suggestion or implication) remains open to debate and re-interpretation. Connotation has, as Miller suggests, "an abiding deniability." A play with connotation is often a way to work around censorship, but by its very nature, it denies the queer visibility the Gaylaxians sought from *Star Trek*'s producers. Rather, the play with connotation, as Miller suggests, teaches only the importance of remaining silent.

"The Host" and "The Outcast," the two *Star Trek: The Next Generation* episodes that brush across the issue of sexual preference, can be seen as similar plays with connotation, often threatened with being swamped by some larger, more "universal" concern. Here, for example, is director Marvin Rush describing the *Star Trek* episode "The Host":

> Male/female, male/male, female/female relationships exist in life in various forms and they're fair game for drama. I think "The Host" was about an aspect of that. But to me it was more about the nature of love, and [whether] the packages makes a difference.[35]

Writing staff supervisor Michael Piller acknowledges that "The Outcast" was a conscious response to the letter-writing campaign but it was, in truth, a "story that addressed the issue of sexual intolerance. . . . [T]hat was really the broader issue."[36]

In "The Host," the *Enterprise*'s doctor, Beverley Crusher, falls in love —with a man. Odan, an alien ambassador, beams aboard, charms the pants off her, and the two become romantically, and, it is strongly suggested, sexually, involved. Only then, after the fact, does Crusher learn that the body she has been sleeping with is actually simply the host while the "man" with whom she has fallen in love is an extraterrestrial symbiont. The host body is dying. The symbiont is temporarily transplanted into Riker's body, the body of a man she considers as a "brother." After much soul-searching, Crusher again falls in love with Odan and it is again suggested that she goes to bed with him. In the final scene, Odan's new host, a woman, arrives to receive the transplant. Odan, in this body as in all of his previous bodies, still desires "Doctor Beverley," but Beverley backs away from embracing him in his female form. "Perhaps it is a human failing but we are not accustomed to those kinds of changes," Dr. Beverley says with a cold stare and a distant voice. "I can't keep up. . . . I can't live with that kind of uncertainty. Perhaps someday our ability to love won't be so limited." Odan kisses her on the wrist and then walks away, before the camera fades away on a cold, expressionless close-up of the good doctor contemplating, no doubt, the "nature of love." "Perhaps it was a human failing," she confessed, safe in the knowledge that on *Star Trek*, human failings like compassion, friendship, emotion, altruism, love, have long been validated in the face of alien challenge. It is, after all, in our failings that we are most decidedly human.

The Gaylaxians were sharply divided about "The Host." Christine, president of the Boston chapter, wrote a letter praising the episode: "The story was powerful, sensitive, well-acted and intelligent, and clearly illustrates *Trek*'s continuing commitment to explore and present important issues regardless of how controversial they might be."[37] Her praise was tempered by her recognition of what could be expected to be said on television rather than what it might be desirable for the program to actually say. *Star Trek*, she suggested, had found a way to explore alternative sexuality without running the "risk that the entire midwest would immediately switch off their TVs." Christine's acceptance of "The Host" thus balances multiple reading formations: one that interprets the program's ideology in relation to Roddenberry's activist image and the other that recognizes the fans as a "powerless elite" that must reconcile its desires with what is practical in reaching a larger viewing public. Similarly, she negotiates between the appreciation of allegory as a form of social commentary and the fans' desire for recognition in terms acceptable within fandom's realist aesthetic. . . .

Not surprisingly, however, given the precarious balance she achieves between these differing reading formations, other group members did not share Christine's endorsement of the episode. The ambiguities of the closing scene particularly provoked discomfort and debate. Why does Crusher pull back from Odan when he appears to her as a woman, yet she was able to sleep with him when he took the form of her "brother"? Is it, as she says, because she can't keep up with the changes or because, as is strongly implied, she can't deal with the possibility of lesbian desire? What is it that the people of the Federation have not yet learned to accept, parasites in host bodies or queer visibility? And, is homosexuality even what's on offer here, given the program's careful efforts to situate Odan as quite literally a man's mind trapped inside a woman's body? Consider, for example, this exchange during one of the interview sessions, a debate that recurred in a similar form each time I discussed this episode with group members:

> *Betty*: I liked it but I wanted it to go on for another half hour. If the third body—the woman had come in fifteen or twenty minutes before the end of the show and Beverley had to deal with her.
> *Lynne*: But they don't have the guts to do that yet. . . .
> *Betty*: If Beverley had to deal with the person she loved in the body of a woman, the whole gay issue would have been raised and you would have lost sight of the issue you raised—is it the shell or the personality that you love?

. . .

Even here, heterosexuality is seen as universal, abstract, while homosexuality is too particular and concrete to carry the weight of such a global concern as "the nature of love." Straights can stand for all lovers, while lesbians are more specialized signifiers.

> *Lynne*: I think Beverley would have responded almost similarly if Odan came back as a young blond male but a total stranger. "I can't do this again." That's the feeling I got. But on top of it all, it's a woman and she's not usually inclined that way. I can't deal with you changing bod-

ies on me. You don't look like you did before. First she had to deal with Riker. My God! Riker's body! Blech! She dealt with that but it took her a good twenty minutes of the episode. She would have needed another twenty minutes of episode to deal with this female body. But I saw the little smile on her face at the end and that's what clued me in that the writer's left it open-ended.

Homosexuality survives as a "little smile," an ambiguous gesture, which is readable as homophobic, foreclosing all future possibilities or as tolerant, "open-ended," and subject to multiple interpretations. So much weight to put on a "little smile" but sometimes that's all you have.

The following season, Star Trek tried again to confront and resolve the "problem" of homosexuality. If "The Host" wasn't really about homosexuality, even if it visually represented the possibility, however fleetingly, on the screen, "The Outcast" was to be the "gay episode." Supervising producer Jeri Taylor explains, " 'The Host' was really more about the nature *of* what is the basis of a love relationship. 'The Outcast,' though, is a gay rights story. It absolutely, specifically and outspokenly dealt with gay issues."[38] "The Outcast" would put the issue behind them once and for all, carefully containing its implications within a single story set on an alien world that had no previous contact with the Federation and, under the circumstances, probably wouldn't want to get into communication again.

The J'naii are an androgynous race who have outlawed the very concept of gender. (The J'naii, predictably enough, were played entirely by women.)[39] Riker meets Soren, a J'naii technician, while working together to rescue a spaceship that has been lost in "null space." The appearance of a woman without gender invites a constant investigation of the wonders of heterosexuality. "What kind of a woman do you find attractive?" she asks Riker. "Tell me, is that the kind of woman all human males prefer?" she asks again. "It is up to the woman to attract the man?" Soren inquires of Dr. Crusher. Repairing a disabled shuttle craft, Riker and Soren discuss their feelings toward each other. "What is involved with two sexes? Mating?" she wants to know, and each time, both her questions and their responses assume that heterosexuality is the only possibility. After all, in a world with two sexes, why settle for only one? "Perhaps it is that complexity which makes the differences in the sexes so interesting," she exclaims, amid Riker's knowing talk about "snips and snails and puppy dog tales" and "sugar and spice and everything nice." Soren confesses that she has, in fact, come to think of herself as female and to have an "unnatural" preference for men, even though such a sexual identity is outlawed in her culture:

> I am taking a terrible risk telling you that. . . . Some have strong inclinations for maleness. Some have urges to be female. I am one of the latter. . . . In our world, these feelings are forbidden. Those who are discovered are shamed and ridiculed. . . . Those of us who have these urges lead secret and guarded lives. We seek each other out. Always hiding, always terrified of being discovered.

The two disobey the laws of her culture and dare to express their "deviant" heterosexual desires for each other, but Soren is made to defend her heterosexuality before the council of Androgynies: "What we do is not different from what you do. . . . What makes you think you can dictate how people love each other?" After much soul-searching, Riker and Worf decide to disobey Star Fleet's Prime Directive and attempt to rescue Soren from the therapy that will "cure" her of her outcast sexuality. For once, on a program famous for its split-second escapes from certain doom, they arrive too late. Soren, who has been cured, rejects Riker's advances and so he flies away aboard the *Enterprise*, leaving her behind. . . .

If allegory depends upon the readers' abilities to fill its silences with their own voices, to complete the statements the text has left unfinished, the fans saw only the gaps and the evasions. Nowhere do any of the characters make explicit reference to the possibility of homosexuality nor do they directly confront homophobia. Homosexuality remains a connotative ghost, still that form of sexual desire that dares not speak its name.

The Gaylaxians recognized that what made this episode particularly dangerous was its insubstantiability, its refusal to state directly and explicitly what its message was intended to be:

> The depiction of Soren's society seemed to be something taken right from Rush Limbaugh's show or Pat Buchanan's campaign literature. If you listen to those people, you'll hear them talking about how the feminist and homosexual political agendas want to destroy the traditional family and make society into a sexless, genderless collection of politically correct clones, and if you don't toe the line, you'll be censored.

Soren's society was a depiction of those people's worst nightmares. It seems to me that if you were of that mindset to begin with, this show did nothing but confirm those unfounded fears, and nothing to challenge them. . . . It was so ambiguous, so valueless and empty, as to leave it open for this interpretation.[40]

The denotative dimensions of the story—the literal level of the narrative —had such force, they feared, that it would completely swamp the connotative meanings of the allegory. What appears on screen, at the most basic denotative level, is an "outspoken" defense of heterosexuality, including that daring moment when Riker and Soren, the actors Jonathan Frakes and Melinda Culea, break all social taboos and kiss each other on the lips, right there on television. . . .

But, pull back from the denotative, take the allegory on its own connotative terms, and what do you have?

If I were a gay teenager trying to come out, this episode would have done nothing for me. I would have left with exactly what I came in with. Yeah—I suppose there are gay people out there. I don't know how or why I'm going to find them and I don't have any kind of sense that things are going to be okay. (Gaylaxian group discussion)

. . .

But then again, given the instability of this allegory, perhaps some people missed the point altogether, perhaps some straight people didn't even realize that the episode was supposed to be about "gay rights." This story was oft-repeated:

There was a discussion where I work in an almost completely straight environment and a lot of people who watched it didn't connect it to the gay issue at all. . . . The thing that was interesting, they were still outraged by what was done to Soren. They felt it was a generic freedom of choice issue. She wasn't allowed to live the life she wanted regardless of what that was. That this might be treated as a gay-related issue was quite a surprise to them. (Gaylaxian group discussion)

What happened when you pointed it out to them? "They argued with it. They still felt that it was more a human rights issue." And they did not perceive that a gay rights issue might also be a human rights issue?

"Well, I couldn't really go into it because I'm only out to half of the group I was talking with and so it wasn't something I could pursue."

And, so, maybe, all the episode said was that heterosexuality ought to exist everywhere in the galaxy, hardly a groundbreaking statement. As staff writer Brannon Braga said, "We were advocating tolerance. What's so risky about making a statement that intolerance is bad?"[41] The allegorical nature of the story allowed the producers to place the risk of "coming out" onto the backs of viewers rather than taking on that responsibility for themselves. "It was a very special episode. There are no subject[s] taboo for this show," Braga brags.[42] Gay fans noted that this was not the same way the series had tackled civil rights issues in the 1960s:

> *Frank*: "Let That Be the Last Battlefield" was a statement against racial discrimination. There was no need to make that statement. *Star Trek* had been making a statement against prejudice from the first episode when they had a multi-racial crew. If they had done "Battlefield" exactly as they did it as a statement against racial prejudice and every person on the ship was white, it would have been insulting—hypocrisy. But that's exactly what "The Outcast" did. They said basically, "we should be accepting and tolerant of people who have different sexual preferences but we aren't going to show any on our show. We aren't going to include any on the crew."

Q for Queer?

> What about non-human species homosexuality? A Klingon male in drag would surely be a highlight of the TV season. Or maybe a lesbian Vulcan, who logically decided that sex with men was unnecessary. Or even a Betazoid chicken hawk after the virginal Wesley Crusher. The *ST:NG Enterprise* has been the home of some homosexual stereotypes. Tasha Yar was at times the ultimate in butch female, not afraid of any man. Data is more anally retentive than even *The Odd Couple*'s Felix Unger. And Worf sometimes wears more leather than an entire issue of *Drummer*.
>
> —Steve K., *The Lavender Dragon*[43]

. . .

If Paramount and Berman thought that "The Outcast" would safely contain the specter of homosexuality on the far-strung planet of the J'Naii, then they misunderstood the power of connotation to grow, like ivy, all over a text once it has been planted there. As D. A. Miller writes, queer connotation has the

> inconvenience of tending to raise this ghost all over the place. For once received in all its uncertainty, the connotation instigates a project of confirmation. . . . Connotation thus tends to light everywhere, to put all signifiers to a test of their hospitality.[44]

The constant promise and deferral of a gay character colored the Gaylaxians' relationship to the series and invited them to constantly read a gay subtext into the episodes. *Star Trek* seemed always on the verge of confessing its characters' sexual preferences, only to back away yet again.

If the producers have trouble thinking of ways to make homosexuality visible within *Star Trek,* if they couldn't seem to find a "good script" to tell that particular story, the Gaylaxians have no trouble locating possibilities. Watch any episode with them and they will show you the spot, the right moment, for a confession of previously repressed desire to come out from hiding:

> *Lynne*: "Geordi realizes that the reason he can't seem to work things out with women is that he's gay . . . Picard goes on shore leave and meets this great woman. Why can't he go on shore leave and meet this great man? It doesn't mean he always prefers men. He can mix it up a little. . . . And it [bisexuality] would probably flourish on board the *Enterprise.* They're real open-minded there.

Soon the entire group is participating within this carnival of outlaw signifiers. . . .

For these fans, the text's silences about characters' sexuality or motives can be filled with homosexual desire, since, after all, in our society, such desire must often go unspoken. Straight fans, on the other hand, are apt to demand conclusive evidence that a character is homosexual and otherwise, read all unmarked characters as straight by default. What's at stake is the burden of proof and the nature of evidence within a culture where homosexuality most often appears within connotation rather than denotation. Such speculations cannot sustain direct challenge and often are not taken literally by those who advance them, but open up a fleeting possibility of imagining a different text existing in the margins of that which Paramount delivers.

Sometimes, the possibilities seem to cohere around a particular character, who appears to embody the richest potential for queer visibility, who builds upon the iconography and stereotypes of queer identity. Here, bids for character sexuality can be more strongly maintained since the text offers precisely the type of evidence that is most commonly presented within popular culture to indicate a character's potential homosexuality. Rumors surrounded the arrival of Tasha Yar as a character in *The Next Generation*'s first season. Maybe this is the queer character Roddenberry had promised: "Tasha Yar—an obvious bisexual character. Considering what she went through as a child, she should be a lesbian" (Betty). Tasha Yar—tough, independent, security chief with short-cropped hair, from a planet where she was repeatedly gang-raped by men, able to fight against any and all adversaries, was the classic Amazon: "She could easily be conceived as being a lesbian" (David). But, as the fans are quick to note, she goes to bed with Data in the program's second episode, "The Naked Now"; "When they decided to straighten her, they used an android. So we ended up heterosexualizing two perfectly wonderful characters. . . . Even if they had left the character alone and not heterosexualized Tasha Yar, we would have been farther ahead than we are now" (David).

The marks of heterosexuality, normally invisible, are made "obvious" by this interpretation, an act of violence committed against otherwise potentially queer characters, a reaction of homosexual panic that seeks to stabilize (or even to deny) their sexuality. Characters' sexualities do not remain unmarked for long within the world of *Star Trek* or, for that matter, the world of popular culture, which insists that characters be undeniably heterosexual even if their sexual preference is totally irrelevant to their narrative actions.[45] "Data has been assigned a sexual orientation, basically" (James). Data has been "heterosexualized." Yar has been "straightened."

Yet, again, how stable is that orientation? "Data is someone where bisexuality can be explored" (James). And, soon, the speculations are all open again.

. . .

Cultural studies' embrace of the model of resistant reading is a logical response to theoretical traditions that spoke of readers only in terms of textually constructed subject positions. Resistant reading, as a model, addresses many important questions about the ideological power of the mass media and the relationship between "the viewer and the viewed." Resistant reading, however, only describes one axis of a more complex relationship between readers and texts. The reading practices characteristic of fandom are never purely and rarely openly resistant to the meanings and categories advanced by program producers. Often, as we have seen, the fans' resistant reading occurs within rather than outside the ideological framework provided by the program and is fought in the name of fidelity to the program concepts. The consummate negotiating readers, fan critics work to repair gaps or contradictions in the program ideology, to make it cohere into a whole that satisfies their needs for continuity and emotional realism. Fandom is characterized by a contradictory and often highly fluid series of attitudes toward the primary text, marked by fascination as well as frustration, proximity as well as distance, acceptance of program ideology as well as rejection. The fans feel a strong identification with the programs, the characters, the producers and their ideological conceptions, even when they feel strong frustration with the failure of the producers to create stories they would like to see told.

. . .

Moreover, we need to identify ways in which resistant reading is not necessarily a sufficient response to dissatisfaction with the images currently in circulation. As many writers have noted, resistant reading risks becoming a catch-all solution for all the problems within popular culture, a way of escaping the need for ideological criticism or research into the political economy of media institutions. A model of resistant reading quickly becomes profoundly patronizing if it amounts to telling already socially marginalized audiences that they should be satisfied with their ability to produce their own interpretations and should not worry too much about their lack of representation within the media itself. Resistant reading can sustain the Gaylaxians' own activism, can become a source of collective identity and mutual support, but precisely because it is a subcultural activity that is denied public visibility, resistant reading cannot change the political agenda, cannot challenge other constructions of gay identity, and cannot have an impact on the ways people outside of the group think about the issues that matter to the Gaylaxians. Slash, or K/S fiction, represents a long-standing tradition in the women's fan-writing community that poses ways of constructing homoerotic fantasies employing the series characters.

Cultural studies' embrace of the model of resistant reading, then, only makes sense in a context that recognizes the centrality of issues of media access and media ownership. Resistant reading is an important survival skill in a hostile atmosphere where most of us can do little to alter social conditions and where many of the important stories that matter to us can't be told on network television. It is, however, no substitute for other forms of media criticism and activism. The Gaylaxians' reception of *Star Trek* points to the importance of linking ethnographic research on resistant readers or subcultural appropriations with a political economy of media ownership and control and with the ideological analysis of program content. If earlier forms of ideological analysis worked from the assumption that texts constructed reading subjects, this new mixture would assume that readers play an active role in defining the texts they consume but: (a) they do so within a social, historical and cultural context that shapes their relative access to different discourses and generic models for making sense of the program materials; (b) they do so in relation to institutional power that may satisfy or defer audience desires; and (c) they do so in regard to texts whose properties may facilitate or resist the readers' interpretive activities. The relationship between readers, institutions, and texts is not fixed but fluid. That relationship changes over time, constantly shifting in relation to the ever-changing balance of power between these competing forces.

PART II

Going Digital

5

"Do You Enjoy Making the Rest of Us Feel Stupid?"

alt.tv.twinpeaks, the Trickster Author, and Viewer Mastery

I had never been online before I came to MIT in 1989. Amy Bruckman, now an important digital researcher, then a new graduate student, was my patient teacher in the ways of the net. I remember complaining when I came back from a month offline that I had more than fifty pieces of email. She smirked and said, "Just wait."

One of the ways I learned about the Internet was trolling the discussion lists for my favorite programs. I was living away from my wife and son that first year and so I had plenty of extra time on my hands. Twin Peaks *was my current fan obsession, and so alt.tv.twinpeaks became the place I went to goof off when I wasn't writing* Textual Poachers *or preparing lecture notes. Since I never planned on writing anything about this community, my notes didn't include contact information for the participants, and it proved impossible after the fact to figure out who said what. For that reason, the names of fans are not identified in this essay.*

At the time, I had not seen any other attempts to do media ethnography via the Internet. I kept thinking about the few dozen letters that Ien Ang drew upon for her book on the television show Dallas *and then comparing them with the dozens of postings an hour I was getting off this list.[1] It is telling that the editor asked me to write some general explanation of Usenet and discussion lists since he feared that many readers would not know what I was talking about. He was right, of course, as I discovered when I presented this paper at the Society for Cinema Studies to a somewhat incredulous audience. Unfortunately, by the time the essay appeared, thanks to the usual delays in academic publishing, the Internet was a household word and there was an explosion of writing about online communities. C'est la vie.*

The focus on male fans and hackers here is also symptomatic of this early moment when researchers, companies, and military bases still dominated the Internet and when there was great concern about whether women would feel comfortable participating in such online discussions. In the end, fandom played an important role in providing a supporting group of friends to help with technical problems and to motivate continued engagement.

Again, my intellectual interests were pushing ahead of my theoretical vocabulary. I now see alt.tv.twinpeaks as an early example of what Pierre Levy would describe as a knowledge community or a collective intelligence, ideas that are developed more fully in "Interactive Audiences" later in this collection.

"Do You Enjoy Making the Rest of Us Feel Stupid?" originally appeared in David Lavery, ed., Full of Secrets: Critical Approaches to Twin Peaks *(Detroit: Wayne State University Press, 1995).*

Many Hackers are expert lock-pickers and carry their "picks" around with them on their key chains. Their pleasure is in "beating the lock." They break, they enter and then they leave. They are not after material goods, but after the thrill of the triumph. . . . A closed system is a challenge. A safe is there to be cracked. A mystery is there to be solved.

—Sherry Turkle, *The Second Self*

Break the code, solve the crime. We've only got four days left.

—Contributor, alt.tv.twinpeaks

Usenet (the User's Network) is an electronic bulletin board shared among computer systems around the world. It is a macro-system that links and coordinates feed from a number of pre-existing communications networks, including UUCP, CSNET, BITENET, and ARPANET. The net system was established to facilitate collaboration between researchers and the exchange of information about the advantages and "bugs" of new technologies. The system has evolved into a great deal more, though its primary users continue to be located at universities, technologically oriented companies, and research organizations. The system now reaches over fifty thousand participants at over two thousand sites in the United States, Canada, Europe, Australia, Japan, and Korea.

Science fiction writers like Orson Scott Card, William Gibson, and Norman Spinrad, among many others, have speculated about the possibilities of a time when government, commerce, and culture are all conducted on "the net" and when most citizens will have access to the system.[2] That day is not yet here. The net system, however, does facilitate discussion of these and many other topics between its scattered (if still highly specialized) users. The system enables subscribers to exchange private electronic mail or to participate in public discussions. The network is organized hierarchically, privileging technologically and scientifically oriented discussion but allowing lower priority space for exchanges centering on current events, hobbies, and cultural interests. A number of the net groups center around popular media texts (ranging from *Tiny Tunes* to *Dr. Demento,* from WWF Wrestling to Nintendo) and genres (science fiction, soap opera, British television, etc.).

Participants in these groups sometimes exchange digitized sounds or computer graphs, but most often they participate in ongoing public debates. Entries may range from a few sentences to ten or more single-spaced pages. Many participants post daily entries (or I should say nightly entries, since a great deal of posting occurs in the evening or early morning hours). Many spend a sizable percentage of their recreational time (and probably a good deal of company time as well) interacting on the net.

A number of the television-oriented groups maintain a volume of a hundred or more postings a day, offering an incredibly rich resource for audience research. We might, for example, contrast this embarrassment of riches with the forty-two letters that form the corpus of Ien Ang's analysis of Dutch viewers of *Dallas.* The problem working with the net becomes not how to attract sufficient responses to allow for adequate analysis but how to select and process materials from the endless flow of information and commentary. What's so exciting is that the net discussions tend to center on those issues that are of the most interest to media researchers: commentary and criticism not only of the specific characters and episodes, but even of specific moments within the aired episodes; attempts to develop aesthetic criteria for the evaluation of television and other popular texts; speculations about media authorship; critiques of ideology; and self-analysis of the netters' own involvement with the broadcast materials. Ethnographic research has often been criticized for its construction of the very audience it seeks to examine, via the organization and structuring of focus groups, rather than engaging with the activity of pre-existing cultural communities as they conduct their daily lives (the focus of more traditional forms of ethnography). Here, the computer net groups allow us to observe a self-defined and ongoing interpretive community as it conducts its normal practices of forming, evaluating, and debating interpretations. These discussions occur without direct control or intervention by the researcher, yet in a form that is legitimately open to public scrutiny and analysis.

The interactive nature of computer net discussion makes it possible to trace the process by which television meanings are socially produced, circulated, and revised. Within moments after an episode is aired, the first posts begin to appear, offering evaluations and identifying issues that will often form the basis for debate and interpretation across the following week. Because this process is ongoing, rather than part of focused and localized interview sessions, computer net discourse allows the researcher to pinpoint specific moments in the shifting meanings generated by unfolding broadcast texts, to locate episodes that generated intense response or that became particularly pivotal in the fans' interpretations of the series as a whole.

Yet we must recognize the social specificity of computer net discourse. I am suspicious of making too easy a move from the particularity of audience response in a concrete context (particularly the highly developed, highly visible response of a fan community) to the sweeping generalizations about semiotic democracy or popular resistance that are the stock and trade of American cultural studies. Examining the nets can tell us a lot about how a particular group of people make sense of television and integrate it into their everyday social interactions; studying the nets cannot by itself provide us with a very good model for a general theory of television spectatorship. Net responses reflect the particular cultural interests and interpretative strategies of their users, who tend to be college-educated, professionally oriented, technologically inclined men, most of whom are involved either with the academy or the computer industry.[3]

This paper will provide a concrete case study suggesting the potential relevance and social specificity of computer net discourse to our ongoing attempts to document and analyze popular reception of television texts. Specifically, I will focus on commentary circulated by one discussion group, alt.tv.twinpeaks, during the fall of 1990, the second season of David Lynch's *Twin Peaks.* I will outline some of the group's reading practices and interpretative strategies (their fixation on resolving narrative enigmas, their development of multiple alternative restagings of the core plotline, their complex relationship to Lynch as author, their appeal to extratextual discourse and intertextual linkages) as well as their perceptions of themselves as sophisticated television viewers and of the series as standing outside the mainstream of American television.[4]

Alt.tv.twinpeaks emerged within just a few weeks of the series' first aired episode and quickly became one of the most active and prolific groups on the system. (One estimate suggests that some twenty-five thousand readers subscribed to alt.tv.twinpeaks, though the vast majority remained "lurkers" who did not actively contribute to the discussion.) The discussion group served many functions for the reception community. One fan provided a detailed sequence of all of the narrative events (both those explicitly related and those implied by textual references) and updated it following each new episode. Another built a library of digitized sounds from the series, while a third generated a collection of favorite quotes that could be used as signature lines at the bottom of postings. Excerpts of cryptic dialogue were reprinted and deciphered. Fans provided reports from local newspapers or summaries of interviews with program stars and directors on local television stations, helping to pool information not yet nationally available. Others compiled lists of the stars' previous appearances, reviews of Lynch's other films (especially *Wild at Heart,* which appeared in the gap between *Twin Peaks'* first and second season), accounts of Lynch's involvement with Julee Cruise's musical career, reactions to Mark Frost's ill-fated *American Chronicles,* assessment of Sherilyn Fenn's *Playboy* pictorial, and an assortment of other events loosely related to the series. Pacific Northwest fans detailed the local geography and culture and fed the group reports about the commercialization of the region where the series was filmed. The net became the vehicle for the exchange of videotapes as well. Fans who missed episodes scrambled to find other local fans who would make them copies; many fans sought to translate PAL tape copies of the European release (with its alternative ending) into American Beta and VHS formats. When ABC put the series on hiatus, the net provided a rallying point for national fan efforts to organize public support for the endangered show. The net circulated addresses and telephone and fax numbers for the network executives and concerned advertisers and ran reports on efforts in different communities to raise fan support. Some fans even wrote their own *Twin Peaks* scripts to form fodder for group discussion during the long weeks between episodes. When the series' return was announced, the net was full of news about celebration parties and further speculations about its likely chances in the ratings. The group, however, spent much of its time in detailed analysis of the series.

As one fan remarked just a few weeks into the series' second season, "Can you imagine *Twin Peaks* coming out before VCRs or without the net? It would have been Hell!" Lynch's cryptic and idiosyncratic series seemed to invite the close scrutiny and intense speculation enabled by the fans' access to these technological resources. Another explained, "Video-recording has made it possible to treat film like a manuscript, to be pored over and deciphered." If we extend this suggestive metaphor, the computer net allowed a scriptural culture to evolve around the circulation and interpretation of that manuscript. In many ways the perfect text for this computer-based culture, *Twin Peaks* combined the syntagmatic complexity of a mystery with the paradigmatic plenitude of the soap. The space between episodes gave ample time for audience speculations while the core narrative moved forward at breakneck pace, continually opening up new enigmas while closing down others, a practice that reached its peak during the first season finale where one fan identified no less than twenty-five different cliff-hangers introduced within a single hour. As one post suggested, "This [*Twin Peaks*] isn't *Murder She Wrote* or Nancy Drew where you get all the clues and have to piece them together before the detective does. It's more like peeling an onion, with new and exciting possibilities etched on each succeeding layer." Characters seemed to undergo dramatic transformations between episodes, to shift from good to evil with only the most minimal warning. The narrative abounded with cryptic messages, codes, and chess problems, riddles and conundrums, dreams, visions, clues, secret passages and locked boxes, shadowy figures peering through dark windows and secondary narratives appearing in the televised soap (*Invitation to Love*) that forms a backdrop to the first season's action. All of these details invited the viewer's participation as a minimal condition for comprehending the narrative and even closer consideration if one had any hopes of solving the compelling narrative hook, "Who killed Laura Palmer?" (or WKLP, as netters started to call it).

The program's coming attractions, with their split second shots and mismatched sounds, mandated the use of the VCR as an analytic tool, required that the image be frozen, frame-advanced, and watched several times. The coming attractions became yet another puzzle that could be eagerly controlled by Lynch's ever-dwindling number of hardcore fans.[5] One fan described his experience of deciphering one such image:

> Looking at the scene I see someone who appears to be wearing an orange shirt. Whoever it was was getting out of a big car, a Cad or a Continental, when he/she is surrounded by squad cars. So, I looked to see who was wearing orange, but could not find anyone. The closest person was Donna . . . Did anyone notice this? Was anyone able to pick out who it might be?

Twin Peaks won the computer netters' admiration for its complexity, its density, its technical precision and virtuosity, its consistency and yet its ability to continually pose problems for interpretation. The group's aesthetic criteria mirror those Sherry Turkle sees as characteristic of Hacker culture. Turkle argues that such criteria reflect the Hacker's close engagement with computer technology and programming but shape their response to a broader range of cultural and social experiences. Turkle notes, for example, the group's preference for the technical precision of Bach over the emotionalism of Beethoven, the complex discursiveness of Escher over the blurry impressionism of Monet, the invented and controlled worlds of science fiction over the social ambiguities of realist fiction. Hackers, Turkle argues, seek texts that pose technical rather than emotional problems, that require decipherment and debugging but may eventually be mastered and brought under cognitive control (196–238). As one fan explained, "I don't care who killed Laura Palmer. I just love the puzzle."

Not surprisingly, these technically oriented viewers embrace the VCR, like the computer, almost as an extension of their own cognitive apparatus. . . . The net discussion was full of passionate narratives describing viewers' slow movement through particular sequences, describing surprising or incongruous shifts in the images. Some fans speculated that Lynch, himself, may have embedded within some single frame a telling clue, planted there just to be located by VCR users intent on solving the mystery: "I was hoping that maybe for a frame or two they'd superimpose someone else's head over BOB's but no such luck." One fan reported, "I finally had a chance to slow-mo through Ronette's dream, and wow! Lots of interesting stuff I'm amazed nobody's mentioned yet! . . . Reviewing this changed my thinking completely. I think BOB is not Laura's killer at all, but was her lover and grieved her death." Others soon joined in the speculation. Does BOB seem, just for an instant, to take on some of the features of, say, Deputy Andy, as one fan asserted? Is he beating Laura or giving her emergency assistance, as two fans debated? What did you make of that shadow that appears for only a split second on the window behind his head, one fan asked? That door frame didn't look very much like the ones we've seen in other shots of the train car, another asserted, but rather more like the doors at the Great Northern. The viewers looked for continuity errors in the text (such as Laura's heart necklace that appears on a metal chain and sometimes on a leather thong, or the recurrent shots of the moon whose cycle does not correspond to the narrative time of the story) or for the aesthetic conventions of this idiosyncratic work (such as the stop lights that mark a stasis in the narrative and the green lights that signal forward movement, at least according to some fan-critics). More often, they were looking for clues that might shed light on the central narrative enigmas.

Fans might protest, as they often did, that those who focused only on the Palmer murder were missing the point of the series. Yet the net discussion consistently centered on the search for answers to narrative questions. The volume intensified each time it appeared that the series was about to unveil one of its many secrets. Not sure what to highlight for discussion, the net lost steam following the resolution of the Palmer murder and only regained momentum as the Windom Earle plot began to unfold. . . . The complexity of Lynch's text justified the viewers' assumption that no matter how closely they looked, whatever they found there was not only intentional but part of the narrative master plan, pertinent or even vital to understanding textual secrets.

The computer net only intensified this process, allowing fans to compare notes, elaborate and refine theories through collaboration with other contributors. All of the participants saw the group as involved in a communal enterprise. Entries often began with "Did anyone else see . . . " or "Am I the only one who thought . . . ," suggesting a need to confirm one's own interpretations through conversation with a larger community of readers, or often, "I can't believe I'm the first one to comment on this," implying that their own knowledge must already be the common property of the group as well as staking out a claim for their own superior knowledge of the shared narrative. Several contributors vowed that "we can solve this if we all put our minds to it," invoking a kind of collective problem-solving quite common in technical fields. . . .

Many of the net contributors watched the series alone, concerned that those who were not initiated within the *Twin Peaks* fan community would not remain appropriately silent, and would disrupt their initial experience of the episode with foolish questions or inane chatter. However, as soon as the episode was completed, they would log onto the net to discuss the events with those already fully initiated into the game, those who shared their passion for breaking the code. Watching the program required their full and uninterrupted attention, but the broadcast was not complete until they had a chance to discuss it with others. One computer net participant described how his participation within the virtual community on the net influenced his face-to-face interactions with local fans:

> I looked forward to the discussions on the net in the coming week, even though I rarely, if ever, participated in them. Often, I would print up the most interesting ones and give them to my friend who had no net access. When we met on the nights when *Twin Peaks* wasn't on, we would often discuss ideas proposed on the net.

Sometimes, those who encountered the net discussion second-hand would log onto their friends' accounts and post suggestions to alt.tv.twinpeaks, further broadening the community's intellectual resources.

Theories about possible murderers emerged with astounding density and even more remarkable diversity within this reception context. In a world where almost everything can count as a clue, including both material explicitly presented within the aired episodes and information from one of the many ancillary texts surrounding the series (interviews, the European release print, the published Laura Palmer diary, the Cooper tapes and autobiography, the Julee Cruise album and music videos, etc.), almost any character could become a prime suspect. There were strong constituencies behind Leland Palmer and Ben Horne, characters *Twin Peaks* seemed to foreground as likely candidates. Others were convinced that Madeline and Laura had switched places and that, as a result, Laura was actually still alive. Another was certain that Josie or the mysterious Asian Man (then believed to be her henchman) was the killer (if only because the series' otherwise unmotivated opening shot—focusing on Josie's enigmatic face—must have some significance.)

More ambitious critics developed elaborate explanations for why the killer was Sheriff Truman, Deputy Andy, Donna, Ronette Pulaski, or Doc Hayward, going well beyond possibilities explicitly raised on the program. . . .

The formulation of such theories is the logical response to a mystery, part of the typical reception of any whodunit, yet rarely has the consumption of a mystery been conducted in such a public fashion. The technology of the net allows what might previously have been private meditations to become the basis for social interaction. Each case made against a possible suspect represented a different formulation of *Twin Peaks'* metatext, a different emplotment of its events, that necessarily changed the meaning of the whole and foregrounded some moments at the expense of others. A world where Laura Palmer is murdered by the kindly doctor who delivered her into the world is a very different place than one where she is murdered by the Horne brothers in their efforts to protect their drug trade or where Laura kills her cousin and assumes her identity. Different theories were grounded in different assumptions about the nature of evil and the trustworthiness of authority. No one was sure how black Lynch's narrative would become. What these competing theories meant was the continued circulation and elaboration of multiple narratives, each of which could be sustained by the aired information, each of which posed a different way of making sense of the series. Each new revelation on the air produced new challenges for some theories while seeming to add ammunition to others. Each clue was re-read multiple times to provide support for each of the metatextual narratives that assumed lives of their own apart from Lynch's text. These theories often proved so compelling to their advocates that even after the program revealed that Leland had been possessed by BOB, fans continued to speculate that BOB might have multiple hosts he floated between, including, of course, their favorite suspect.

Soon the elaboration of these theories became so complicated that only a few could play the game, while others watched with a mixture of fascination and irritation. Such a mixed reaction is suggested by one contributor:

Tell me! Tell me! How many times are people watching *TP?* Do you take notes on every subject as you are watching? Or, when a question comes up you drag out each of the episodes, grab a yellow pad, some popcorn and start watching? Do you have a photographic memory? . . . Do you enjoy making the rest of us feel stupid? Does anyone share my frustration?

Within the informational economy of the net, knowledge equals pres-tige, reputation, power. Knowledge gains currency through its circula-tion on the net, and so there is a compulsion to be the first to circu-late new information and to be among the first to possess it. Net eti-quette requires the posting of "spoiler warnings" before contributions that contain information that might give away forthcoming plot devel-opments or "spoil" the pleasure for viewers who have not yet seen the most recent episode, allowing viewers to make a rational choice be-tween their desire for mastery over the program universe and the imme-diacy of a first viewing. As the mystery drew to a close on *Twin Peaks*, some hardcore net fans began to produce their own speculations about the likely outcomes with "Possible Spoiler Warning," or in one case, "Probable Spoiler Warning," granting only slightly less authority to their musings than to the actual aired material. Such postings point to the extraordinary degree of investment some fans made in their predic-tions, the certainty with which they promoted particular interpretations of the characters and their motives.

Elsewhere, I have examined the metatextual speculations character-istic of the female media fan community, focusing specifically on the process by which fans comprehend and move beyond the many texts of *Star Trek*.[6] On one level, the activities of the two fan communities parallel each other: both engage in repeated rereading of a common narrative, as well as group discussion, as a means of building upon narrative excesses and resolving gaps and contradictions; both groups draw not only on the material explicitly presented but also on ancillary texts, extratextual commentary, and fan speculations as a way of build-ing an increasingly complex map of the program universe and its in-habitants.

On other levels, the two groups' activities are strikingly different. The female *Star Trek* fans focus their interest on the elaboration of par-adigmatic relationships, reading plot actions as shedding light on char-acter psychology and motivations. The largely male fans in the *Twin Peaks* computer group essentially reversed this process, focusing on mo-ments of character interaction as clues that might help to resolve plot questions. The male fans' fascination with solving the mystery justified their intense scrutiny and speculation about father-daughter relations, sexual scandals, psychological and emotional problems, and romantic entanglements. . . .

One can argue that these differences in response merely reflect differences in the generic traditions surrounding the two series, that one reads buddy shows (like *Star Trek*) in terms of their relationships and mysteries (like *Twin Peaks*) in terms of their syntagmatic complexities. In both cases, however, the program is open to alternative readings. If *Twin Peaks* was a mystery, it was also a soap opera and many female fans of the series focused on the bonding between Harry Truman and Dale Cooper as their central interest in the series. Computer net discussions of *Star Trek*, on the other hand, tend to treat the characters as autonomous problem-solvers rather than looking at their interrelationships; Trekkers on the net devote attention to discussions of technical problems and plot holes, rather than on the social and emotional lives of the series protagonists.[7]

Female fans often use the program materials as a basis for gossip, appealing to conceptions of *Star Trek*'s "emotional realism" as a justification for drawing on personal experiences to support their interpretations. Significantly, this strategy was almost entirely absent from computer net discourse.[8] *Twin Peaks* fans hid behind the program, moving through a broad network of texts, but revealing little of themselves in the process. The series gave them something to discuss among themselves that allowed netters to deflect rather than explore personal questions. Rather than focusing on personal revelation, interpretation became the occasion for displaying professional expertise (as in the case of one regular contributor who drew on her psychology background to shed insight into Multiple Personality Disorders and other mental health issues viewed as relevant to the series). The netters pooled their knowledge, shared their mastery, yet held this process at a distance from their emotional lives and personal experiences.

The rules of female fan interpretative practice dictate that explanations must first be sought within the fictional world of the narrative before resorting to explanations based on extratextual knowledge of authorship or the production process. . . . *Twin Peaks'* computer net fans, on the other hand, consistently appealed to knowledge of generic expectations or assumptions about Lynch as author as the primary basis for their speculations about likely plot developments. Lynch's authorial

identity emerged in the net discourse as both that of a wizard programmer who has tapped into the network of previously circulating cultural
materials and jerry-rigged them into a more sophisticated narrative system and that of a trickster who consistently anticipates and undermines
audience expectations. These appeals to authorship justified these fans'
fascination with the soap opera dimensions of the series, providing a
high-culture rationale for their preoccupation with what is, after all,
"only a television program."

   The first conception of Lynch, that of the master programmer, led
series enthusiasts to search for an Ur-text or texts that might provide
the key to decoding his particular narrative: "crack the code and solve
the crime." Lynch's predilection for casting roles with actors already
familiar from other contexts (including heavy use of the casts of *The
Mod Squad, West Side Story,* and from his own stock company from
previous films) and his allusions to other texts (from Romantic poetry
to film noir and popular music) gave credence to the fans' efforts to find
the solution by looking beyond textual boundaries. Some, repeating the
logic of auteurists elsewhere, sought the answers in Lynch's own films,
tracing repeated motifs and character names or playing with the previous associations of cast members. This impulse also led to a close
scrutiny of the Laura Palmer secret diaries, written by Lynch's daughter
(who, as the fans repeatedly reminded each other, was shocked to learn
who had committed the crime).[9] Others ransacked the lyrics and liner
notes of Julee Cruise's album (which had been written and produced by
Lynch and included music used in the series) or *Industrial Symphony
#1,* a music performance tape which included Cruise and a good deal
of the program iconography. Yet others cast a still broader net, pulling
in plots invoked by the series (*Vertigo, Laura, The Third Man, Double
Indemnity,* even *Breathless, The Magic Flute, Heathers,* and *The Search-
ers*). Fans hoped to find the text that contained a key to unraveling
Twin Peaks' many secrets: "Why go to all the trouble of creating the
similarities to [*Vertigo* and *Laura*] if they're not going to use the plot
line???" And sometimes the fans hit pay dirt. For example, one fan's
discovery that Whitley Strieber's *Communion* asserted that owls are
often screen memories for alien encounters allowed the group to predict
the program's introduction of a science fiction subtext and to guess why
"the owls [were] not what they seemed." Another drew on Charles
Dickens's *The Mystery of Edwin Drood* to determine that the mysterious Japanese gentleman bidding on Ghostwood Estates was Catherine

Martell in disguise, a plot twist they recognized weeks before her masquerade was uncovered on the show.

Such remarkable predictions of otherwise unlikely developments led to periodic speculations that Lynch monitored the nets and shaped the program in response to fan debates: "Back in Lit. class we talked about how Dickens wrote his books in installments and sometimes wound up changing his original plan because of the feed-back he to got. . . . I wonder how much we are writing our own show?" There was for a brief time a hoax on the net; someone submitted entries claiming to be David Lynch. Later, "Lynch" stopped posting because of his "unjust suspicions" of other netters who demanded that he somehow prove his identity.[10]

The conception of Lynch as a trickster played an equally powerful role in the fans' speculations. As soon as the netters came to accept a previously outlandish line of speculation that solution began to seem too obvious, too clichéd to be the real answer, and the search for alternatives began again: "It seemed too obvious to be true. Lynch is one devious guy." "There are not clichés here. You will *not* get what you expect." "If David Lynch doesn't fuck with reality in his shows, who will?" "Wouldn't it be just like Lynch to hint at the solution to the mystery in last night's episode, then have the police decide not to follow up on it?" Lynch's perversity and unpredictability were constantly appealed to as a means of justifying the fans' equally outrageous speculations about lesser suspects: "Since nice well-balanced people are not a hallmark of David Lynch, Donna must be into something incredibly sleazy." The myth of the trickster author allowed the fans to keep alive the case that the whole series might be Cooper's dream as he confronts his failure to prevent the murders in Pittsburgh or that Sheriff Truman might really be the mastermind behind the region's drug traffic. "With Lynch, I don't think you can rule out any possibilities." As one fan explained, evoking an analogy between Lynch and an equally tricky writer, Edgar Allan Poe:

> Poe and Lynch both mock the kind of rationality that assumes that one air-tight explanation will account for all details . . . Look for someone we Really have not suspected at all, Could not suspect at all, Look for dozens of questions to remain unanswered, for the series to end with hundreds of plot threads, dangling into a TV vacuum. . . .

The fans' pleasure lay simultaneously in their mastery over the text (their ability to successfully predict the next turn of its convoluted plot) and their vulnerability to Lynch's trickery (their inability to guess what is likely to happen next). Matching wits against Lynch became the ideal test of their own intellectual rigor and creative impulses, a chance to demonstrate their knowledge and mastery at a task that refused to yield easily to their probings. While most critics were pushing the producers the resolve the Palmer murder before they lost all of their viewers, the computer net fans only wanted to see the enigmas expand, wanted to forestall closure in order to prolong their pleasure in playing with puzzles. One fan posted a joke that perfectly captured their pleasurable agony over the deferral of narrative resolution: "A robber walks into a bank and says to the teller, 'Give me all your money or I'll tell you who killed Laura Palmer.'" Another described the experience in more personal terms:

> I love what Lynch is doing to me as a viewer. It's a kind of a wonderful masochism. Part of me wishes the answer could never be revealed . . . I am so hoping that when what is really going on in *Twin Peaks* is fully and completely revealed, perhaps at the end of one more season after this, that it will be so shocking and unexpected that it will turn our faces white as a sheet and then the series will end.

While many critics complained that the series had become so complex as to be incomprehensible, the computer net fans feared it was becoming too simple and predictable, selling out to the lowest common denominator, betraying the promise it offered as the ultimate problem set. Many of them gained a special prestige from their ability to understand this program that proved incoherent and unapproachable to many of their friends and family members. The fans wanted its complexities to proliferate so they could spend more hours trying to work through the problems it posed.

> It will be a sad sight indeed if WKLP is neatly tied up and put to rest on November 10. If the WKLP mystery could continually be held out like a carrot on a stick, a tantalizing temptation, so close but yet so far away, for the entire season I think I would go insane. But it would be a good kind of insanity. An insanity I could curl up with and keep for my own

and revel in as a companion to my weirdness. May WKLP remain an eternal mystery, I gotta have some fun you know.

Many hoped that the Laura Palmer mystery was simply the beginning of what promised to be an ever more complicated narrative, one that could expand outward in many different directions: "We have only just seen the tip of a very large iceberg . . . I suspect we may be witnessing the creation of a masterpiece of filmmaking." No matter how incoherent the series might seem to average television viewers, the fans remained convinced that it all made sense on some higher level, not yet fully recognizable, that would be more profound than any one had previously suspected. . . .

What these fans admired about Lynch was that he remained true to what they perceived as his "vision": that he kept the problem complex despite pressure to simplify it for mass consumption, and that he did so at the expense not only of commercial success, but in the face of increased critical attacks. One fan proclaimed with a kind of suicidal glee, "Quite clearly, *Twin Peaks* is about to explode in a fiery ball of weirdness." What they feared most was that Lynch might be simply improvising the scripts as he went along, that there was no master plan within which all the bits of data could be reassembled, that there was no answer to the puzzle that they were all brainstorming to solve:

> Am I the only one experiencing a crisis of faith? I waken in the middle of the night in a cold sweat imagining a world in which no one knows who killed Laura Palmer. I imagine Lynch and Frost just making it up as they go along, snickering about attempts to identify the killer when none exists. I see them ultimately making an arbitrary choice of culprits, a totally unsatisfying conclusion to the mystery. Are we being treated to an excruciatingly slow fuck destined to end in a whimper of an orgasm? Don't get me wrong. I'm not complaining, there are worse things in life. . . .

Others acknowledged that, given the intensity of their interest, the plot's resolution could only be a letdown:

> After so much build up, so much analysis, so much waiting and so many false clues, how can any answer totally satisfy the anticipation that has

built up. If WKLP is firmly resolved on the 11/10 episode we will all be in for a huge let down. Even those who guessed right will only celebrate and gloat briefly and then be left empty inside.

Disappointment seemed inevitable. If Lynch did not betray them, then the medium of TV would. As one fan warned at then end of the first season: "The series is destined to lose most of its edge-of-reality feeling, if for no other reason than it has to keep going, speaking from a little box and protecting its market share. TV consumes all." Underlying their celebration of the program was a profound skepticism about American popular culture and a contempt for most of television.

> The primary qualification for a network programming position is the ability and willingness to ultimately force any show into a standard-form, three-lines-or-less mold, regardless of how well it really fits there. The sorts of things that *Twin Peaks* has—a non-trivial plot that requires multiple episodes to resolve; clues, events presented that such that their significance might take a few minutes, a few hours, or even a few days to sink in, instead of being tube fed to the audience point by agonizing point; characters that are complex and interesting and don't always segregate well into "good guys" and "bad guys"' high quality, non-mundane production values, the attitude that a single show can be quirky and bizarre and obscure and funny and dramatic and horrifying and satirical and exciting and thought-provoking and more, all at once . . . —these possibilities are utterly alien to the folks in "TV-Land" (due perhaps to the belief that such things would be over the heads of the short attention spans, limited mental capacities, and defective comprehensional abilities that they assume their viewers possess).

For these viewers, what made the program so exceptional was the demand *Twin Peaks* made upon the spectator, the justification its narrative complexity offered for their own preferred activities. "What other show would motivate that level of criticism? Yes, it failed to meet your expectations, but would you have expected so much from *Three's Company?*" The fact that the program was more difficult to follow than most network series simply made their mastery over its material that much more impressive. One fan described what it took to become a fan of the series:

I think you have to like things that challenge the mainstream; you have to like wandering down a twisted path without concern for the fact that there might be a quicker and more direct way. You have to be a bit of a movie/TV buff to appreciate some of the subtle, inside jokes. It also helps increase enjoyment being able to exchange dialogue and ideas with you folks here on the net.

If *Twin Peaks* was an exceptional television series, then they were an exceptional audience who possessed all the cultural competencies necessary to fully appreciate its greatness: "*TP* is not a passive work, like all too much of television and film; it is an active process of participation—almost like a sport . . . All is never absolutely clear in *TP* and I for one hope that it remains that way . . . What's the interest in a program (or in a world) where everything is known and certain?"[11]

Paradoxically, the more authority fans ascribed to the author, the more suspicious they become of that authority. So much was riding on their conception of Lynch's masterfulness that their anxiety intensified as the series unfolded. If Lynch as author justified their fannish activity, rationalized the time and attention devoted to his text, what would happen if the text was meaningless—or rather, if they all found meaningful originated within the reception community rather than the author? For some, the revelation of a supernatural or science fiction dimension in the series made their previous efforts futile and destroyed the pleasure of the game. For others, however, these new twists were embraced as opening the text to even more baffling enigmas, creating a cosmic labyrinth where WKLP was simply the opening to a maze that led toward the Black and White Lodges. . . .

The netters hoped that *Twin Peaks* would be "full of secrets": that it would provide fodder for their speculations for years to come. For these fans, the computer had become an integral part of their experience of the series and the many fan metatexts that circulated on alt.tv .twinpeaks were as compelling as the aired episodes themselves. The computer provided a way of linking their own, admittedly obsessive, fixation upon *Twin Peaks*' enigmas to a broader social community of others who shared similar fascinations and frustrations. Participating in this virtual community became a way of increasing the intensity and density of those speculations, of building up other fans' explorations and expanding upon their theories. Both the mode and content of this television talk originated not only within the complexities of Lynch's texts but also within the traditions and interests of computer culture. Lynch's *Twin Peaks* might have been able to exist in a world without VCRs and the net; ABC's preferred text certainly could. But the fans' could not. For that reason, alt.tv.twinpeaks has survived the hoopla about the series, has survived for several years beyond its cancellation. The international circulation of the series helped sustain the group's activities, with American fans acting as expert guides and bemused witnesses to the viewers of the series in Europe, Australia, and Asia (via the international linkages the net provides). The group watched with renewed interest the release of *Fire Walk with Me,* the Lynch feature film that gave new nuances to their previous accounts of Laura Palmer's life and death. The group's output has dwindled, down to thirty or forty postings a week, compared to the one hundred to two hundred entries a day at its peak, but it still reflects the ongoing efforts of the interpretive community to master a series that they feel uniquely realized the potentials of network television and fully exploited the potentials of computer communication.

6

Interactive Audiences?
The "Collective Intelligence" of Media Fans

If "Star Trek Rerun, Reread, Rewritten" represented my first public airing of the ideas in Textual Poachers, *"Interactive Audiences" was my first attempt to lay out the reconceptualization of fandom that would shape* Convergence Culture. *The goal I set for myself with "Interactive Audiences" was to write about fans without once mentioning Michel de Certeau. We should change our theory every five thousand miles just like we change oil in our cars. New injections improve performance and keep us from clogging up the system. I am frustrated that despite a growing number of younger scholars writing about fans, many still operate primarily in relation to the paradigms from the late 1980s and early 1990s. There are so many other potential ways of looking at the topic.*

When my friend Christopher Weaver handed me a copy of Pierre Levy's Collective Intelligence, *I realized that this approach addressed many of the questions I had trouble talking about in* Textual Poachers —*specifically the social dimensions of fan communities. Levy gave us a way of thinking about fandom not in terms of resistance but as a prototype or dress rehearsal for the way culture might operate in the future. Levy describes his vision of "collective intelligence" as an "achievable utopia"—not something that grows inevitably from the new configuration of technologies but rather something we must work toward and fight to achieve. Fandom is one of those spaces where people are learning how to live and collaborate within a knowledge community. We are trying out through play patterns of interaction that will soon penetrate every other aspect of our lives. Levy, in short, gives us a model for a fan-based politics.*

"Interactive Audiences?" first appeared in Dan Harries, ed., The New Media Book *(London: British Film Institute, 2002). Some dimensions of*

the convergence culture argument emerged in two other essays, "The Stormtroopers and the Poachers: Cultural Convergence in a Digital Age," in Phillipe Le Guern, ed., Les cultes médiatiques: culture fan et oeuvres cultes *(Rennes, France: Presses universitaires de Rennes, 2002), and "Quentin Tarantino's Star Wars? Digital Cinema, Media Convergence and Participatory Culture," in David Thorburn and Henry Jenkins, eds.,* Rethinking Media Change: The Aesthetics of Transition *(Cambridge, MA: MIT Press, 2003). (I should acknowledge that there are significant terminological shifts and rethinking between these three essays.)*

"You've got three seconds. Impress me."

An advertisement for Applebox Productions depicts the new youth consumer: his scraggly dishwater blonde hair hangs down into his glaring eyes, his chin is thrust out, his mouth is turned down into a challenging sneer, and his finger posed over the remote. One false move and he'll zap us. He's young, male, and in control. No longer a couch potato, he determines what, when, and how he watches media. He is a media consumer, perhaps even a media fan, but he is also a media producer, distributor, publicist, and critic. He's the poster child for the new interactive audience.

The advertisement takes for granted what cultural studies researchers struggled to establish throughout the 1980s and 1990s—that audiences were active, critically aware, and discriminating. Yet, this advertisement promises that Applebox Productions has developed new ways to overcome his resistance and bring advertising messages to this scowling teen's attention. The interactive audience is not autonomous; it still operates alongside powerful media industries.

If the current media environment makes visible the once invisible work of media spectatorship, it is wrong to assume that we are somehow being liberated through improved media technologies. Rather than talking about interactive technologies, we should document the interactions that occur among media consumers, between media consumers and media texts, and between media consumers and media producers. The new participatory culture is taking shape at the intersection between three trends:

   1. New tools and technologies enable consumers to archive, annotate, appropriate, and recirculate media content;

2. a range of subcultures promote Do-It-Yourself (DIY) media production, a discourse that shapes how consumers have deployed those technologies; and

3. economic trends favoring the horizontally integrated media conglomerates encourage the flow of images, ideas, and narratives across multiple media channels and demand more active modes of spectatorship.

In this essay, I will try to describe how these three trends have altered the way media consumers relate to each other, to media texts, and to media producers. In doing so, I hope to move beyond the either-or logic of traditional audience research—refusing to see media consumers as either totally autonomous from or totally vulnerable to the culture industries. It would be naive to assume that powerful conglomerates will not protect their own interests as they enter this new media marketplace, but at the same time, audiences are gaining greater power and autonomy as they enter into the new knowledge culture. The interactive audience is more than a marketing concept and less than "semiotic democracy."

Collective Intelligence

In *Collective Intelligence,* Pierre Levy offers a compelling vision of the new "knowledge space," or what he calls "the cosmopedia," that might emerge as citizens more fully realize the potentials of the new media environment. Rejecting technological or economic determinism, Levy sees contemporary society as caught in a transitional moment, the outcome of which is still unknown, but which has enormous potentials for transforming existing structures of knowledge and power. His book might best be read as a form of critical utopianism framing a vision for the future ("an achievable utopia"), offering an ethical yardstick for contemporary developments. Levy explores how the "deterritorialization" of knowledge, brought about by the ability of the net and the Web to facilitate rapid many-to-many communication, might enable broader participation in decision-making, new modes of citizenship and community, and the reciprocal exchange of information. Levy draws a productive distinction between organic social groups (families, clans, tribes), organized social groups (nations, institutions, religions, and corporations), and self-organized groups (such as the virtual communities of the Web). He links the emergence of the new knowledge space to the breakdown of geographic constraints on communication, of the declining loyalty of individuals to organized groups, and of the diminished power of nation-states to command the exclusive loyalty of their citizens. The new knowledge communities will be voluntary, temporary, and tactical affiliations, defined through common intellectual enterprises and emotional investments. Members may shift from one community to another as their interests and needs change, and they may belong to more than one community at the same time. Yet, they are held together through the mutual production and reciprocal exchange of knowledge. As Levy explains,

> the members of a thinking community search, inscribe, connect, consult, explore. . . . Not only does the cosmopedia make available to the collective intellect all of the pertinent knowledge available to it at a given moment, but it also serves as a site of collective discussion, negotiation, and development. . . . Unanswered questions will create tension within cosmopedic space, indicating regions where invention and innovation are required.[1]

Online fan communities might well be some of the most fully realized versions of Levy's cosmopedia, expansive self-organizing groups focused around the collective production, debate, and circulation of meanings, interpretations, and fantasies in response to various artifacts of contemporary popular culture. Fan communities have long defined their memberships through affinities rather than localities. Fandoms were virtual communities, "imagined" and "imagining" communities, long before the introduction of networked computers.[2] The history of science fiction fandom might illustrate how knowledge communities emerged. Hugo Gernsbeck, the pulp magazine editor who has been credited with helping to define science fiction as a distinctive genre in the 1920s and 1930s, was also a major advocate of radio as a participatory medium. Gernsbeck saw science fiction as a means of fostering popular awareness of contemporary scientific breakthroughs at a moment of accelerating technological development.[3] The letter column of Gernsbeck's *Astounding Stories* became a forum where laypeople could debate scientific theories and assess new technologies. Using the published addresses, early science fiction fans formed an informal postal network,

circulating letters and amateur publications. Later, conventions facilitated the face-to-face contact between fans from across the country and
around the world. Many of the most significant science fiction writers
emerged from fandom. Given this history, every reader was understood
to be a potential writer, and many fans aspired to break into professional publication; fan ideas influenced commercially distributed works
at a time when science fiction was still understood predominantly as a
micro-genre aimed at a small but passionate niche market. The fan-
issued Hugo Award (named after Gernsbeck) remains the most valued
recognition a science fiction writer can receive. This reciprocity among
readers, writers, and editors set expectations as science fiction spread
into film and television. *Star Trek* fans were, from the start, an activist
audience, lobbying to keep its series on the air and later advocating specific changes in the program content to better reflect its own agendas.
Yet, if fans were the primary readers for literary science fiction, they
were only a small fraction of the audience for network television. Fans
became, in John Tulloch's words, a "powerless elite," unable to alter the
series content but actively reshaping the reception context through
grassroots media production.[4] *Star Trek* fandom, in turn, was a model
for other fan communities to create forums for debating interpretations,
networks for circulating creative works, and channels for lobbying the
producers.

Fans were early adopters of digital technologies. Within the scientific
and military institutions where the Internet was first introduced, science
fiction has long been a literature of choice.[5] Consequently, the slang and
social practices employed on the early bulletin boards were often directly modeled on science fiction fandom. Mailing lists that focused on
fan topics took their place alongside discussions of technological or scientific issues. In many ways, cyberspace is fandom writ large.

The reconstitution of these fandoms as digital enclaves did not come
without strenuous efforts to overcome the often overtly hostile reception fan women received from the early Internet's predominantly male
population. Operating outside of those technical institutions, many female fans lacked computer access and technical literacy. Heated debates
erupted at conventions as fans were angered at being left behind when
old fan friends moved online. At the same time, as Sue Clerc notes, fan
communities helped many women make the transition to cyberspace;
the group insured that valued members learned to use the new technologies, since "for them, there is little benefit to net access unless many of

their friends have it."[6] Fan women routed around male hostility, developing Web communities "that combine the intimacy of small groups with a support network similar to the kind fan women create off-line." Discussion lists, mailing groups, Web rings, and chatrooms each enabled fan communication.

Nancy Baym has discussed the important functions of talk within online soap fandom: "Fans share knowledge of the show's history, in part, because the genre demands it. Any soap has broadcast more material than any single fan can remember."[7] Fans inform each other about program history or recent developments they may have missed. The fan community pools its knowledge because no single fan can know everything necessary to fully appreciate the series. Levy distinguishes between shared knowledge (which would refer to information known by all members of a community) and collective intelligence (which describes knowledge available to all members of a community). Collective intelligence expands a community's productive capacity because it frees individual members from the limitations of their memory and enables the group to act upon a broader range of expertise. As Levy writes, within a knowledge community, "no one knows everything, everyone knows something, all knowledge resides in humanity."[8] Baym argues:

> A large group of fans can do what even the most committed single fan cannot: accumulate, retain, and continually recirculate unprecedented amounts of relevant information. . . . [Net list] participants collaboratively provide all with the resources to get more story from the material, enhancing many members' soap readings and pleasures.[9]

Soap talk, Baym notes, allows people to "show off for one another" their various competencies while making individual expertise more broadly available. Fans are motivated by epistemaphilia—not simply a pleasure in knowing but a pleasure in exchanging knowledge. Baym argues that fans see the exchange of speculations and evaluations of soaps as a means of "comparing, refining, and negotiating understandings of their socioemotional environment."[10] Matthew Hills has criticized audience researchers for their preoccupation with fans' meaning production at the expense of consideration of their affective investments and emotional alliances.[11] Yet, as Baym's term "socioemotional" suggests, meanings are not some abstracted form of knowledge, separated from our pleasures and desires, isolated from fandom's social bonds.

When fans talk about meaningful encounters with texts, they are describing what they feel as much as what they think. . . . Fan speculations may, on the surface, seem to be simply a deciphering of the aired material, but increasingly speculation involves fans in the production of new fantasies, broadening the field of meanings that circulate around the primary text. . . .

Levy contrasts his ideal of "collective intelligence" with the dystopian image of the "hive mind," where individual voices are suppressed. Far from demanding conformity, the new knowledge culture is enlivened by multiple ways of knowing. This collective exchange of knowledge cannot be fully contained by previous sources of power—"bureaucratic hierarchies (based on static forms of writing), media monarchies (surfing the television and media systems), and international economic networks (based on the telephone and real-time technologies"—that depended on maintaining tight control over the flow of information. The dynamic, collective, and reciprocal nature of these exchanges undermines traditional forms of expertise and destabilizes attempts to establish a scriptural economy in which some meanings are more valuable than others.[12]

The old commodity space was defined through various forms of decontextualization, including the alienation of labor, the uprooting of images from larger cultural traditions so that they can circulate as commodities, the demographic fragmentation of the audience, the disciplining of knowledge, and the disconnect between media producers and consumers. The new information space involves multiple and unstable forms of recontextualization. The value of any bit of information increases through social interaction. Commodities are a limited good and their exchange necessarily creates or enacts inequalities. But meaning is a shared and constantly renewable resource and its circulation can create and revitalize social ties. If old forms of expertise operated through isolated disciplines, the new collective intelligence is a patchwork woven together from many sources as members pool what they know, creating something much more powerful than the sum of its parts.

How Computers Changed Fandom

For Levy, the introduction of high-speed networked computing constituted an epistemological turning point in the development of collective intelligence. If fandom was already a knowledge culture well before the Internet, then how did transplanting its practices into the digital environment alter the fan community? The new digital environment increases the speed of fan communication, resulting in what Matthew Hills calls "just in time fandom."[13] If fans once traded ideas through the mails, they now see the postal service as too slow—"snail mail" —to satisfy their expectations of immediate response. Hills explains, "The practices of fandom have become increasingly enmeshed with the rhythms and temporalities of broadcasting, so that fans now go online to discuss new episodes immediately after the episode's transmission time or even during ad-breaks perhaps in order to demonstrate the 'timeliness' and responsiveness of their devotion."[14] Where fans might have raced to the phone to talk to a close friend, they can now access a much broader range of perspectives by going online.

This expectation of timeliness complicates the global expansion of the fan community, with time lags in the distribution of cultural goods across national markets hampering full participation from fans that will receive the same program months or even years later. International fans often complain that they are additionally disadvantaged because their first-time experience of the episodes is spoiled by learning too much from the online discussions.

The digital media also alters the scope of communication. Fandoms centering on Asian popular culture, such as Japanese anime or Hong Kong action films, powerfully exploit the Internet's global reach. Japanese fans collaborate with American consumers to insure the underground circulation of these cultural products and to explain cultural references, genre traditions, and production histories.[15] Anime fans regularly translate and post the schedule of Japanese television so that international fans can identify and negotiate access to interesting programs. American fans have learned Japanese, often teaching each other outside of a formal educational context, in order to participate in grassroots projects to subtitle anime films or to translate manga (comics). Concerned about different national expectations regarding what kinds of animation are appropriate for children, anime fans have organized their own ratings groups. This is a new cosmopolitanism—knowledge sharing on a global scale.

As the community enlarges and reaction time shortens, fandom becomes much more effective as a platform for consumer activism. Fans can quickly mobilize grassroots efforts to save programs or protest unpopular developments. New fandoms emerge rapidly on the Web—in some cases before media products actually reach the market. As early participants spread news about emergent fandoms, supporters quickly develop the infrastructure for supporting critical dialogue, producing annotated program guides, providing regular production updates, and creating original fan stories and artwork. The result has been an enormous proliferation of fan Web sites and discussion lists. . . . As fandom diversifies, it moves from cult status toward the cultural mainstream, with more Internet users engaged in some form of fan activity.

This increased visibility and cultural centrality has been a mixed blessing for a community used to speaking from the margins. The speed and frequency of communication may intensify the social bonds within the fan community. In the past, fans inhabited a "week-end only world," seeing each other in large numbers only a few times a year at conventions.[16] Now, fans may interact daily, if not hourly, online. Geographically isolated fans can feel much more connected to the fan community and home-ridden fans enjoy a new level of acceptance. Yet, fandom's expanded scope can leave fans feeling alienated from the expanding numbers of strangers entering their community. This rapid expansion outraces any effort to socialize new members. For example, fandom has long maintained an ethical norm against producing erotica about real people rather than fictional characters. As newer fans have discovered fan fiction online, they have not always known or accepted this prohibition, and so there is a growing body of fan erotica dealing with celebrities. Such stories become a dividing point between older fans committed to traditional norms and the newer online fans who have asserted their rights to redefine fandom on their own terms.

Online fan discussion lists often bring together groups who functioned more or less autonomously offline and have radically different responses to the aired material. Flame wars erupt as their taken-for-granted interpretive and evaluative norms rub against each other. In some cases, fans can negotiate these conflicts by pulling to a metalevel and exploring the basis for the different interpretations. More often, the groups splinter into narrower interests, pushing some participants from public debates into smaller and more private mailing lists.

Levy describes a pedagogical process through which a knowledge community develops a set of ethical standards and articulates mutual goals. Even on a scale much smaller than Levy's global village, fandoms often have difficulty arriving at such a consensus. While early accounts of fandom stressed its communitarian ideals, more recent studies have stressed recurring conflicts. Andre MacDonald has described fandom in terms of various disputes—between male and female fans, between fans with different assumptions about the desired degree of closeness of the producers and stars, between fans who seek to police the production of certain fantasies and fans who assert their freedom from such constraints, between different generations of fans, and so forth.[17] MacDonald depicts a community whose utopian aspirations are constantly being tested against unequal experiences, levels of expertise, access to performers and community resources, control over community institutions, and degrees of investment in fan traditions and norms. Moreover, as Nancy Baym suggests, the desire to avoid such conflicts can result in an artificial consensus that shuts down the desired play with alternative meanings.[18] Levy seemingly assumes a perfect balance between mechanisms for producing knowledge and for sustaining affiliations. Yet, MacDonald and Baym suggest a constant tension between these two goals, which can reach a crisis as list memberships have expanded alongside the exponential growth of net subscribers. . . .

Networked computing has also transformed fan production. Web publication of fan fiction, for example, has almost entirely displaced printed zines. Fanzines arose as the most efficient means of circulating fan writing.[19] Fan editors charged only the costs of reproduction, seeing zines as a vehicle for distributing stories and not as a source of income. In some fandoms, circuits developed for loaning individually photocopied stories. In other cases, readers and editors came to see zines as aesthetic artifacts, insisting on high-quality reproduction and glossy color covers. Fans have increasingly turned to the Web to lower the costs of production and to expand their reading public. Fans are also developing archives of older zine stories, helping to connect newer fans with their history. . . .

Digital technologies have also enabled new forms of fan cultural production. Photoshop collage has become popular as a means of illustrating fan fiction, and now digital art may go to auction at cons (conventions) alongside illustrations done in pen and ink, colored pencil, or oil. For a time, mp3s of fan-generated music (filk) could be readily downloaded alongside commercial favorites through Napster. . . . Fan artists have been part of the much larger history of amateur film and video production. George Lucas and Steven Spielberg were themselves amateur filmmakers as teenagers, producing low-budget horror or science fiction movies. *Star Wars,* in turn, has inspired Super 8 film-makers since its release in the early 1970s. Some British fan clubs produced original episodes of *Doctor Who,* sometimes filming in the same gravel quarries as the original series. As the videocassette recorder became more widely available, fans re-edited series footage into music videos, using popular music to encapsulate the often-unarticulated emotions of favorite characters.[20] As fan video makers have become more sophisticated, some fan artists have produced whole new storylines by patching together original dialogue.

The World Wide Web is a powerful distribution channel, giving what were once home movies a surprising degree of public visibility. Publicity materials surface while these amateur films are still in production, most of the films boast lavish movie posters, and many of them include downloadable trailers to attract would-be viewers impatient with download times. *Star Wars* fans were among the first to embrace these new technologies, producing at last count more than three hundred Web movies.[21] These fans exploited the various merchandise surrounding this blockbuster film franchise for raw materials to their homegrown movies. . . . These fan filmmakers have used home computers to duplicate effects Lucasfilm had spent a fortune to achieve several decades earlier; many fan films create their own light saber or space battles. . . .

Knowledge Culture Meets Commodity Culture

Levy distinguishes between four potential sources of power—nomadic mobility, control over territory, ownership over commodities, and mastery over knowledge—and suggests a complex set of interactions and negotiations between them. The emergent knowledge cultures never fully escape the influence of the commodity culture, any more than commodity culture can totally function outside the constraints of territoriality. But knowledge cultures will, he predicts, gradually alter the ways that commodity culture operates. Nowhere is that transition clearer than within the culture industries, where the commodities that circulate become resources for the production of meaning: "The distinctions between authors and readers, producers and spectators, creators and interpretations will blend to form a reading-writing continuum, which will extend from the machine and network designers to the ultimate recipient, each helping to sustain the activities of the others."[22]

Creative activity, he suggests, will shift from the production of texts or the regulation of meanings toward the development of a dynamic environment, "a collective event that implies the recipients, transforms interpreters into actors, enables interpretation to enter the loop with collective action."[23] Room for participation and improvisation are being built into new media franchises. Kurt Lancaster, for example, has examined how commercial works (including computer, role-playing, and card games) surrounding the cult science fiction series *Babylon 5* facilitate a diverse range of fan performances, allowing fans to immerse themselves in the fantasy universe.[24] . . . Cult works were once discovered; now they are being consciously produced, designed to provoke fan interactions. The producers of *Xena: Warrior Princess,* for example, were fully aware that some fans wanted to read Xena and Gabrielle as lesbian lovers and thus began to consciously weave "subtext" into the episodes. As Levy explains, "The recipients of the open work are invited to fill in the blanks, choose among possible meanings, confront the divergences among their interpretations."[25]

To be marketable the new cultural works will have to provoke and reward collective meaning production through elaborate back stories, unresolved enigmas, excess information, and extratextual expansions of the program universe.[26] The past decade has seen a marked increase in the serialization of American television, the emergence of more complex appeals to program history, and the development of more intricate story arcs and cliffhangers. To some degree, these aesthetic shifts can be linked to new reception practices enabled by the home archiving of videos, net discussion lists, and Web program guides. These new technologies provide the information infrastructure necessary to sustain a richer form of television content, while these programs reward the enhanced competencies of fan communities.

Television producers are increasingly knowledgeable about their fan communities, often soliciting their support through networked computing. *Babylon 5* producer J. Michael Straczinski actively courted the science fiction fan community long before his proposed series was approved for production. He cited the fan buzz to demonstrate its market potential, and the fans lobbied local stations to purchase the syndicated series. The series producer, known affectionately by his user name, JMS, went online daily, responding to questions about his complex and richly developed narrative. Kurt Lancaster estimates that JMS may have made more than 1,700 posts to the fan community, sometimes actively engaging in flame wars with individual fans as well as conducting what he saw as a continuing seminar on the production of genre television.[27] While JMS sought to be more accessible to fans, he found it difficult to shed his authority or escape a legal and economic system designed, in part, to protect corporate interests from audience appropriation. His lawyers warned him that he would have to leave the group if there was danger that he would be exposed to fan speculations that might hold him hostage to potential plagiarism suits. Such restrictions reimpose the hierarchy of commodity culture over the informal reciprocality of the knowledge culture.

While JMS is perhaps unique in the degree of his exposure to fans, other producers have shown a similar awareness of online fan discourse. For example, when the WB Network postponed the season finale of *Buffy the Vampire Slayer* in the wake of the Columbine shootings, producer Joss Whedon made a notorious public call for Canadian fans to "bootleg that puppy" and distribute it via the Web to American viewers. Fans, in turn, rallied to Whedon's defense when the religious right launched a letter-writing campaign against the introduction of a lesbian relationship involving series regulars.[28] By contrast, *Survivor* producer Mark Burnett engaged in an active disinformation campaign to thwart audience efforts to predict the winner of its million-dollar competition, burying false leads in the official Web site awaiting discovery by fan hackers. When longtime World Wrestling Federation announcer Jerry Lawler was fired, he brought his side of his disputes with Vince McMahon directly to online fans. Some of these producers sought to deceive, others to inform the fan community, but each showed an awareness of how online discourse reframed the reception context for television programs.

For many media producers, who still operate within the old logic of the commodity culture, fandom represents a potential loss of control over their intellectual property. The efforts of the recording industry to dismantle Napster demonstrated that the traditional media companies were prepared to spend massive sums in legal action against new forms of grassroots distribution. The recording industry explicitly framed the case as a chance to "educate" the public about corporate intellectual property rights and thus avoid future "piracy."[29] Television producers, film studios, and book publishers have been equally aggressive in issuing "cease and desist" letters to fan Web sites that transcribe program dialogue or reproduce unauthorized images. If new media has made visible various forms of fan participation and production, then these legal battles demonstrate the power still vested in media ownership.

The horizontal integration of the entertainment industry—and the emergent logic of synergy—depends on the circulation of intellectual properties across media outlets.[30] Transmedia promotion presumes a more active spectator who can and will follow these media flows. Such marketing strategies promote a sense of affiliation with and immersion in fictional worlds. The media industry exploits these intense feelings through the marketing of ancillary goods, from T-shirts to games, with promises of enabling a deeper level of involvement with the program content. However, attempts to regulate intellectual property undercut the economic logic of media convergence, sending fans contradictory messages about how they are supposed to respond to commercial culture.[31] . . . Often, the conflict boils down to an issue of who is authorized to speak for a series, as when a Fox television executive justified the closing of *Simpsons* fan sites by saying: "We have an official Web site with network approved content and these people don't work for us." It is perhaps symptomatic of this highly charged legal culture that fandom.com, a company created to support fan community activities and thwart "cyberbullying," almost immediately began issuing "cease and desist" letters to other sites that used the term "fandom." Ultimately, fandom.com was forced to back down, but only after it had totally undercut its claims to be "by and for fans."

Levy sees industry panic over interactive audiences as short-sighted: "By preventing the knowledge space from becoming autonomous, they deprive the circuits of commodity space . . . of an extraordinary source of energy." The knowledge culture, he suggests, serves as the "invisible and intangible engine" for the circulation and exchange of commodities.[32] The online book dealer Amazon.com has linked bookselling to the fostering of online book culture. Readers are encouraged to post critical responses to specific works or to compile lists of their favorite books. Their associates program creates a powerful niche marketing system: Amazon patrons are offered royalties for every sale made on the basis of links from their sites. Similarly, the sports network ESPN sponsors a fantasy baseball league, a role-playing activity in which sports fans form teams, trade players, and score points based on the real-world performance of various athletes. Such activities give an incentive for viewers to tune into ESPN for up-to-the-minute statistics.[33]

Attempts to link consumers directly into the production and marketing of media content are variously described as "permission-based marketing," "relationship marketing," or "viral marketing" and are increasingly promoted as the model for how to sell goods, cultural and otherwise, in an interactive environment. Jupiter Communications notes that 57 percent of consumers visit a new site based on word of mouth.[34] As one noted industry guide explains, "Marketing in an interactive world is a collaborative process with the marketer helping the consumer to buy and the consumer helping the marketer to sell."[35] Researchers are finding that fandom and other knowledge communities foster a sense of passionate affiliation or brand loyalty that insures the longevity of particular product lines.[36] In viral marketing, such affiliations be-come self-replicating as marketers create content that consumers want to circulate actively among their friends. Even unauthorized and vaguely subversive appropriations can spread advertising messages, as occurred through Internet spoofs of the Budweiser "whazzup" commercials.

Building brand loyalty requires more than simply coopting grassroots activities back into the commodity culture. Successful media producers are becoming more adept at monitoring and serving audience interests. The games industry, which sees itself as marketing interactive experiences rather than commodities, has been eager to broaden consumer participation and strengthen the sense of affiliation players feel towards their games.[37] LucasArts has integrated would-be *Star Wars* gamers into the design team for the development of their massively multiplayer online game. A Web page was created early in the design process and ideas under consideration were posted for fan feedback. Kurt Squire describes the benefits of this "participatory design" process: "Ordinary users, who are ordinarily left out of the design process, can bring their expertise using products to the conversation, and help ensure more usable products. This ends up saving money for the designers, who can spend less energy in user/customer support. And, of course, this process results in more usable products, which benefits everyone."[38] Game companies often circulate their game engines as shareware, seeking to unleash the creative potential of their consumers. In some cases, fan-designed "mods" or game worlds (such as *Counterstrike*) have been integrated into the commercial releases. Maxis, the company that manages the *Sims* franchise, encourages the grassroots production and trading of "skins" (new character identities), props, and architectural structures, even programming code. *Sims* creator Will Wright refers to his product as a "sandbox" or "doll house," viewing it more as an authoring environment where consumers can play out their own stories than as a "hard-rails" game. Ultimately, Wright predicts, two-thirds of *Sims* content will come from consumers.[39]

It remains to be seen, however, whether these new corporate strategies of collaboration and consultation with the emerging knowledge communities will displace the legal structures of the old commodity culture. How far will media companies be willing to go to remain in charge of their content or to surf the information flow? In an age of broadband delivery, will television producers see fans less as copyright infringers and more as active associates and niche marketers? Will global media moguls collaborate with grassroots communities, such as the anime fans, to insure that their products get visible in the lucrative American market?

From Jammers to Bloggers

In his 1993 essay "Culture Jamming: Hacking, Slashing and Sniping in the Empire of Signs," Mark Dery documented emerging tactics of grassroots resistance ("media hacking, informational warfare, terror-art and guerilla semiotics") to "an ever more intrusive, instrumental technoculture whose operant mode is the manufacture of consent through the manipulation of symbols."[40] In citizens band (CB) radio slang, the term "jamming" refers to efforts to "introduce noises into the signal as it passes from transmitter to receiver." Culture jammers refused to be "passive shoppers" and insisted on their right to insert alternative ideas into the meme-stream. . . .

Dery's essay records an important juncture in the history of DIY media. Over the past several decades, emerging technologies—ranging from the photocopier to the home computer and the video cassette recorder—have granted viewers greater control over media flows, enabled activists to reshape and recirculate media content, lowered the costs of production, and paved the way for new grassroots networks. Recognizing that their revolution would not be televised, the 1960s counterculture created an alternative media culture, using everything from rock to underground newspapers, from poster art to people's radio, to communicate outside the corporately controlled media, and in the process, student leaders proposed theories of participatory culture that would influence subsequent activists. The DIY aesthetic got a second wind in the

1980s as punk rockers, queer activists, and third-wave feminists, among others, embraced photocopied zines, stickers, buttons, and T-shirts as vehicles for cultural and political expression.[41] These groups soon recognized the radical potential of videotape for countersurveillance and embraced the "digital revolution" as an extension of earlier movements toward media democracy.[42]

Many of the groups Dery describes, such as Adbusters, ACT UP, Negativeland, The Barbie Liberation Army, Paper Tiger Television, and the Electronic Disturbance Community, would happily embrace his "culture jammer" banner. Yet, Dery overreached in describing all forms of DIY media as "jamming." These new technologies would support and sustain a range of different cultural and political projects, some overtly oppositional, others more celebratory, yet all reflecting a public desire to participate within, rather than simply consume, media. Culture jammers want to opt out of media consumption and promote a purely negative and reactive conception of popular culture. Fans, on the other hand, see unrealized potentials in popular culture and want to broaden audience participation. Fan culture is dialogic rather than disruptive, affective more than ideological, and collaborative rather than confrontational. Culture jammers want to "jam" the dominant media, while poachers want to appropriate their content, imagining a more democratic, responsive, and diverse style of popular culture. Jammers want to destroy media power, while poachers want a share of it.

"The territory mapped by this essay ends at the edge of the electronic frontier," Derry wrote, expressing optimism about the emerging political and cultural power grassroots media activists might enjoy in a context where media flows are multidirectional.[43] Yet, he also cautions that the media industries will find alternative means of marginalizing and disenfranchising citizen participation. . . . Returning to this same terrain at the end of the decade, it is clear that new media technologies have profoundly altered the relations between media producers and consumers. Both culture jammers and fans have gained greater visibility as they have deployed the Web for community building, intellectual exchange, cultural distribution, and media activism. Some sectors of the media industries have embraced active audiences as an extension of their marketing power, have sought greater feedback from their fans, and have incorporated viewer-generated content into their design processes. Other sectors have sought to contain or silence the emerging knowledge culture. . . . The old rhetoric of opposition and cooptation assumed a world where consumers had little direct power to shape media content and where there were enormous barriers to entry into the marketplace, whereas the new digital environment expands their power to archive, annotate, appropriate, and recirculate media products. . . . Levy describes a world where grassroots communication is not a momentary disruption of the corporate signal but the routine way that the new media system operates: "Until now we have only reappropriated speech in the service of revolutionary movements, crises, cures, exceptional acts of creation. What would a normal, calm, established appropriation of speech be like?"[44]

Perhaps, rather than talking about culture jammers, we might speak of bloggers. The term "blog" is short for "Web log," a new form of personal and subcultural expression involving summarizing and linking to other sites. In some cases, bloggers actively deconstruct pernicious claims or poke fun at other sites; in other cases, they form temporary tactical alliances with other bloggers or with media producers to insure that important messages get more widely circulated. These bloggers have become important grassroots intermediaries—facilitators, not jammers, of the signal flow. Blogging describes a communication process, not an ideological position.

As Levy writes:

The new proletariat will only free itself by uniting, by decategorizing itself, by forming alliances with those whose work is similar to its own (once again, nearly everyone), by bringing to the foreground the activities they have been practicing in shadow, by assuming responsibility —globally, centrally, explicitly—for the production of collective intelligence.[45]

Bloggers take knowledge in their own hands, enabling successful navigation within and between these emerging knowledge cultures. One can see such behavior as cooptation into commodity culture insofar as it sometimes collaborates with corporate interests, but one can also see it as increasing the diversity of media culture, providing opportunities for greater inclusiveness, and making commodity culture more responsive to consumers. In an era marked both by the expanded corporate reach of the commodity culture and the emerging importance of grassroots knowledge cultures, consumer power may now be best exercised by blogging rather than jamming media signals.

7

Pop Cosmopolitanism
Mapping Cultural Flows in an Age of Media Convergence

On the way to the north Georgia mountain cabin where I go many summers to write, I stopped at a grocery store in Clayton and overheard a conversation between the grocery clerk and a customer ahead of me in line. The grocery clerk, a white girl with a broad south-ern accent, was trying to explain why she had a Japanese name on her employee badge and found herself talking about an alternative identity she assumes through "cosplay," the practice of anime fans dressing up like favorite characters. Drawing a blank from her listener, she tried to explain what anime is and found herself referencing children's shows like Pokemon *and* Yu-Gi-Oh! *Again, the adult man looked at her with limited comprehension but gestured toward his son, who was newly at-tuned to the exchange and happy to acknowledge his own interests by pulling* Yu-Gi-Oh! *cards out of his pocket. Finally, the confused man asks, "How in the world did you ever get interested in that?" I might have pointed him toward the issues of* Shojin Jump, *the Japanese comics magazine, which was on sale in a small-town grocery store that didn't manage to carry* Entertainment Weekly, Time, *or* Newsweek. *The father may have been baffled but his son was growing up in a world where Asian media products were readily at hand. When the customer left, I signaled that I was a fellow "otaku," that is, a fan of Japanese media, and she opened up to me about her local club's plans to go to a major anime convention in Atlanta in a few weeks, and about rumors that there might be another anime fan working at the Wendy's down the street. She is what this essay calls a pop cosmopolitan, someone whose embrace of global popular media represents an escape route out of the parochialism of her local community.*

"Pop Cosmopolitanism" was my attempt to situate my work on par-

ticipatory culture and media convergence in a global context. I have spent much of my life focused almost entirely on American popular culture and have been reluctant to write about other people's culture. Then I woke up one morning and realized that globalization had profoundly altered the nature of American popular culture. As I suggest here, to write about American popular culture today demands a global framework.

"*Pop Cosmopolitanism*" *first appeared in Marcelo M. Suarez-Orozco and Desiree Baolian Qin-Hillard, eds.,* Globalization: Culture and Education in the New Millennium *(Berkeley: University of California Press, 2004).*

If there is a global village, it speaks American. It wears jeans, drinks Coke, eats at the golden arches, walks on swooshed shoes, plays electric guitars, recognizes Mickey Mouse, James Dean, E.T., Bart Simpson, R2-D2, and Pamela Anderson.

—Todd Gitlin, *Media Unlimited* (2001)[1]

The twain of East and West have not only met—they've mingled, mated, and produced myriad offspring, inhabitants of one world, without borders or boundaries, but with plenty of style, hype, and attitude. In Beijing, they're wearing Levis and drinking Coke; in New York, they're sipping tea in Anna Sui. While Pizzicato Five is spinning heads in the U.S., Metallica is banging them in Japan.

—Jeff Yang, *Eastern Standard Time* (1997)[2]

Bert and Bin Laden: Rethinking Cultural Imperialism in an Age of Media Convergence

The story made its rounds in the fall of 2001: a Filipino-American high school student created a Photoshop collage of *Sesame Street*'s Bert interacting with terrorist leader Osama Bin Laden as part of a series of "Bert Is Evil" images he posted on his homepage. Others depicted Bert as a Klu Klux Klansman or having sex with Pamela Anderson. In the wake of September 11, a Bangladesh-based publisher scanned the Web for Bin Laden images that could be printed on anti-American signs, posters, and T-shirts. CNN reporters recorded the unlikely image of a mob of angry Pakistanis marching through the streets waving signs depicting Bert and Bin Laden. American public television executives spotted the CNN footage and threatened to take legal action: "The people responsible for this should be ashamed of themselves."[3]

This story illustrates several themes that will be central to my argument: first, it suggests the rapid flow of images across national borders in an age of media convergence, a flow that is facilitated both by commercial strategies (such as the localization and global distribution of *Sesame Street* and CNN) and by grassroots tactics (such as the use of Photoshop to appropriate and manipulate these images and the Web to distribute them). Second, it suggests that those media flows are apt to be multidirectional, creating temporary portals or "contact zones" between geographically dispersed cultures (in this case, Bangladesh and San Francisco). Third, it suggests the unpredictable and contradictory meanings that get ascribed to those images as they are decontextualized and recontextualized at the sites of consumption. Finally, the story suggests the increased centrality of teens and youth to the global circulation of media in an era where a teen's Web site can become the center of an international controversy.

I have spent my career studying American popular culture, adopting an approach based on older notions of national specificity. In recent years, however, it has become increasingly difficult to study what's happening to American popular culture without understanding its global context. I mean this not simply in the predictable sense that American popular culture dominates (and is being shaped for) worldwide markets, but also in the sense that a growing proportion of the popular culture that Americans consume comes from elsewhere, especially Asia. This essay represents a first stab at explaining how and why Asian popular culture is shaping American entertainment.

Our analysis must start with the concept of media convergence. Most industry discourse about convergence begins and ends with what I call the black box fallacy: sooner or later all media is going to be flowing through a single black box in our living rooms and all we have to do is figure out which black box it will be. Media convergence is not an endpoint; rather, it is an ongoing process occurring at various intersections between media technologies, industries, content, and audiences. Thanks to the proliferation of channels and the increasingly ubiquitous nature of computing and telecommunications, we are entering an era where media will be everywhere and we will use all kinds of media in relation to each other. We will develop new skills for managing that information, new structures for transmitting information across channels, new creative genres that exploit the potentials of those emerging information structures, and new modes of education to help students understand their impact on their world. Media convergence is more than simply the digital revolution; it involves the introduction of a much broader array of new media technologies that enable consumers to archive, annotate, transform, and recirculate media content. Media convergence is more than simply a technological shift; it alters the relationship between existing technologies, industries, markets, genres, and audiences. This initial wave of media changes exerts a destabilizing influence, resulting in a series of lurches between exhilaration and panic. Yet, media convergence is also sparking creative innovation in almost every sector of popular culture; our present media environment is marked by a proliferation of differences, by what Grant McCracken calls Plenitude.[4]

In a forthcoming book, I will describe and document the social, cultural, political, legal, and economic ramifications of media convergence.[5] In this essay, I will be focusing on the interplay between two forces:

Corporate convergence—the concentration of media ownership in the hands of a smaller and smaller number of multinational conglomerates who thus have a vested interest in insuring the flow of media content across different platforms and national borders.

Grassroots convergence—the increasingly central roles that digitally empowered consumers play in shaping the production, distribution, and reception of media content.

These two forces—the top-down push of corporate convergence, the bottom-up pull of grassroots convergence—intersect to produce what might be called global convergence, the multidirectional flow of cultural goods around the world. Ulf Hannerz is describing global convergence when he writes: "[World culture] is marked by an organization of diversity rather than by a replication of uniformity. . . . The world has become one network of social relationships and between its different regions there is a flow of meanings as well as of people and goods."[6]

Global convergence is giving rise to a new pop cosmopolitanism.[7] Cosmopolitans embrace cultural difference, seeking to escape the gravitational pull of their local communities in order to enter a broader sphere of cultural experience. The first cosmopolitans thought beyond the borders of their village; the modern cosmopolitans think globally. We tend to apply the term to those who develop a taste for international food, dance, music, art, or literature, in short, those who have achieved distinction through their discriminating tastes for classical or high culture. Here, I will be using the term "pop cosmopolitanism" to refer to the ways that the transcultural flows of popular culture inspires new forms of global consciousness and cultural competency. Much as teens in the developing world use American popular culture to express generational differences or to articulate fantasies of social, political, and cultural transformation, younger Americans distinguishing themselves from their parents' culture through their consumption of Japanese anime and manga, Bollywood films and Bhangra, and Hong Kong action movies. This pop cosmopolitanism may not yet constitute a political consciousness of America's place in the world (and in its worst forms, it may simply amount to a reformation of orientalism), but it opens consumers to alternative cultural perspectives and the possibility of feeling what Matt Hills calls "semiotic solidarity" with others worldwide who share their tastes and interests.[8] . . . Pop cosmopolitanism cannot be reduced to either the technological utopianism embodied by Marshall McLuhan's "global village" (with its promises of media transcending the nation-state and democratizing cultural access) or the ideological anxieties expressed in the concept of media imperialism (with its threat of cultural homogenization and of "the West suppressing the Rest," as Ramaswami Harindranath describes it).[9]

The media imperialism argument blurs the distinction between at least four forms of power: economic (the ability to produce and distribute cultural goods), cultural (the ability to produce and circulate forms and meanings), political (the ability to impose ideologies), and psychological (the ability to shape desire, fantasy, and identity). Within this formulation, Western economic dominance over global entertainment both expresses and extends America's status as a superpower nation; the flow of cultural goods shapes the beliefs and the fantasies of worldwide consumers, reshaping local cultures in accordance with U.S. economic and political interests. The classic media imperialism argument ascribed almost no agency to the receiving culture and saw little reason to investigate actual cultural effects; the flow of goods was sufficient to demonstrate the destruction of cultures.[10] Ethnographers have found that the same media content may be read in radically different ways in different regional or national contexts, with consumers reading it against the backdrop of more familiar genres and through the grid of familiar values. Even within the same context, specific populations (especially the young) may be particularly drawn toward foreign media content, while others may express moral and political outrage. Most will negotiate with this imported culture in ways that reflect the local interests of media consumers rather than the global interests of media producers.

To be sure, there is probably no place on the planet where you can escape the shadow of Mickey Mouse. Entertainment is America's largest category of exports. The Global Disney Audiences Project, for example, deployed an international team of scholars to investigate the worldwide circulation of Disney goods. They found that in eleven of the eighteen countries studied, 100 percent of all respondents had watched a Disney movie, and many of them had bought a broad range of other ancillary products.[11] But, while still strong, the hold of American-produced television series on the global market has slipped in recent years.[12] Local television production has rebounded and domestic content dominates the prime evening viewing hours, with American content used as filler in the late-night or afternoon slots. Hollywood faces increased competition from other film-producing nations, including Japan, India, and China, which are playing ever more visible roles within regional, if not yet fully global markets. Major media companies, such as Bertelsman, Sony, and Universal Vivendi, contract talent worldwide, catering to the tastes of local markets rather than pursuing nationalistic interests; their economic structure encourages them not only to be the intermediaries between different Asian markets but also to bring Asian content into Western countries. Many American children are more familiar with the characters of Pokemon than they are with those from the Brothers Grimm or Hans Christian Anderson, and a growing portion of American youth are dancing to Asian beats. With the rise of broadband communications, foreign media producers will distribute media content directly to American consumers without having to pass through U.S. gatekeepers or rely on multinational distributors. At the same time, grassroots intermediaries will play an increasingly central role in shaping the flow of cultural goods into local markets.

Adopting a position that if you can't beat them, merge with them, the American entertainment industry has become more aggressive in recruiting or collaborating with Asian talent. Sony, Disney, Fox, and Warner Brothers have all opened companies to produce films in Chinese, German, Italian, Japanese, and other languages aimed both at their domestic markets and at global export. American television and film increasingly is remaking successful products from other markets, ranging from *Survivor* and *Big Brother,* which are remakes of successful Dutch series, to *The Ring,* a remake of a Japanese cult horror movie, or *Vanilla Sky,* a remake of a Spanish science fiction film. Many of the cartoons shown on American television are actually made in Asia (increasingly in Korea), often with only limited supervision by Western companies.

These shifts complicate any simple mapping of the relationship between economic, political, and cultural power. We still must struggle with issues of domination and with the gap between media have and have-not nations, but we do so within a much more complicated landscape. . . . The result is not so much a global culture that eradicates local differences but rather a culture that continually produces local differences in order to gain a competitive advantage within the global marketplace. Arjun Appadurai writes, "Electronic mediation and mass migration . . . seem to impel (and sometimes compel) the work of the imagination. Together, they create specific irregularities because both viewers and images are in simultaneous circulation. Neither images nor viewers fit into circuits or audiences that are easily bound within local, national, or regional spaces."[13]

Pokemon *and* Iron Chef: *Strategies of Corporate Convergence*

The flow of Asian goods into Western markets has been shaped through the interaction of three distinctive kinds of economic interests: (1) national or regional media producers who see the global circulation of their products not simply as expanding their revenue stream but also as a source of national pride; (2) multinational conglomerates who no longer define their production or distribution decisions in national terms but seek to identify potentially valuable content and push it into as many markets as possible; and (3) niche distributors who search for distinctive content as a means of attracting upscale consumers and differentiating themselves from those offering things already on the market. For example, in the case of world music, international media companies such as Sony identify international artists and market them aggressively in their local or regional markets. As those artists are brought westward, the companies make a commercial decision whether they think they will open mainstream, in which case they retain distribution rights within the United States, or niche, in which case they subcontract with a boutique label or third-party distributor.[14]

In a compelling analysis of the impact of Japanese transnationalism on popular culture, Koichi Iwabuchi draws a distinction between the circulation of cultural goods that are essentially "odorless," bearing few traces of their cultural origins, and those that are embraced for their culturally distinctive "fragrance."[15] In some cases, mostly where they are targeting niche or cult audiences, these goods are strongly marked as coming from some exotic elsewhere; in other cases, especially where they are targeting the mainstream, their national origins are masked and the content retrofit to American tastes.

As Iwabuchi has documented, Japanese media industries sought ways to open Western markets to their "soft goods," or cultural imports based on the overseas success of their hardware and consumer electronics. Seeking global distribution for locally produced content, Japanese corporations such as Sony, Sumitomo, Itochu, and Matsushita bought into the American entertainment industry. They saw children's media as a sweet spot in Western societies. Much as Hollywood's ability to compete in international markets rests on its ability to recoup most of its production costs from domestic grosses, the success of Japanese-made comics and animation meant that these goods could enjoy competitive prices as they entered into Western markets. . . . In Japan, more than 200 animation programs are aired on television each week and about 1,700 animated films (short or feature length) are produced for theatrical distribution each year. Japanese media producers had created a complex set of tie-ins linking their comics, animated films, and television series to toys, which allows them to capitalize quickly on successful content and bring it to the largest possible audience. They hoped to export this entire apparatus—the programs, the comics, and the toys—to the West. In the domestic market, anime and manga appeal to a broad cross section of the public, but as they targeted the West, Japanese media companies targeted children as the primary consumers of their first imports. As this generation matured, the companies anticipated that they would embrace a broader range of Japanese-made media.

Illustrating the deodorization process, Anne Allison shows how *Mighty Morphin Power Rangers* was stripped of any specific connotations of Asianness and remade for distribution in the West, not simply through redubbing the dialogue, but by recasting the characters with multiracial American actors and reshooting some of the footage in southern California.[16] She contrasts the *Power Rangers*' success with the relative failure of *Sailor Moon,* which made fewer efforts at retooling for American tastes and remained less clearly compatible with American genre conventions. While the success of these exports can be ascribed to their "freshness" and distinctiveness, that difference was understood more in terms of genre innovation than of their Japanese origins. *Pokemon* was more open about its Japanese roots yet still underwent modifications, such as changing dumplings into doughnuts, to make it more accessible to the U.S. market.[17] . . . By contrast, Allison argues American cultural exports typically retain recognizable ties back to the United States, a claim supported by the findings of the Global Disney Audiences Project, which found that the majority of consumers in a worldwide survey saw Disney as distinctly American or Western in its cultural values and orientation.[18]

Allison overlooks, however, the degree to which the national origins of children's programs are being blurred worldwide: children's programs are more apt to be dubbed into local languages even in countries where subtitling is the norm for adult fare, and many forms of localization occur in American children's programming as it enters those markets. *Sesame Street* is an obvious example. Consumers worldwide know *Sesame Street* but they don't recognize Bert or Big Bird because the Muppets are redesigned for local tastes. The American-based Children's Television Workshop works closely with local media companies to generate new content appropriate to local cultures and languages while setting content and technical standards that must be met by any *Sesame Street* franchise.[19] The difference between the remaking of *Mighty Morphin Power Rangers* for the American market and *Sesame Street* for the Japanese market may be less clear-cut than Allison proposes, based on the degree of control the producing country exercises and the degree to which local audiences are aware of the transformations that have occurred. . . .

For an example of how "fragrance" may enhance commercial prospects, consider the cult success of *Iron Chef.* Produced by Fuji International Television, the series entered North America in the mid-1990s through Asian-language television stations, where it developed a cult following among channel-surfing pop cosmopolitans.[20] The Food Network brought the series to an even broader audience. On the one hand, much of its appeal comes from its clever appropriations from Asian martial arts traditions. The Chairman, played by Kaga Takeshi, lives in a castle and rules over an army of "Iron Chefs." American fans express a fascination with the ornate decor and costumes, the pomp and circumstance surrounding the cooking competitions, the mystique of clan loyalties, and the preparation of foods with exotic and unfamiliar ingredients. While the series was dubbed for its Food Network broadcast, the mysterious Chairman speaks Japanese with English subtitles. Opening segments situate the chosen ingredients within Japanese history and culture. At the same time, the show frequently pits Japanese cooks against representatives of other world cuisines, with recurring characters embodying Chinese, French, and Italian traditions. Each week, the rival chefs have to prepare a broad range of dishes based on an assigned ingredient, sometimes distinctly Japanese, sometimes foreign; the cooking battles are often a struggle between chefs committed to a traditional Japanese approach and those who assimilate and transform Western approaches. *Iron Chef* balances two distinctive kinds of audience interests: on the one hand, the high camp surrounding its martial arts theatricality, and on the other, a growing public fascination with international cuisine at a time when once-exotic ingredients are more widely available in Western grocery stores.[21] Confident that they understood its appeal, UPN sought to remake it for an American audience, recasting William Shatner as the illusive Chairman, employing U.S.-based chefs, and displacing its martial arts borrowings with references to professional wrestling. As UPN entertainment division head Tom Noonan explained, "Candidly, this show isn't about wasabi or pudding or sushi. It's about the Iron Chefs that compete against each other in this sort of intense, very theatrical, over-the-top, gladiator-like style."[22] The series was widely seen as a failure to successfully Americanize Asian content. As the *San Jose Mercury* explained, "something's lost during the translation."[23]

At the moment, Japanese style is marketed as a distinctive "fragrance" to niche or cult audiences and "deodorized" for broader publics, but this distinction is starting to break down as American consumers develop a preference for those qualities they associate with Japanese cultural productions. Much of this process of recontextualizing Japanese content, at the moment, is occurring on the grassroots levels.

The "Desi" and the "Otaku": Tactics of Grassroots Convergence

Cosmopolitans and locals, Hannerz notes, have a common interest in preserving cultural differences in the face of pressures toward homogeneity. The locals care little about diversity per se but want to hold onto their own traditions. The cosmopolitans recognize that they will not get the diversity they crave "unless other people are allowed to carve out special niches for their cultures and keep them."[24] Grassroots convergence serves the needs of both cosmopolitans and locals. A global communication network allows members of diasporic communities to maintain strong ties back to their motherlands, insuring access to materials and information important to their cultural traditions and preserving social connections with those they left behind.[25] Cosmopolitans use networked communication to scan the planet in search of diversity and communicate with others of their kind around the world.

This section documents the role of grassroots intermediaries in shaping the flow of Asian cultural goods into Western markets. Specifically, we will consider two kinds of cultural communities: the role of the South Asian diasporic community (the "desi") in preparing the way for Bollywood films and Bhangra music, and the role of Western fans (or the "otaku") in insuring the translation and circulation of Japanese anime and manga. In both cases, grassroots cultural production and distribution demonstrated a demand for Asian content that preceded any systematic attempts to commercially distribute it in the West. Yet, we underestimate the impact of these grassroots intermediaries if we see them as markets or even marketers; they also play a central role in shaping the reception of those media products, emphasizing rather than erasing the marks of their national origin and educating others about the cultural traditions they embody.

The westward flow of Indian media content reflects successive generations of South Asian immigration. Immigrant grocery stores became the initial points of distribution for Hindi videos, which enabled a nostalgic reconnection with the world left behind.[26] Bhangra emerged in the club cultures of Europe and North America, building upon regional traditions from India, but expanded to reflect points of contact with reggae, hip hop, and techno within an increasingly globalized youth culture.[27] As Sunaina Marr Maira writes, "A uniquely Indian American subculture allows second-generation youth to socialize with ethnic peers while reinterpreting Indian musical and dance traditions through the

lens of American popular culture."[28] Cultural shows on college campuses and festivals in local neighborhoods enabled participants to perform and attendees to reaffirm ethnic identities.[29] Combining classic
dance and current club styles, the cultural shows construct India as both
timeless and contemporary, as both a world away and right in one's
own backyard, reflecting the conflicted character of diasporic culture. In
Boston, Los Angeles, and elsewhere around the country, theaters (still
mostly ma-and-pa operations) are opening that exclusively show Hindi-
language films. The United States and Britain now account for 55 percent of international Bollywood ticket sales.[30]

Pop cosmopolitans are increasingly being drawn toward Indian fashion, music, and cinema, surfing the circuits of distribution that enabled
first- and second-generation immigrants to maintain ties within the diaspora. Perhaps they stumbled into an immigrant grocery store in search
of ingredients for a favorite curry and left with a few videos. Perhaps
they caught some Bhangra at a local club. Perhaps an Indian-born
friend invited them to one of the culture shows. Perhaps they happened
onto a Bollywood Web site or flipped across an Indian-language cable
station.

In this context, it is hardly surprising that Indian styles are increasing
appropriated by Western performers, such as Madonna's use of henna
and Indian religious iconography in her "Ray of Light" tour or Baz
Luhrman's imitation of a Bollywood aesthetic in *Moulin Rouge*. These
Western appropriations have further increased American awareness of
the richness and vitality of Indian popular culture, as suggested by the
surprising box office success of Mira Nair's film *Monsoon Wedding*.[31]
Seeking to tap British interest in all things Bollywood, Andrew Lloyd
Webber commissioned *Bombay Dreams*, an original stage musical with
an all-Asian cast and with music by distinguished Bollywood composer
A. R. Rahman.[32] As Webber explained, "There are more people seeing
Bollywood musicals on screens on any given night than there are people
watching plays in the West End."[33] American and British film companies are helping to finance the production of Hindi-language films with
expectations that they will do well not only in Asia but in the West.
Summing up these trends, Indian-American filmmaker Kavita Munjai
claims, "The young generation is flocking to see Hindi blockbusters.
India is the flavour of the day in America now."[34]

As Maira notes, the "desis" display deeply ambivalent feelings toward
Indo-chic, sometimes proud to see their national culture gain greater

visibility, sometimes uncomfortable with the way Western consumers misunderstand or misuse these traditions, and sometimes uncertain whether their own hybrid identities give them any stable position from which to police the authenticity of these new transcultural appropriations.[35] What does it mean that Indo-chic flourishes at a moment when, post September 11, there is also a rise in "Paki-bashing"? Does the decontextualized consumption of cultural goods necessarily lead to a greater understanding between what remain distinct and largely isolated ethnic populations? Does the ability to dance to the Other's music lead to any real appreciation of the Other's social condition or political perspective? Conflicts arise from the fact that the "desi" and the pop cosmopolitans are consuming at cross-purposes: one seeking to make peace with their parent culture, even as they carve out a place for themselves in the new world; the other seeking to escape the constraints of their local culture and tap into the coolness they now associate with other parts of the world.

The pop cosmopolitan walks a thin line between dilettantism and connoisseurship, between orientalistic fantasies and a desire to honestly connect and understand an alien culture, between assertion of mastery and surrender to cultural difference. These same paradoxes and contradictions surface when we turn our attention to American fans of Japanese anime, the "otaku." "Otaku" is a Japanese term used to make fun of fans who have become such obsessive consumers of pop culture that they have lost all touch with the people in their immediate vicinity. American fans have embraced the shameful term, asserting what Matt Hills calls a "semiotic solidarity" with their Japanese counterparts;[36] constructing their identity as "otaku" allows them to signal their distance from American taste and their mastery over foreign content. While a minority of "otaku" are Asian or Asian-American, the majority have no direct ties back to Japan. Sean Leonard, the president of the MIT Anime Society, whose interest stemmed from his initial exposure to Japanese children's programming, is typical of many of his generation:

> I first discovered anime around when I was in 10th grade. I started hearing and watching a little *Sailor Moon,* which aired periodically on USA. What really got me into it, though, was when a Mexican friend of mine lent me the first ten episodes of *Fushigi Yuugi* (The Mysterious Play), fansubbed. It's a really cool shoujo series, and it was totally different, and totally more complex, than anything else I had seen before. I

resolved that I really liked anime and that I would pursue it. Shortly thereafter, I decided to look at anime from an academic perspective: I wanted to figure out its history, its creators, its principles, and all of that stuff.[37]

Initially, anime, like Bollywood videos, entered this country through small distributors who targeted Asian immigrants. Fans would venture into ethnic neighborhoods in search of content; they turned to a handful of Japanese bookstores in New York and San Francisco for manga, which had not yet been translated or distributed in North America.[38] The Web enabled fans to start their own small-scale (and sometimes pirate) operations to help import, translate, and distribute manga and anime. As Leonard explains, "Fansubbing [amateur subtitling] has been critical to the growth of anime fandom in the West. If it weren't for fans showing this stuff to others in the late 70s–early 90s, there would be no interest in intelligent, 'high-brow' Japanese animation like there is today." On college campuses, student organizations build extensive libraries of both legal and pirated materials and host screenings designed to educate the public about anime artists, styles, and genres. The MIT Anime Society, for example, hosts weekly screenings from a library of more than 1,500 films and videos.[39] Since 1994, the club has provided a Web site designed to educate Americans about anime and anime fan culture. Last year, it also launched a newsletter with interviews, commentary, and reviews.

Increasingly, larger commercial interests are capitalizing on this growing "otaku" culture. Disney, for example, has purchased the American rights to the films of Hayao Miyazaki (*Princess Mononoke, Spirited Away*), redubbed them with the voices of American film stars, and insured their distribution across North America. The Cartoon Network features a wide array of anime series as part of its late night "adult swim" programming. ADV Films, the major importer of anime series for the American market, has announced the launch of a twenty-four-hour Anime network.[40] Tokyopop, a San Francisco–based company, will publish four hundred volumes of translated manga for American consumption this year. Shueisha, the Japanese comics publisher, launched a monthly English-language version of its successful weekly *Shonen Jump,* predicting that it would be selling one million copies a month in the American market within the next three years. It is a striking mark of the growing competence and confidence of American manga fans that

Shonen Jump is being published Japanese style—with text designed to be read from back to front and right to left—rather than flipping the pages.[41]

Ethnographers who have studied this subculture disagree about the degree to which otaku seek any actual connection with real-world Japan or simply enter into an imaginary world constructed via anime genres. As Susan Napier writes, "The fact that anime is a Japanese . . . product is certainly important but largely because this signifies that anime is a form of media entertainment outside the mainstream, something 'different.' "[42] Napier suggests that fans are attracted to the strange balance of familiar and alien elements in Japanese animation, which openly appropriates and remakes Western genre conventions. Some anime fans do cultivate a more general knowledge of Japanese culture. They meet at sushi restaurants, and some clubs build partnerships via the Internet with sister organizations in Japan. Members often travel to Japan in search of new material or to experience that fan culture more directly; some study Japanese language in order to participate in various translation projects. As American fans go online and establish direct contact with their Japanese counterparts, it creates an opening for other kinds of conversation. Discussion lists move fluidly from anime- and manga-specific topics to larger considerations of Japanese politics and culture. These different degrees of cultural engagement are consistent with what Hannerz has told us about cosmopolitanism more generally: "[In one kind], the individual picks from other cultures only those pieces which suit himself. . . . In another mode, however, the cosmopolitan does not make invidious distinctions among the particular elements of the alien culture in order to admit some of them into his repertoire and refuse others; he does not negotiate with the other culture but accepts it as a package deal."[43] What cosmopolitanism at its best offers us is an escape from parochialism and isolationism, the beginnings of a global perspective, and the awareness of alternative vantage points.

The Mangaverse *and the Animatrix: Forms of Corporate Hybridity*

American films and television programs become absolutely mainstream as they are introduced into Japan, China, or India. They come with massive marketing campaigns that make it hard for anyone anywhere on the planet to remain unaware that they have Jedi in their midst. Historically, imported media products have been marginalized in the American market. European cinema shows only at art cinema venues; British comedies are packaged for elite public broadcasting audiences, and Asian content gets absorbed into the outer reaches of the cable dial. Foreign media gets introduced on the fringes of an expanded menu of options without touching the mainstream. But at least some Asian media is gaining unprecedented visibility and influence. *Pokemon* and *Yu-Gi-Oh!* are unavoidable aspects of contemporary children's culture. *Crouching Tiger, Hidden Dragon* played at the multiplexes. And Madonna's borrowings from Bhangra made it into the top 40 charts. As these trends continue, major American media companies seek new models of collaboration with international artists. We might describe these developments as corporate hybridity. Hybridity has often been discussed as a strategy of the dispossessed as they struggle to resist or reshape the flow of Western media into their culture.[44] Here, hybridity can be seen as a corporate strategy, one that comes from a position of strength rather than vulnerability or marginality, one that seeks to control rather than contain transcultural consumption.

Christina Klein has examined the distinctly transnational status of *Crouching Tiger, Hidden Dragon*.[45] Its director, Ang Lee, was born in Taiwan but educated in the United States; this was the first film Lee had produced on Chinese soil. Its financing came from a mixture of Japanese- and American-based media conglomerates. The film was produced and co-written by Lee's long-term collaborator, the American James Schamus. The cast included performers drawn from across the Chinese diaspora—Zhang Ziyi (Mainland China), Chang Chen (Taiwan), Chow Yun-Fat (Hong Kong), and Michelle Yeoh (Malaysia). Lee describes *Crouching Tiger* as a "combination platter," stressing its borrowings from multiple cultural traditions. Schamus agrees: "We ended up making an eastern movie for western audiences and in some ways a more western movie for eastern audiences."[46]

We are apt to see more "combination platter" movies as Hollywood assimilates a generation of Hong Kong directors, technicians, and performers it recruited following Chinese reunification. Exploiting political turmoil and economic disarray in Hong Kong, American media companies raided what had emerged as a powerful competitor worldwide. On the surface, this recruitment parallels similar moments in film history when Hollywood sought to buy out competing national cinemas or to imitate styles and genres, which had proven successful in the global marketplace. Yet, it is one thing to absorb Arnold Schwarzenegger or Mel Gibson, another to absorb Jet Li or Chow Yun-Fat. Their marked ethnic and racial differences could not be easily ignored as Hollywood sought to create Western vehicles for these Eastern stars. In some cases, the films tap orientalist fantasies, as when Chow Yun-Fat is cast in *Anna and the King* or Michelle Yeoh appears as a seductive foreign agent in *Tomorrow Never Dies*. In other cases, the films deal explicitly with themes of cultural relocation and assimilation, as in Jackie Chan's *Shanghai Noon* or *Rumble in the Bronx*. Director John Woo has maintained similar themes and styles but relocated them to Western genres and performers (*Face/Off, Mission: Impossible 2*). More recently, however, Woo has drawn on his outsider perspective to revisit key moments in American cultural history, exposing the forgotten role played by Navahos in transmitting messages during World War II in *Windtalkers.*

American media producers are similarly responding to the growing popularity of anime and manga by soliciting Japanese-style content to augment their existing franchises, bringing a distinctly Asian style to bear on characteristically American content. In 2002, for example, Marvel Comics experimented with a new *Mangaverse* title, which reimagined and resituated its stable of superheroes within Japanese genre traditions: Spiderman is a ninja, the members of the Avengers assemble into a massive robot, and the Hulk turns into a giant green monster.[47] Initially conceived as a one-shot novelty, *Mangaverse* proved so successful that Marvel has launched an entire new production line, Tsunami, which will produce manga-style content for the American and global market, mostly working with Asian or Asian-American artists.[48] . . .

The Matrix is perhaps the most successful and visible example of this absorption of Japanese pop culture influences into the American mainstream. The directors, the Wachowski Brothers, hired Japanese manga artists to do the film's storyboards and Hong Kong martial arts choreographer Yuen Wo Ping to stage the action sequences, hoping to produce a live-action counterpart to *Ghost in the Shell* and *Akira*. In anticipation of the release of *The Matrix Reloaded*, Warner Brothers commissioned the Animatrix, a series of short animated prequels created by Yoshiaki Kawajiri, Takeshi Koike, Mahiro Maeda, and a range of other distinguished Asian animators, which could be downloaded from the Web.[49]

These examples of corporate hybridity depend on consumers with the kinds of cultural competencies that could only originate in the context of global convergence, requiring not simply knowledge of Asian popular culture but an understanding of its similarities with and differences from parallel traditions in the West. These products allow pop cosmopolitans to demonstrate their mastery, counting on them to teach other audience members how to decode the works. At the same time, the *Mangaverse* and the Animatrix provide an opening for fans of more mainstream franchises to savor the "fragrance" of Asian popular culture, potentially expanding the market for cultural imports.

Pedagogical Implications

Many current efforts toward multicultural education start from assumptions of ethnic purity or cultural authenticity at odds with the current moment of global convergence. Our classrooms are increasingly internationalized, though ties to mother countries break down over multiple generations. Our students come from mixed racial or ethnic families that owe allegiance to multiple cultural traditions; they may have strong identifications with youth subcultures that cut across national and racial borders; they may engage in patterns of intercultural consumption that heighten their awareness of other traditions and practices. Children's media have been central to current corporate strategies of global convergence, but youth have played central roles as grassroots intermediaries facilitating the flow of Asian popular culture into the American marketplace. As such, they already inhabit a different kind of cultural landscape than their parents' generation, a space betwixt and between different national or ethnic traditions that includes an awareness of Asian perspectives.

Darrell Hamamoto, a professor of Asian-American Studies, told *USA Today* that this trend toward "Asiaphilia" will do little to alter the stereotyping of Asian-Americans: "It's all superficial and there's no depth to it. Beneath this adoration of all things yellow, all things Asian, comes this condescension. In its most benign form, it's patronizing and in its most severe form, it's a killer."[50] He may well be right. There is no guarantee that pop cosmopolitanism will lead to any real understanding between different cultures, since, as Hannerz notes, it often involves the selective appropriation and repurposing of other cultural traditions for one's own interests: "Cosmopolitanism often has a narcissistic streak." Yet, Hannerz also warns against too easy a dismissal of cosmopolitanism as a kind of dilettantism, suggesting that the "surrender" of oneself to a foreign culture enables fresh perceptions upon which a deeper understanding can be built. While the uneven flow of cultural materials across national borders often produces a distorted understanding of national differences, it also represents a first significant step towards global consciousness.

Pop cosmopolitanism is generating its own intelligentsia, its own critics, historians, translators, and educators. These fans and consumers are also producing their own vernacular theories of globalization, their own understandings of the role Asian content plays in American cultural life, their own explanations for why this material is becoming so accessible to them. Educators need to recognize that these patterns of consumption generate a hunger for knowledge, a point of entry into a larger consideration of cultural geography and political economy. What kinds of educational intervention build upon that hunger and push it toward a greater understanding of America's place in the world? What kinds of pedagogical interventions might displace orientalist stereotypes with a more nuanced account of cultural difference and national specificity?

Shigeru Miyagawa's multimedia project *Star Festival* offers one glimpse of what this kind of intervention might look like. *Star Festival* offers a virtual environment in which students can explore and learn more about contemporary Japanese culture and society. Based on Miyagawa's own personal history, the project depicts a Japanese-American professor's return to the city where he was born and his attempts to resolve internal questions about his cultural identity. The Professor has dropped his personal digital assistant (PDA) and the player has recovered it; while searching through the city for its owner, the player learns things about Miyagawa's family history and about the cultural traditions that drew him back to Japan. What emerges is a picture not of a pristine Asian culture cut off from Western life but one that exists in dialogue with American influences. In one key sequence, we visit a shop that constructs papier-mâché figures used in cultural festivals. Alongside more traditional Japanese icons, we see re-creations of Tarzan, Superman, John Wayne, Rambo, and an array of other Western pop culture figures. *Star Festival*'s curricular guide identifies a range of classroom activities that students at varied grade levels can complete as they work their way through the CD-ROM. Some involve learning more about

Japanese cultural traditions, such as origami or fish printing. Others involve learning more about the player's own mixed cultural and racial identities, such as constructing a family tree and documenting one own family's migrations. Miyagawa sees the project as not simply enabling students to learn more about Japan but also to learn more about themselves and to develop a greater respect for the diversity of cultural identities within the current classroom.

Pedagogical interventions need not be that elaborate. Teachers can bring examples of Asian pop cultural materials into their classrooms, drawing on the expertise of students to spark debates about what these materials mean and what kinds of cultural changes they represent. For example, I introduced my MIT students to Sheila Chandra's album *Weaving My Ancestor's Voices*. Chandra, whose mother was Indian and father Irish, has produced a new kind of pop music based on the fusion of elements drawn from classical Indian and Celtic musical traditions. I played some selections from the album for my students, read her liner-note explanation of how she was trying to use music to make sense of her mixed cultural heritage, and asked them what they thought. One Indian-born student with a strong background in classical music objected: "I can't listen to it. It sounds all wrong to me." A second-generation "desi" retorted, "But the music sounds the way we feel. We feel all wrong." This exchange sparked a larger discussion of how these hybrid forms of music express the conflicts and contradictions of inhabiting a diasporic culture. As the conversation expanded to include students who were not from Asia, further differences in perspective emerge. One second-generation "desi" had dismissed Bollywood films as "corny" and "amateur" compared to Hollywood blockbusters, while a pop cosmopolitan celebrated their vibrancy and originality. Suddenly, students were debating who has the right to judge the merits of these films and what criteria should be applied. If carefully supervised to ensure a climate of mutual respect, such classroom discussions can focus attention on the different investments students make in these imported cultural materials depending on their own personal backgrounds and intellectual interests, which in turn paves the way for a larger consideration of the uneven flow of cultural influences across national borders, of the cultural traditions from which these materials originate, of the different factors that promote or threaten diversity worldwide, and of the larger history of exchanges between East and West that might take us from the Silk Road to the World Wide Web. The goal should not be to push aside taste for popular culture in favor of preference for a more authentic folk culture or a more refined high culture, but rather to help students build upon what they have already learned about cultural difference through their engagement with Asian media imports and to develop a more sophisticated understanding of how these materials reflect the current "garage sale" state of global culture.[51]

8

Love Online

"Love Online" was first drafted in a hotel room in Omaha, Nebraska, while I was waiting for my son to get back from one of his first dates with his online girlfriend. (All of this makes sense if you read the essay, I promise.) Every detail I included was carefully cleared with my son, who wanted his story to be told. Each time that the article has been reprinted, I have gone back to him to make sure he is still comfortable with what I say about him. People who have read my work over the past two decades have had a chance to watch my son grow up. Later in this collection, they will have a chance to read "The Monsters Next Door," which was to have been my son's first publication. "Love Online" first appeared in Technology Review *in October 2002.*

When my son Henry was fifteen, we made a trip from Cambridge to Omaha so that he could meet his girlfriend face to face for the first time. Though they met online, this is not the story of a virtual relationship; their feelings were no less real to them than the first love of any other teenager, past or present.

When I was suffering the first pangs of unrequited adolescent longing, there weren't a lot of girls in my immediate vicinity who would risk the stigma involved in going out with me. One summer I met a few girls at a camp for honors students but our relationships withered once we returned to our own schools and neighborhoods. My son, finding slim pickings at school, cast a wider net, seeking kindred spirits wherever they dwelt in a neighborhood as big as cyberspace itself. Online, he had what it took—good communication skills.

He met Sarah in an online discussion group; they talked through private email; after getting to know her a little he finally got the courage to phone her. They dated in chat rooms. They sent each other virtual candy, flowers, and cards downloaded off various Web sites.

They spoke of "going out," even though they sat thousands of miles apart.

Sarah's father often screened her telephone calls and didn't want her to talk with boys. He didn't pay the same degree of attention to what she did online. He quickly ran up against the difference between his expectations of appropriate courtship and the realities of online love. He felt strongly that boys should not talk to his daughter on the telephone or ask her out on dates unless they were personally known to him. Henry had to go through the ritual of meeting him on the telephone and asking his permission to see her before we could make the trip.

Long-distance communication between lovers is hardly new. The exchange of love letters was central to the courtship of my grandparents (who were separated by the First World War) and of my parents (who were separated by my father's service after the Second World War). By the time my wife and I were courting, we handed our love letters back and forth in person and read them aloud to each other. Our courtship was conducted face to face or through late-night telephone conversations. The love letter was a residual form—though we still have a box of yellowing letters we periodically reread with misty-eyed nostalgia.

Sarah and Henry's romantic communications might seem, at first, more transient, bytes passing from computer to computer. Yet, he backlogged all of their chats and surprised Sarah with a printout. In this fashion, he preserved not only the carefully crafted love letters but the process of an evolving relationship. It was as if my wife and I had tape-recorded our first strolls in the park together.

Henry and Sarah would not have met outside the virtual communities the Internet facilitates. But they were both emphatic that purely digital communication could not have sustained their relationship. The first time Sarah confirmed that she shared my son's affections, she spoke her words of love on a chat room without realizing that he had been accidentally disconnected. By the time he was able to get back online, she had left in frustration. Wooing must be difficult if you can't even be sure the other party is there.

The medium's inadequacies are, no doubt, resulting in significant shifts in the vocabulary of love. In cyberspace, there is no room for the ambiguous gestures that characterized another generation's fumbling first courtships. In a multi-user domain, one doesn't type, "Henry smiles. He moves his hand subtly toward her in a gesture that might be averted at the last moment if she seems not to notice or to be shocked."

The language of courtly love emerged under similar circumstances: distant lovers putting into writing what they could not say aloud.

They may have met online but they communicated through every available channel. Their initial exchange of photographs produced enormous anxiety as they struggled to decide what frozen image or images should anchor their more fluid online identities. In choosing, my son attempted to negotiate between what he thought would be desirable to another fifteen year old and what wouldn't alienate her conservative parents.

The photographs were followed by other tangible objects, shipped between Nebraska and Massachusetts. These objects were cherished because they had achieved the physical intimacy still denied the geographically isolated teens. Henry sent her, for example, the imprint of his lips, stained in red wine on stationery. In some cases, they individually staged rituals they could not perform together. Henry preserved a red rose he purchased for himself the day she first agreed to go steady. Even in an age of instant communication, they still sent handwritten notes. These two teens longed for the concrete, for being together in the same space, for things materially passed from person to person.

Barring that, they cherished their weekly telephone calls. Talking on the telephone helped make Sarah real for Henry. When his friends at school challenged his inability to "produce" his girlfriend for inspection and asked how he knew she wasn't a guy, he cited their telephone conversations. Even for these teens, the fluidity of electronic identities posed threats. Once, early in their relationship, Henry jokingly told Sarah that they went to the same school, never imagining that she would believe him. The results were both farcical and tragic as she searched in vain for her mystery date.

After a while, they started to fear that they might break up without ever having seen each other in the flesh, and they didn't want it to end that way. After some pleading, I agreed to accompany Henry on the trip.

Henry and Sarah first "met" in an airport. He almost didn't recognize her since she was so different from the single photograph she had sent. From the start, their interaction was intensely physical. Henry said that what had given him the most pleasure was being able to play with her hair, and Sarah punched him in the arm so many times he was black and blue. Sarah's mother and I watched two slouching teens shuffle through the terminal, learning to walk in rhythm.

As would-be dramatists, they wondered what they should say at that first meeting. Sarah solved the problem by shouting "Sony PlayStation" across the crowded airport. The two of them had a running debate about the relative merits of different game systems. Their first date was to an arcade where Sarah made good her long-standing boasts and beat him at *Street Fighter II* before Henry got his revenge on *NFL GameDay*. Sarah made the state finals in a video-game competition, so it was no surprise this proved central to the time they spent together. Sarah's mother purchased some new games and—ever the chaperone—brought the game system down to the parlor from Sarah's room so they could play together.

If we are going to talk, from Cambridge to Omaha, with people we've never met before, we need something to talk about. For Henry and Sarah, that common culture consisted not only of different games and game systems, but also a shared enthusiasm for professional wrestling. They met on rec.sport.pro-wrestling, brought together by a shared interest in the Undertaker, a star of the World Wrestling Federation. They both were participants in an electronic pro wrestling role-playing game. Henry brought a cardboard sign with him to a televised wrestling event, pushed his way through the crowd, and got on camera so he could send Sarah a broadcast message.

Popular culture also helped to bridge the awkward silences in my exchanges with Sarah's parents. I had wondered what a media scholar from "the People's Republic of Cambridge" would say to two retired Air Force officers from Nebraska. As Sarah's mother and I sat in the arcade, trying to dodge religion and politics, we found common ground discussing *Star Trek,* the original *Saturday Night Live* cast, and of course, *Mutual of Omaha's Wild Kingdom.*

Henry and Sarah broke up sometime after that trip—not because they had met online or because the real-life experience hadn't lived up to their expectations but because they were fifteen, their interests shifted, and they never really overcame her father's opposition. Henry's next relationship was also online—with a girl from Melbourne, Australia, and that experience broadened his perspective on the world, at the price of much sleep as they negotiated time differences. Now twenty-one, he has gone through his normal share of other romantic entanglements, some online, more face to face (with many of the latter conducted, at least in part, online to endure the summer vacation separation).

We've read more than a decade of press coverage about online relationships—much of it written since my son and I made this trip together. Journalists love to talk about the aberrant qualities of virtual sex. Yet, many of us embraced the Internet because it has fit into the most personal and banal spaces of our lives. Focusing on the revolutionary aspects of online courtship blinds us to the continuities in courtship rituals across generations and across media. Indeed, the power of physical artifacts (the imprint of lips on paper, the faded petals of a rose), of photographs, of the voice on the telephone, gain new poignancy in the context of these new relationships. Moreover, focusing on the online aspects of these relationships blinds us to the agility with which teens move back and forth across media. Their daily lives require constant decisions about what to say on the phone, what to write by hand, what to communicate in chat rooms, what to send by email. They juggle multiple identities—the fictional personas of electronic wrestling, the constructed ideals of romantic love, and the realities of real bodies and real emotions.

9

Blog This!

*Since January 2001, I have been writing a monthly column,
"Digital Renaissance," for the print (initially) and then the online edition of* Technology Review. *The columns are short and topical, responding to a range of developments at the intersection between technology
and culture. The core readership for these columns has some affiliation
with MIT or has a strong interest in science and technology. Increasingly I have used the column to rehearse arguments that will later
find their way into my academic writing. I have included a selection of
my favorite of these columns throughout the book. Many more got reworked and incorporated into* Convergence Culture.

*"Blog This," I said, and not unexpectedly, the blogging community
followed that instruction. I simply wasn't prepared for the consequences.
What happened next illustrates the gap that remains between traditional journalism and blogging. As someone who writes journalistically,
I often have no say over the titles and subtitles assigned to my work and
do not see them before the article is posted (or at least I didn't at the
time this column was written). The editor, in this case, made an unfor-
tunate analogy between bloggers surviving following the dot bomb and
cockroaches surviving a nuclear holocaust. The blogging community
quite rightly objected to being compared to cockroaches and didn't see
past that opening to realize that wasn't the perspective the essay itself
took. When I learned of their complaints, I immediately asked my editors to change the text on at least the online edition since I did not want
my name attached to such a slur. But when they changed it, a number
of bloggers wrote back angry that I made them look silly: when people
followed their links to the article it no longer contained the offending
words.*

*"Blog This!" was written at a point just before blogging really gained
national attention, before bloggers overthrew Trent Lott, before they
raised money to send their own reporters to Baghdad, and before they*

took on 60 Minutes *for its fraudulent coverage of George W. Bush's National Guard service. Today, the claim that bloggers might be important grassroots intermediaries seems almost indisputable, whereas at the time I wrote this, many found my assertions far-fetched or overstated. Any skepticism here was a result of having to appease my editor, who felt the public wouldn't really believe that bloggers represented an emerging force in American media culture—though, once again, I got hit by bloggers for not being a true believer in their cause.*

"Blog This!" first appeared in Technology Review *in February 2002.*

A few months ago, I was at the Camden PopTech conference, and the guy sitting next to me was typing incessantly into his wireless laptop, making notes on the speakers, finding relevant links and then hitting the send key—instantly updating his Web site. No sooner did he do so than he would get responses back from readers around the country. He was a blogger.

Bloggers are turning the hunting and gathering, sampling and critiquing the rest of us do online into an extreme sport. We surf the Web; these guys snowboard it. Bloggers are the minutemen of the digital revolution.

"Blog" is short for "Web log." Several years ago, heavy Web surfers began creating logs—compendia of curious information and interesting links they encountered in their travels through cyberspace. Improvements in Web design tools have made it easier for beginners to create their own Web logs and update them as often as they wish—even every five minutes, as this guy was doing. Blogs are thus more dynamic than older-style home pages, more permanent than posts to a net discussion list. They are more private and personal than traditional journalism, more public than diaries.

Blogger.com, one of several sites at the heart of this phenomenon, now lists more than 375,000 registered users, adding 1,300 more each day. Users range broadly—from churches that have found blogging an effective tool for tending to their congregations' spiritual needs, to activists who see blogging as a means of fostering political awareness, to fans who use blogs to interact with other enthusiasts. Most often, bloggers recount everyday experiences, flag interesting stories from online publications, and exchange advice on familiar problems. Their sites go by colorful names like *Objectionable Content,* the *Adventures of the*

Accordion Guy in the 21st Century, or *Eurotrash,* which might leave you thinking that these are simply a bunch of obsessed adolescents with too much time and bandwidth.

Yet something more important may be afoot. At a time when many dot coms have failed, blogging is on the rise. We're in a lull between waves of commercialization in digital media, and bloggers are seizing the moment, potentially increasing cultural diversity and lowering barriers to cultural participation.

What will happen to democracy in the current media environment, where power is concentrated in the hands of a few publishers and networks? Media scholar Robert McChesney warns that the range of voices in policy debates will become constrained. The University of Chicago Law School's Cass Sunstein worries that fragmentation of the Web is apt to result in the loss of the shared values and common culture that democracy requires. As consumers, we experience these dual tensions: turn on the TV and it feels like the same programs are on all the channels; turn to the Web and it's impossible to distinguish the good stuff from the noise. Bloggers respond to both extremes, expanding the range of perspectives and, if they're clever, creating order from the informational chaos.

At the risk of egotism on my part, let's imagine what happens when bloggers get hold of the online version of "Digital Renaissance." Some may post links to the column calling me a pretentious ass. Others, if I am lucky, may feel that I have some interesting insights. My arguments for grassroots media may be taken up by conservative and progressive sites alike but framed differently depending on the bloggers' own ideological agendas. Once this column appears, my authorial control ends and theirs begins. As these words move through various contexts, they assume new associations and face direct challenges, but they also gain broader circulation.

Ultimately, our media future could depend on the kind of uneasy truce that gets brokered between commercial media and these grassroots intermediaries. Imagine a world where there are two kinds of media power: one comes through media concentration, where any message gains authority simply by being broadcast on network television; the other comes through grassroots intermediaries, where a message gains visibility only if it is deemed relevant to a loose network of diverse publics. Broadcasting will place issues on the national agenda and define core values; bloggers will reframe those issues for different publics and ensure that everyone has a chance to be heard.

It may seem strange to imagine the blogging community as a force that will shape the information environment almost as powerfully as corporate media. We learn in the history books about Samuel Morse's invention of the telegraph but not about the thousands of operators who shaped the circulation of messages, about Thomas Paine's *Common Sense* but less about the "committees of correspondence" through which citizens copied and redistributed letters across the colonies, about the publication of Harriet Beecher Stowe's abolitionist blockbuster *Uncle Tom's Cabin* but not about the teenagers who used toy printing presses to publish nationally circulated newsletters debating the pros and cons of slavery. In practice, the evolution of most media has been shaped through the interactions between the distributed power of grassroots participatory media and the concentrated power of corporate/governmental media.

As the digital revolution enters a new phase, one based on diminished expectations and dwindling corporate investment, grassroots intermediaries may have a moment to redefine the public perception of new media and to expand their influence.

So blog this, please.

10

A Safety Net

"A Safety Net" was written a month or so after September 11 and it should be read alongside Re:Constructions, *the Web page that was constructed by members of the MIT comparative media studies community the weekend following the disaster. For a discussion of the creation of this Web site, see "Applied Humanism: The Re:Constructions Project,"* Cinema Journal, *Spring 2004.*

"A Safety Net" first appeared in Technology Review *in December 2001.*

Nineteen sixty-two. In the same year as the Cuban missile crisis, the United States Air Force launched a research collaboration with the Rand Corporation designed to provide a reliable system of communication in the case of an enemy attack on North America. Drawing on research at MIT and elsewhere, Rand engineer Paul Baran proposed a packet-switching network that would enable the rapid rerouting of data throughout a decentralized communications system. Baran's instructions were to ensure "minimum essential communications" and thus guarantee "second strike" capability; he proposed an even more robust system allowing contact among as many as a hundred networked computers. Baran's proposal was an important landmark in the Internet's prehistory.

September 11, 2001. The attacks on the World Trade Center and the Pentagon launched the first American "war" of the digital age, the first military crisis during which a significant portion of the American public had Net access. One might ask, then, how well the Internet functioned as an emergency communications network. In the years since Baran's proposal, the Net has become something larger than what the Rand researchers might have imagined—a vast network linking the civilian population rather than a modest system that ensures data flow between bunkers. "War," for the moment, anyway, means something significantly different as well—a shift from nightmares of nuclear attack to the reality of terrorist actions. And the communications that have turned out to be the most essential in the wake of those actions are not those aimed at coordinating a swift military strike, but rather those that express the loss and fear of the civilian population.

From a purely technical perspective, the system worked better than anyone might have anticipated. While the World Trade Center housed an important relay system for cell phones, and its destruction thus left many New Yorkers without telecommunications, there was no significant national disruption of the computer networks. In the hour following the attacks, many national news Web sites were swamped by a sudden surge in traffic. But within a few hours, they had stripped down their front pages and expanded the number of mirror sites. And the Net itself never faltered. Countless emails—in many cases, final messages—were sent from the World Trade Center when the victims of the attack were unable to reach their loved ones by telephone, and many more were sent by people around the country seeking any kind of information about friends or family who were unaccounted for following the buildings' collapse.

Americans returned to network television in the days following the tragedy, reassured by the familiar voices of the news anchors, overwhelmed by the repeated images of the airplane striking the second tower, engulfed in expressions of nationalism. The networks offered non-stop coverage without commercial interruption for more than ninety hours, the longest single block of news coverage in the history of American broadcasting, and viewership was at a record high. Yet the Net and the Web served personal needs that these more public channels of information could never touch.

In recent years, some have expressed doubt that online communities are real communities with hearts and souls. They surely would not have expected the enormous outpouring of grief and caring that flowed through the Internet in the days following September 11. My colleagues describe how their friends and families began to circulate poetry as part of the process of coping with their feelings of powerlessness and anxiety. Net groups reached out to their members in New York and Washington, DC, or found themselves confronting feelings of enormous loss over the deaths of people they had only met online and never knew face to face. Fan discussion lists organized to donate blood or otherwise support the relief efforts. In my own case, my email to my parents was recirculated to more distant family members or people in their church community.

And in this manner, messages—both profound and trivial—flowed from one enclave to another. Intellectuals sent analyses, churches prayers, militants hate mail, pacifists cries for peace, and companies spam. Netscape demonstrated the reductive click-here menu-driven triviality of commercial interactivity, asking respondents to decide whether they felt sad, shocked, or angry at what had occurred. We may never know how many people received the insightful words of Afghan-American author Tamim Ansary, who warned us that we could not bomb his homeland back to the Stone Age because after decades of occupation it was already there, or the rather distasteful parody of Osama bin Laden set to the verse of Doctor Seuss's *How the Grinch Stole Christmas*. Despite the seeming exhaustiveness of the television newscasts, many used the Web to read foreign coverage and thus gain a better perspective on the United States' position in the world. Many circulated petitions or words of protest or calls to arms, returning to an ideal of grassroots democratic participation that stands in stark contrast to the ideas about military authority and elite decision-making that shaped the original Rand studies.

This was a new kind of national crisis and it demanded a new kind of emergency communications system. What Americans needed was a safety net, not an information superhighway. I think they found it was already there.

PART III

Columbine and Beyond

11

Professor Jenkins Goes to Washington

In his book Anxious Intellects: Academic Professionals, Public Intellectuals, and Enlightenment Values, *John Michael argues that public intellectuals in effect construct the publics they address, often seeing them as embodiments of their personal and professional fantasies.[1] I have spent a lot of time thinking about his argument and have concluded that the opposite is also true: publics construct intellectuals in their own images and to serve their own needs. The scholars who have the greatest impact in the public sphere are those who leave themselves open to diverse appropriations.*

"Professor Jenkins Goes to Washington" began life as an email I wrote to my immediate friends and colleagues describing what I went through when I was called to Washington to testify before the U.S. Senate Commerce Committee about youth and media violence. At the end of the email, I included as an afterthought the suggestion that they should feel free to pass it on to anyone they thought might be interested. No sooner did I hit the send key than responses started to come in—from hundreds of people all over the country, most of them removed in several degrees of separation from anyone I knew. A new wave would come whenever the post made it onto another discussion list. I heard from orthodox rabbis and pagans, members of the National Rifle Association and prisoners at Angola, science fiction writers, rock stars, and academics. By the next day messages were coming from around the world and the story was being picked up by mainstream publications. The message's routing cut across traditional ideological and geographic boundaries, reaching people who would agree with each other about very little else other than that Congress was misguided in its response to popular culture. I only hit the send key once, but many previously unknown allies took it upon themselves to ensure my email's

circulation, just as many others hit the delete key or made a conscious decision not to pass it along.

In the process, my identity was appropriated. While the title of the essay was intended as an in-joke, "Professor Jenkins" began to take on mythic proportions. A little known techno composer sampled my testimony off C-Span and turned it into a song called "Goth Control," transforming through his remixing and reverberation what I described here as a hesitant and faltering speech into one that felt much more resounding. The American Civil Liberties Union used several quotes from the speech on their next desk calendar. Brad King and John Borland devote the better part of a chapter of their history of computer game culture to my testimony, offering the following somewhat unflattering description: "From a distance, catching a glimpse of him across the campus of the Massachusetts Institute of Technology in Boston, Jenkins might be mistaken for a 'grandfather' gamer. He is balding slightly and carries a little extra paunch in the stomach underneath a pair of suspenders. He has a slight shuffle when he walks and has the soft voice and gentle mannerisms of a therapist."[2] Another news story recently labeled me "perhaps the most prominent scholar in the country devoted to examining pastimes often deemed profoundly frivolous."[3] A writer for the hip Web zine Penny Arcade *described Professor Jenkins as "the last line of defense against the hordes of irrational, knee-jerk parents groups and anti-game zealots."[4] I honestly don't know who this "Professor Jenkins" character is—he doesn't even look very much like me— but I play him on television and when he speaks, people listen. I have come to accept this mythology as serving certain political purposes.*

This version of "Professor Jenkins Goes to Washington" appeared in Harper's *in July 1999. A full version of the testimony I entered into the Congressional Record can be found at http://web.mit.edu/comm-forum/ papers/jenkins_ct.html. I used the visibility this piece created to open up dialogue with teachers and educators about how our schools were responding to the aftermath of the Columbine school shootings in Littleton, Colorado. The work that emerged from that dialogue includes "The Politics and Pleasures of Popular Culture: A Study Guide," co-authored with Cynthia Jenkins, which appeared in* Telemedium, *Spring 2003; "Lessons from Littleton: What Congress Doesn't Want to Hear about Youth and Media,"* Independent Schools, *Winter 2000; and "The Uses and Abuses of Popular Culture: Raising Children in the Digital Age,"* The College Board Review, *January 2000. More recently, I wrote a foreword for Geraldine Bloustein's* Girl Making *(Berghahn Books, 2004) describing my experiences going into schools after Columbine and speaking with students about their perceptions of the incident.*

This is the story of how a mild-mannered MIT professor ended up being called before Congress to testify about "selling violence to our children" and what it is like to testify.

Where to start? For the past several months, ever since my book from *Barbie to Mortal Kombat: Gender and Computer Games* appeared, I've been getting calls to talk about video game violence. It isn't a central focus of the book, really. We were trying to start a conversation about gender, about the opening up of the girls' game market, about the place of games in "boy culture," and so forth. But all the media wants to talk about is video game violence. Here is one of the most economically significant sectors of the entertainment industry, the real beachhead in our efforts to build new forms of interactive storytelling as part of popular, rather than avant-garde, culture, but the media only wants to talk about violence.

These stories always follow the same pattern. I talk with an intelligent reporter who gives every sign of getting what the issues are all about. Then, the story comes out and there's a long section discussing one or another of a seemingly endless string of anti–popular culture critics and then a few short comments by me rebutting what they said. A few times, I got more attention but not most. But these calls came at one or two a week all fall and most of spring term.

Then, with the Littleton shootings, they increased dramatically. Suddenly, we are finding ourselves in a national witch-hunt to determine which form of popular culture is to blame for the mass murders, and video games seemed like a better candidate than most. So, I am getting calls back to back from the *Los Angeles Times*, the *New York Times*, the *Christian Science Monitor*, the *Village Voice*, *Time*, etc. I am finding myself denounced in the *Wall Street Journal* op-ed page for being a fuzzy-headed liberal who blames the violence on "social problems" rather than media images.

And then the call came from the U.S. Senate to see if I would be willing to fly to Washington with just a few days' notice to testify before the Senate Commerce Committee hearings. I asked a few basic questions, and each of the answers filled me with greater dread. It turned out that the people testifying were all anti–popular culture types, ranging from Joseph Lieberman to William Bennett, or industry spokesmen. I would be the only media scholar who did not come from the "media effects" tradition, and the only one who was not representing popular culture as a "social problem." My first thought was that this was a total setup, that I had no chance of being heard, that nobody would be sympathetic to what I had to say, and gradually all of this came to my mind as reasons to do it and not reasons to avoid speaking. It felt important to speak out on these issues.

A flashback: When I was in high school, I wore a trench coat (beige, not black), hell, in elementary school I wore a black vampire cape and a medallion around my neck to school. I was picked on mercilessly by the rednecks who went to my school and I spent a lot of time nursing wounds, both emotional and some physical, from an essentially homophobic environment. I was also a sucker for Frank Capra movies—*Mr. Smith Goes to Washington* most of all—and films like *1776* that dealt with people who took risks for what they believed. I had an amazing high school teacher, Betty Leslein, who taught us about our government by bringing in government leaders for us to question (among them Max Cleland, who was then a state legislature and is now a member of the Commerce Committee) and sent us out to government meetings to observe. I was the editor of the school paper and got into fights over press censorship. And I promised myself that when I was an adult, I would do what I could to speak up about the problems of free speech in our schools. Suddenly, this was a chance.

I also had been reading Jon Katz's amazing coverage on the Web of the crackdown in schools across America on free speech and expression in the wake of the shootings. Goth kids harassed for wearing subcultural symbols and pushed into therapy. Kids suspended for writing the wrong ideas in essays or raising them in class discussions. Kids pushed offline by their parents. And I wanted to do something to help get the word out that this was going on.

So, it didn't take me long to say yes.

I was running a major conference the next day and then I would have one day to pull together my written testimony for the Senate. I didn't have much in my own writings I could draw on. I pulled together what I had. I scanned the Web. I sent out a call for some goth friends to tell me what they felt I should say to Congress about their community, and a number of them stayed up late into the night sending me information.

And I pulled an all-nighter to write the damn thing that was really long because I didn't have time to write short. And then, I worked with my colleague, Shari Goldin, to get it proofed, edited, revised, and sent off to Congress. And to make arrangements for a last-minute trip.

When I got there, the situation was even worse than I had imagined. The Senate chamber was decorated with massive posters of video game ads for some of the most violent games on the market. Many of the ad slogans are hyperbolic—and self-parodying—but that nuance was lost on the senators, who read them all dead seriously and with absolute literalness. Most of the others testifying were professional witnesses who had done this kind of thing many times before. They had their staff. They had their props. They had professionally edited videos. They had each other for moral support. I had my wife and son in the back of the room. They are passing out press releases, setting up interviews, being tracked down by the major media, and no one is talking to me. I try to introduce myself to the other witnesses. David Grossman, the military psychologist who thinks video games are training our kids to be killers, won't shake my hand when I wave it in front of him. I am trying to keep my distance from the media-industry types because I don't want to be perceived as an apologist for the industry—even though, given the way this was set up, they were my closest allies in the room. This is set up so you can either be anti–popular culture or pro-industry, and the thought that as citizens we might have legitimate investments in the culture we consume was beyond anyone's comprehension.

The hearings start and one by one the senators speak. There was almost no difference between Republicans and Democrats on this one. They all feel they have to distance themselves from popular culture. They all feel they have to make "reasonable" proposals that edge up toward censorship but never quite cross the constitutional lines. It is political suicide to come out against the dominant position in the room.

One by one, they speak. Hatch, Lieberman, Bennett, the Archbishop from Littleton. . . . Bennett starts to show video clips that removed from context seem especially horrific. The fantasy sequence from *The Basketball Diaries* reduced to 20 seconds of Leonardo DiCaprio blasting away kids. The opening sequence from *Scream* reduced to its most visceral elements. Women in the audience are gasping in horror. The senators cover their faces with mock dread. Bennett starts going on and on about "surely we can agree upon some meaningful distinctions here, between *Casino* and *Saving Private Ryan*, between *The Basketball Diaries* and

192 | *Professor Jenkins Goes to Washington*

Clear and Present Danger . . ." I am just astonished by the sheer absurdity of this claim, which breaks down to a pure ideological distinction that has neither aesthetic credibility nor any relationship to the media effects debate. *The Basketball Diaries* is an important film; *Clear and Present Danger* is a right-wing potboiler! Scorsese is bad but Spielberg is good?

Meanwhile, the senators are making homophobic jokes about whether Marilyn Manson is "a he or a she" that I thought went out in the 1960s. These strike me as precisely the kind of intolerant and taunting comments that these kids must have gotten in school because they dressed differently or acted oddly in comparison with their more conformist classmates.

By this point, we reach the hour when the reporters have to call in their stories if they are going to make the afternoon edition and so they are heading for the door. It's down to the C-Span camerawoman and a few reporters from the game industry trade press.

And then I am called to the witness stand. Now, the chair is something nobody talks about. It is a really, really low chair and it is really puffy so you sit on it and your butt just keeps sinking and suddenly the tabletop is up to your chest. It's like the chairs they make parents sit in when they go to talk to elementary school teachers. The senators on the other hand sit on risers peering down at you from above. And the whole power dynamics is terrifying.

Grossman starts to attack me personally, claiming that a "journalism" professor and a "film critic" has no knowledge of social problems. It takes me a while for the attacks to sink in because they are so far off the mark. I am not a journalism professor and I am not a film critic. I am a media scholar who has spent more than fifteen years studying and writing about popular culture, and I do think I have some expertise at this point on how culture works, how media is consumed, how media panics are started, how symbols relate to real-world events, how violence operates in stories, etc. And that's what I was speaking about.

I am doing OK with all of this. I am surprisingly calm while the other people speak, and then Senator Brownback calls my name, and utter terror rushes through my body. I have never felt such fear. I try to speak and can hardly get the words out. My throat is dry. I reach for a glass of water and my hands are trembling so hard that I spill water all over the nice table. I am trying to read and the words are fuzzing out on the page. Most of them are handwritten anyway by this point because I kept revising and editing until the last minute. And I suddenly can't read my writing. Cold sweat is pouring over me. I have visions of the cowardly lion running down the halls in Oz escaping the great blazing head of the Wizard. But there's no turning back and so I speak and gradually my words gain force and I find my voice and I am debating the Congress about what they are trying to do to our culture. I take on Bennett about his distorted use of *The Basketball Diaries* clip, explaining that he didn't mention this was a film about a poet, someone who struggles between dark urges and creativity, and that the scene was a fantasy intended to express the rage felt by many students in our schools and not something the character does, let alone something the film advocates. I talked about the ways these hearings grew out of the fear adults have of their own children and especially their fear of digital media and technological change. I talked about the fact that youth culture was becoming more visible but its core themes and values had remained pretty constant. I talked about how reductive the media effects paradigm is as a way of understanding consumers' relations to popular culture. I attacked some of the extreme rhetoric being leveled against the goths, especially a line in *Time* from a GOP hack that we needed "goth control," not "gun control." I talked about the stuff that Jon Katz had been reporting about the crackdown on youth culture in schools across the country, and I ended with an ad-libbed line, "Listen to your children, don't fear them." Then, I waited.

Senator Brownback decided to take me on about the goths, having had some staff person find him a surprisingly banal line from an ad for a goth nightclub that urged people to "explore the dark side." And I explained what I knew about goths, their roots in Romanticism and in the Aesthetic movement, their nonviolence, their commitment to acceptance, their strong sense of community, their expression of alienation. I talked about how symbols could be used to express many things and that we needed to understand what these symbols meant to these kids. I spoke about Gilbert and Sullivan's *Patience* as a work that spoke to the current debate, because it spoofed the original goths, the Aesthetics, for their black garb, their mournful posturing, and said that they were actually healthy and well-adjusted folks underneath but they were enjoying playing dark and soulful. The senator tried repeating his question as if he couldn't believe I wasn't shocked by the very concept of giving yourself over to the "dark side." And then he gave up and shuffled me off the stand.

The press swarmed around the anti-violence speakers but didn't seem to want to talk to me. I just wanted to get out of there. I felt no one had heard what I had to say and that I had been a poor messenger because I had stumbled over my words. But several people stopped me in the hallway to thank me. And dozens more have sent me email since having seen it on C-Span or heard it on the radio or seen the transcript on the Web or heard about it from friends. And suddenly I feel better and better about what happened. I spoke out about something that mattered to me in the halls of national power and people out there had heard my message, not all of them certainly, but enough.

I know the fight isn't over—at least I hope it isn't. There will be more chances to speak, but I felt like I had scored some victory just by being there and speaking. Someone wrote me that it was all the more powerful to have one rational voice amid a totally lopsided panel of extremists. People would see this was a witch-hunt of sorts. I'd like to believe that.

The key thing was that I got a statement into the record that was able to say more than I could in five minutes, and people can now read it on the Web.

What follows is the text of my oral remarks, which are rather different from the written statement because I was still doing research and writing on the airplane:

I am Henry Jenkins, Director of the MIT comparative media studies program. I have published six books and more than fifty essays on various aspects of popular culture. My most recent books, *The Children's Culture Reader* and *From Barbie to Mortal Kombat: Gender and Computer Games,* deal centrally with the questions before this committee. I am also the father of a high school senior and the housemaster of an MIT dormitory housing 150 students. I have spent my life talking with kids about their culture and I have come here today to share with you some of what I have learned.

The massacre at Littleton, Colorado, has provoked national soul-searching. We all want answers. But we are only going to find valid answers if we ask the right questions. The key issue isn't what the media are doing to our children but rather what our children are doing with the media. The vocabulary of "media effects," which has long dominated such hearings, has been challenged by numerous American and international scholars as an inadequate and simplistic representation of media consumption and popular culture. Media effects research most often empties media images of their meanings, strips them of their contexts, and denies their consumers any agency over their use.

William Bennett just asked us if we can make meaningful distinctions between different kinds of violent entertainment. Well, I think meaningful distinctions require us to look at images in context, not looking at 20-second clips in isolation. From what Bennett just showed you, you would have no idea that *The Basketball Diaries* was a film about a poet, that it was an autobiographical work about a man who had struggled between dark urges and creative desires, that the book on which it was based was taught in high school literature classes, and that the scene we saw was a fantasy which expressed his frustrations about the school, not something he acts upon and not something the film endorses.

Far from being victims of video games, Eric Harris and Dylan Klebold had a complex relationship to many forms of popular culture. They consumed music, films, comics, video games, television programs. All of us move nomadically across the media landscape, cobbling together a personal mythology of symbols and stories taken from many different places. We invest those appropriated materials with various personal and subcultural meanings. Harris and Klebold were drawn toward dark and brutal images that they invested with their personal demons, their antisocial impulses, their maladjustment, their desires to hurt those who had hurt them.

Shortly after I learned about the shootings, I received email from a sixteen-year-old girl who shared with me her Web site. She had produced an enormous array of poems and short stories drawing on characters from popular culture and had gotten many other kids nationwide to contribute. Though they were written for no class, these stories would have brightened the spirit of writing teachers. She had reached into contemporary youth culture, including many of the same media products that have been cited in the Littleton case, and found there images that emphasized the power of friendship, the importance of community, the wonder of first romance. The mass media didn't make Harris and Klebold violent and destructive and it didn't make this girl creative and sociable but it provided them both with the raw materials necessary to construct their fantasies.

Of course, we should be concerned about the content of our culture and we all learn things from the mass media. But popular culture is only one influence on our children's imaginations. Real life trumps media images every time. We can shut down a video game if it is ugly, hurtful, or displeasing. But many teens are required to return day after day to schools where they are ridiculed and taunted and sometimes physically abused by their classmates. School administrators are slow to respond to their distress and typically can offer few strategies for making the abuse stop. As one Littleton teen explained, "Every time someone slammed them against a locker or threw a bottle at them, they would go back to Eric and Dylan's house and plot a little more."

We need to engage in a rational conversation about the nature of the culture children, consume but not in the current climate of moral panic. I believe this moral panic is pumped up by three factors.

1. Our fears of adolescents. Popular culture has become one of the central battlegrounds through which teens stake out a claim on their own autonomy from their parents. Adolescent symbols from zoot suits to goth amulets define the boundaries between generations. The intentionally cryptic nature of these symbols often means adults invest them with all of our worst fears, including our fear that our children are breaking away from us. But that doesn't mean that these symbols carry all of these same meanings for our children. However spooky-looking they may seem to some adults, goths aren't monsters. They are a peaceful subculture committed to tolerance of diversity and providing a sheltering community for others who have been hurt. It is, however, monstrously inappropriate when GOP strategist Mike Murphy advocates "goth control," not "gun control."

2. Adult fears of new technologies. The *Washington Post* reported that 82 percent of Americans cite the Internet as a potential cause for the shootings. The Internet is no more to blame for the Columbine shootings than the telephone is to blame for the Lindbergh kidnappings. Such statistics suggest adult anxiety about the current rate of technological change. Many adults see computers as necessary tools for educational and professional development. But many also perceive their children's online time as socially isolating. However, for many "outcasts," the online world offers an alternative support network, helping them find someone out there somewhere who doesn't think they are a geek.

3. The increased visibility of youth culture. Children fourteen and under now constitute roughly 30 percent of the American population, a demographic group larger than the baby boom itself. Adults are feeling more and more estranged from the dominant forms of popular

culture, which now reflect their children's values rather than their own. Despite our unfamiliarity with this new technology, the fantasies shaping contemporary video games are not profoundly different from those that shaped backyard play a generation ago. Boys have always enjoyed blood-and-thunder entertainment, always enjoyed risk-taking and rough-housing, but these activities often took place in vacant lots or backyards, out of adult view. In a world where children have diminished access to play space, American mothers are now confronting directly the messy business of turning boys into men in our culture and they are alarmed at what they are seeing. But the fact that they are seeing it at all means that we can talk about it and shape it in a way that was impossible when it was hidden from view.

We are afraid of our children. We are afraid of their reactions to digital media. And we suddenly can't avoid either. These factors may shape the policies that emerge from this committee, but if they do, they will lead us down the wrong path. Banning black trench coats or abolishing violent video games doesn't get us anywhere. These are the symbols of youth alienation and rage—not the causes.

Journalist Jon Katz has described a backlash against popular culture in our high schools. Schools are shutting down student net access. Parents are cutting their children off from online friends. Students are being suspended for displaying cultural symbols or expressing controversial views. Katz chillingly documents the consequences of adult ignorance and fear of our children's culture. Rather than teaching children to be more tolerant, high school teachers and administrators are teaching students that difference is dangerous, that individuality should be punished, and that self-expression should be constrained. In this polarized climate, it becomes *impossible* for young people to explain to us what their popular culture means to them. We're pushing this culture further and further underground and thus further and further from our understanding.

I urge this committee to listen to youth voices about this controversy and have submitted a selection of responses from young people as part of my extended testimony.

Listen to our children. Don't fear them.

12

Coming Up Next!
Ambushed on Donahue

The first time "Professor Jenkins" appeared was something of an accident—an email that jumped tracks and made its way into the public record. The second time, I did it on purpose, adopting his voice and persona in order to get my message heard by a larger public. Salon asked me to write about my experiences on the television talk show Donahue. *Adopting a somewhat more comic version of this persona helped me crystallize the terms of the debate for readers. I didn't want to take myself too seriously here; I had, after all, proven once again to be inarticulate under pressure, and what I was describing had more than a few farcical elements. I was starting to think I could have a second career as an intellectual tackling dummy—letting myself get beaten up by various powerful institutions and then writing about the experience.*

For the record, I had profoundly mixed feelings about being placed in a position of defending Grand Theft Auto 3. *Hardcore gamers argue that* Grand Theft Auto 3*'s open-ended narrative and richly detailed environment has advanced the art of game design. I would argue that the technical advances represented by GTA3 hold open enormous potentials for games to become a medium that encourages serious reflection about choice and consequences, a question to which I return in "The War between Effects and Meanings" (also in this collection).*

Having said this, the game's innovative potential does not excuse its ugly assumptions about race and gender. In its public statement against Grand Theft Auto 3, *the National Organization for Women asks: "The game is just a fantasy some say. But how many young men fantasized about picking up and beating to death a hooker before a video game suggested the idea? . . . Is this our definition of 'fun' now? Is this how we 'play'?"[1] Representatives of the Haitian-American community raised similar concerns about the game's sequel,* Grand Theft Auto: Vice City, *where a protagonist explains his motives: "My mission in the game is to kill the Haitians, I hate these Haitians! We'll take them out, we'll take them down!" Given the enormous commercial success of the franchise (one survey found the game had been played by 70 percent of American teenage boys), there should be a serious public debate about the way it represents the contemporary urban experience, much as there would be a discussion if such images surfaced in a book, film, or television series. As I note below, I feel about GTA3 the same way generations of film scholars have felt about* Birth of a Nation—*it's a work that includes lots of disturbing and distasteful aspects but represents a huge step forward in the evolution of the medium. Perhaps, as with* Birth of a Nation, *the tension between formal innovation and reactionary politics will help to push debates about the medium itself to a higher level and inspire other artists to offer their own responses to the issues it depicts.*

   "Coming Up Next! Ambushed on Donahue*" appeared in* Salon *in September 2002.*

On the long drive back from Secaucus, I kept thinking about all the things I should have said. I had just gotten my ass whupped on *Donahue*. Looking for comfort, I called my mother on the cell. She thought my suit looked good and my hair was combed straight. Somehow, it didn't help.

I am the director of MIT's new comparative media studies program. I've been writing about video games for more than a decade, have testified before the Senate Commerce Committee and the Federal Communications Commission, have conducted workshops with game designers, spoken to PTA meetings and the American Library Association, and been interviewed by more reporters than I can count. I agreed to appear on *Donahue* to talk about games because I knew I should have owned the issue. But I blew it.

The first thing I told my wife after I got off the phone from my first conversation with the *Donahue* producers was that I was flying to New York to get beaten up on national television. She asked if she should have my head examined.

But the producers were so, so reassuring. They wanted to have an intelligent discussion, to avoid sensationalism, to give me a chance to make my arguments. They would have some representatives of the games industry and someone from one of the media reform groups. One producer almost convinced me that *Donahue* was a serious news discussion program.

I really wanted to believe. I remember Phil Donahue publicizing the issue of sexual harassment in the workplace long before Anita Hill; I remember his program as one of the first to allow gays, lesbians, and bisexuals to talk openly about discrimination. I recalled how he quit the talk-show business in disgust and how they lured him back with the promise that he could be a progressive alternative to O'Reilly. There were signs all over the Boston subway telling us "Donahue's Back. Be Thinkful."

That ungrammatical slogan should have been the first clue that something was wrong with the new *Donahue*. But I had also watched the opening episode: Phil was trying so hard to escape the "wimp" label that he was practically frothing at the mouth. *Donahue* was mimicking the style of reactionary talk television as if that style didn't carry its own insidious political messages. Marlo Thomas's hubby had been lured to the dark side of the Force.

So, yeah, I should have known better. I did know better, sorta. I did it anyway. And after the fact, the only person I could kick was myself. I was ambushed, and forgot how to fight back.

I knew what the activists opposed to gaming violence would say—that computer games are too violent and are bad for young people. I was ready to tear them apart on the evidence. Despite all of the publicity about school shootings, the rate of juvenile violent crime in the United States is currently at a thirty-year low. When researchers interview people serving time for violent crimes, they find that they typically consume *less* media than the general population, not more. A 2001 surgeon general's report concluded that the strongest risk factors for school shootings centered around the quality of the child's home life and their mental stability, not their media exposure.

The field of "media effects" research includes around three hundred studies of media violence. But most of those studies are inconclusive. Many have been criticized on methodological grounds, particularly because they attempt to strip complex cultural phenomena down to simple variables that can be tested in the laboratory. Most found a correlation, not a causal relationship, which means they could simply be demonstrating that aggressive people like aggressive entertainment.

Only about thirty of those studies deal with video games specifically. And if you actually read the reports, most responsible researchers are careful to qualify their findings and are reluctant to make sweeping policy recommendations. None of them buy a simple monkey-see, monkey-do hypothesis. But the activists strip aside any qualifications, simplifying their conclusions and mulching together all of those contradictory findings. What they want is the aura of scientific validation, since that provides cover to all of their liberal allies who wouldn't support the Moral Majority but love to sound off about cultural pollution.

Activists exploit any data point and any tragic event as grist for their cause. They will cite studies that show that eight-year-olds have difficulty separating out fact from fiction and use them to justify restricting seventeen-year-olds' access to violent entertainment. Ninety percent of American boys play video games, so it's a pretty good bet that if the killer is an adolescent boy, they can find the proof that he was a gamer.

Parents are demanding that the government do something even if it's wrong, and once we reach that point, we tend to do all the wrong things. This is doubly dangerous. First, constitutional protections make it unlikely that the government is going to take decisive action against the media industries. So all of the fears get redirected onto the kids who play these games. We may not have an epidemic of youth violence in this country but lots of adults are ready to lock up teenage boys and throw away the key. Second, every moment our government focuses on the wrong problems, they take away time and resources that could be used to combat the actual causes of youth violence. Banning games doesn't put a stop to domestic violence, doesn't ensure that mentally unstable kids get the help they need, doesn't stop bullying in the hallways, and doesn't deal with the economic inequalities and racial tensions that are the real source of violence in American culture.

But, during my fifteen minutes on *Donahue,* I never got to say any of this. I was intellectually ready for this discussion, but nothing prepared me emotionally. I was the captain of my high school debate team, but debating on *Donahue* is a whole different ball game. The first thing you've got to do is throw away the note cards.

I walked tall into the studio, having been reassured once again by the producer that they weren't planning any cheap shots. They lied.

No sooner do I sit down then I glance at the teleprompter and get a preview of what Donahue had in store for me: "I want to show you a picture. This is thirteen-year-old Noah. While reenacting the video game *Mortal Kombat,* he was stabbed to death by his friend." I hear the producer coach Donahue on how to speak with Noah's mother so that it looks like she called spontaneously when they really had prearranged the call. I hear him reassure Daphne White, spokeswoman for the Lion and the Lamb Project and my sparring partner for the show, that he has some especially gristly footage from *Grand Theft Auto 3* at the ready and she clucks with glee. And then, whoosh, we are going live in, five, four, three, two, one, seconds—and you're ON THE AIR. I stare blankly into the camera as a freight train comes barreling toward me.

I hear Donahue explaining about how some school kids got shot in the back of their heads because their slayers had learned about "kill zones" from a video game. I find myself wondering why anyone would imagine a kid needed to play *Quake* to learn that you can kill someone by shooting them in the back of the head when just moments before, MSNBC was interviewing a former Mafia hit man.

Then, the first question goes to White, who uses it to remind viewers that she is a concerned mother. Never mind that I am a father and have raised a son successfully through his teenage years. On *Donahue,* activists are moms and intellectuals are presumed to be childless.

White explains how parents across the country had purchased *Grand Theft Auto 3* for their children without any idea of its distasteful contents. Hello! The game is called *Grand Theft Auto 3*. It's rated M for Mature Audiences—not appropriate for children under seventeen—"violence, blood, strong language." The hit men and prostitutes are right there on the package. If you are a thoughtful—er, I mean, "thinkful"—parent, how much more information do you need before alarm bells start going off in your head?

White notes that the Federal Trade Commission had cited overwhelming evidence that video games were aggressively marketed to youth. The same FTC study found that 83 percent of all video game purchases were either made by parents or by parents and children together. Moms and dads still control the purse strings on what remain high-ticket items in most family budgets. As parents, my wife and I took responsibility for knowing something about the media we bought our son. We didn't expect the storekeeper to protect us from ourselves.

And suddenly, it's my turn. I had composed a little speech debunking the evidence but it seemed beside the point because her last speech was backed by nothing more than her personal distaste for *Grand Theft Auto 3*. Uncomfortable with the black-and-white framing of the discussion, I search for middle ground, praising the Lion and the Lamb Project for helping parents to make informed choices. And I really meant it.

Education, not regulation, is going to ensure that parents get to decide what kind of media their children consume. Maybe we could all work together to improve the quality of resources available to parents.

But seeking middle ground was a classic liberal mistake. On these *Crossfire*-style programs, any compromise is read as weakness. Make no mistake about it, everything here works to exaggerate the differences between you and the person sitting on the other side of the table. It isn't a conversation, a discussion, or even a debate by any classical standards. You are opponents, whether you want to be or not. The producers actually keep you in separate rooms before they bring you on the air. They encourage you to interrupt each other and to show as much passion as possible, because what they want is controversy and entertainment. The producers rattle your cages until your blood is pumping and you want *them* to go down. They flash up captions underneath your image and you have no say over how they shorthand your position. When you cede a point, you can almost hear the folks on your own side booing.

Then, Donahue spooks moms with a clip from *GTA3*. You can tell he enjoys it: "We're going to kill a cop, or more than one cop, and a prostitute. . . . This is gratuitous violence here. We're beating, beating. We'll get a little blood here in a minute. The blood, you'll see. Look at this." He shows it over and over like we were watching the Zapruder film. Of course, any violence we see was staged by the show's producers, this being a game and not a movie. If Donahue really believed watching these scenes was harmful to minors, why was he showing them without parental warnings during what used to be considered the family hour? Pay no attention to the man behind the curtain.

Then, he asks me to justify what we just saw. Where does one start? The idea that we are going to get rid of violent entertainment is preposterous. Every storytelling medium in the history of mankind has included violent themes and stories, because we depend on stories to help us sort through our conflicting values and our mixed feelings about aggression. We turn to violent entertainment for the same reason moral reformers turn toward apocalyptic rhetoric—because it gives us a sense of order in a world that otherwise can seem totally chaotic. We fantasize about a lot of things we'd never want to do in real life, and through fantasy we bring those impulses momentarily under control. What is bad about a lot of games isn't that they are violent but that they trivialize violence. They tell us little about our inner demons because they fall back too quickly on tried-and-true formulas. Without fail, the works that moral reformers cite are not the ones that are formulaic but those that are thematically rich or formally innovative. It is as if the reformers responded to the work's own provocation to think about the meaning of violence but were determined to shut down that process before it ever gets started.

If you want to actually change the quality of popular culture, the best way to do it is not to throw rocks from the sidelines but to get involved in thinking through the creative challenges confronting the games industry. And that's what I've been doing, speaking at trade shows, doing workshops with individual companies, trying to figure out how to develop a richer and more complex vocabulary for representing violence in games.

And that's where *Grand Theft Auto 3* enters the picture. I feel about *GTA3* the same way I feel about the film *Birth of a Nation*—it's a work that includes lots of distasteful aspects but I respect, even admire it, as a huge step forward in the evolution of computer games as a medium. There are elements in the game that are hard to defend—your health can be replenished by "powerups" gained from visiting prostitutes; you are encouraged to club passers-by with baseball bats just to watch their blood splatter. No one, not even the people who made this game, think it's the best plaything for small children. This game was made for adults. People over the age of eighteen, by the way, constitute 61 percent of the total market for computer games.

GTA3 is a story about a mobster, not unlike such critically praised works as *The Godfather, Goodfellas,* and *The Sopranos.* Maybe not as good, but asking some of the same questions. You have escaped from prison. What kind of life are you going to build for yourself?

Contrary to what Donahue said, you don't score points by killing people. This isn't a virtual shooting gallery. Unlike earlier video games that give you no way forward except to slaughter everything that moves, this game offers an enormously expansive and responsive landscape. Certain plot devices cue you about possible missions, but nothing stops you from stealing an ambulance and racing injured people to the hospital or grabbing a fire truck and putting out blazes or simply walking around town. This open-ended structure puts the burden on you to make choices and explore their consequences. If you choose to use force, you are going to attract the police. The more force, the more cops. Pretty soon, you're going down. *GTA3* is only as violent as we choose to make it, and, used wisely, the game can tell us a lot about our own antisocial impulses. White dismissed all of this as "purely technical."

Assuming the role of host, White asks me whether I can identify video games that fully meet my ideals and I yammer like an idiot. I should have said that the medium has not achieved its full potential but any number of games in recent years have tried to offer more morally complex and emotionally demanding representations of aggression, loss, and suffering, everything from *Black & White,* where your moral choices get mapped onto the physical landscape of the game, to *The Sims,* where game characters mourn those who have died, or *Morrowind,* where how other characters treat you reflects your history of violent actions. Over the past year or so, the games industry has assembled the building blocks that can lead toward a much more complex portrayal of violence, but no one has put them altogether yet. None of this is apt to look much like progress to someone who believes that teens should only inhabit an imaginary world where the lamb shalt lay down with the lion and Barney shalt hug the Teletubbies.

After the commercial break comes the prearranged phone call from Noah's poor mother, then a call from a fourteen-year-old girl who is told that she doesn't represent the core of the video game market, and then a hostile question from Donahue, who attempts to reduce my efforts to reform the video game industry from within to the issue of whether I have ever taken money from the games industry.

The moral reformers always want to peg me as an apologist for the video game industry. I won't lie—the games industry likes what I have to say and they shove the media my way whenever they get a chance. Lately, I've even engaged in some sponsored research to help explore how games could be used to improve the quality of American education. Sponsorship covers the expenses of the research. Trust me, if I wanted to sell my mind to the highest bidder, I could command a whole lot higher price. What motivates me is, more or less, the same thing that drives Daphne White—a concern for American youth. This debate always gets presented as though there were only two sides—mothers battling to protect their kids and the cigar-chomping entertainment industry bosses who prey on American youth. This formulation allows no space to defend popular culture from any position other than self-interest. When Congress calls witnesses, it calls the usual reform groups and then allows the industry to name a few spokespeople. When Donahue sets up a discussion, his producers do the same. I enter the room already tainted with having been recommended by the industry. Meanwhile, the media effects researchers find themselves beholden to social conservatives. There are only two seats at the table.

Even though I am sometimes disappointed with their content, I refuse to give up on games. White kept harping on the fact that *GTA3* was the top-selling game in the country, as if it were representative of the industry as a whole. If we went only a few more notches down the charts, we would have found games like *Harry Potter, Star Wars, The Sims, Civilization 3, Spiderman,* and *Rollercoaster Tycoon.* M-rated games make only about 9 percent of the gross revenue from the American games industry. The game industry is more diverse than it was a decade ago, the technology and storytelling more sophisticated, the market more far-reaching, but the reformers keep beating the same dead horses. White and her allies describe games as commodities no more valuable and every bit as dangerous as cigarettes. I call games an art, and challenge game designers to live up to their responsibilities as artists and storytellers.

Only after the fact does it occur to me that most of the research dollars our program has accepted to look at games and education come from Microsoft, the same company that partially owns MSNBC and cuts Phil Donahue's paycheck. You got to love living in an age of media concentration!

By this point, however, I am caught looking like a kid with his hand in the cookie jar, trying to explain to someone who really couldn't care less how contemporary universities get funded.

Sometimes it was three against one. At others two against one. Sometimes, Phil even tossed me a lifeline. But at all points, it was me struggling with my own emotional responses. I should have picked a point, preferably a simple one, and hammered it over and over like White did. Instead, I was self-censoring, getting bogged down in the complexities, uncertain what distortion to correct. Most people watching the show probably read me the way the producers wanted—as a pointy-bearded civil libertarian and a paid corporate apologist trying to talk down to a concerned mom.

And then, it's over. As I exit the studio, I hear Donahue grumble to his producer that those *GTA3* clips seemed a whole lot more bloody when he was watching them before the show.

I wanted to tell them that media *does* have influence but media is most powerful when it reinforces our existing beliefs and behaviors, least powerful when it seeks to change them. Advertising, for example, is pretty effective at getting us to try a new product, but ultimately, if the product turns our teeth a funny color, we are unlikely to buy it again no matter how much marketing gets thrown at it. We typically test media representations against our direct experience and dismiss them when they don't ring true. I wanted to tell them that if you look closely at the personal background of those kids who have been involved in school shootings, you will find a history of real-world aggression and violence. They don't need games to teach them to hate and hurt; they learned that at home or at school.

I wanted to tell them about spending an afternoon brainstorming about games with the Royal Shakespeare Company and discovering that they were all *GTA3* fans. I wanted to tell them what I learned when I went around the country talking with teens about school violence—that the adults were focused in the wrong places if what they wanted to do was to stop kids from hurting each other. I wanted to talk about the importance of media literacy education not simply for teens but for their parents.

I wanted to tell them lots of things but it was over.

I was driving back to Cambridge, my tail between the legs, and all I could think about as we got bogged down in the repair work on I-95 were all of the things I should have said.

When I got home in the wee hours of the morning, I found that I had already started to receive hateful emails from the *Donahue* dittoheads.

"You are obviously not a mother trying to raise teenagers you stupid freaking moron idiot."

"I'd like to take that stupid X Box and crack that moron from MIT over the head with it."

"By the way, Moron, get a shave."

Guess Mom was wrong about the hair.

Donahue's Back. Be Thinkful.

13

The War between Effects and Meanings

Rethinking the Video Game Violence Debate

The Limbaugh decision described here turned into a rally-ing point for both sides in the ongoing culture war over video games and youth violence. On the one hand, Judge Limbaugh's ruling paved the way for more local ordinances, more lawsuits and public protests against violent titles. The attacks on Grand Theft Auto 3 *emerged in the immediate aftermath of this decision. On the other hand, academics and civil libertarians were joining forces to try to overturn a dangerous precedent—the complete dismissal of any claims that video and com-puter games expressed meanings or were protected by the First Amend-ment. As an advisor to the Free Expression Network, I was one of more than thirty international media scholars who signed an amicus brief that helped to overturn the Limbaugh ruling. I still feel that signing the brief and helping to recruit other signatories was the right decision, but I remain troubled by the terms with which the brief addressed the Lim-baugh ruling. The brief focused its energies on debunking the media effects research that was explicitly cited by the County of St. Louis in support of its regulations. Yet, it did not make an affirmative case that games constituted a meaningful form of expression. "The War between Effects and Meanings" constructs an argument for why games—and game violence—are meaningful.*

The essay also grew out of my need to explain what some were see-ing as a contradiction in my own actions. I was one of the leaders of the Education Arcade, an initiative to explore the pedagogical value of computer and video games. I was arguing that games could be im-portant resources for teaching science and history, yet I was also argu-

ing that games did not "teach" children to kill, a claim central to the reform group's attacks on games. Here, I show the difference between the educational models underlying the two sets of claims. The intended readers of this piece were high school teachers and administrators, though I have presented talks based on this essay before a broad range of audiences, including university media students, media literacy activists, and games industry executives.

"The War between Effects and Meanings" first appeared in Independent Schools *in Summer 2004. It is one of several essays I wrote in response to the Limbaugh decision. See also "Power to the Players," which appeared in* Technology Review *in June 2002.*

Suppose a federal judge was asked to determine whether books were protected by the First Amendment. Instead of seeking expert testimony, examining the novel's historical evolution, or surveying the range of the local bookstore, the judge chose four books, all within the same genre, to stand for the entire medium. Teachers and librarians would rise up in outrage. So, where were you when they tried to take the games away?

On April 19, 2002, U.S. District Judge Stephen N. Limbaugh, Sr., ruled that video games have "no conveyance of ideas, expression or anything else that could possibly amount to speech" and thus enjoy no constitutional protection. Limbaugh had been asked to evaluate the constitutionality of a St. Louis law that restricted youth access to violent or sexually explicit content. Constitutional status has historically rested on a medium's highest potential, not its worst excesses. Limbaugh essentially reversed this logic—saying that unless all games expressed ideas, then no game should be protected.

The judge didn't look hard for meaning in games, having already decided (again, contrary to well-established legal practice) that works whose primary purpose was to entertain could not constitute artistic or political expression. St. Louis County had presented the judge with videotaped excerpts from four games, all within a narrow range of genres, and all the subject of previous controversy. . . .

Gamers have expressed bafflement over how Limbaugh can simultaneously claim that video games do not express ideas and that they represent a dangerous influence on American youth. Reformers, in turn, are perplexed that the defenders of games can argue that they have no direct consequences for the people who consume them and yet warrant constitutional protection. To understand this paradox, we have to recognize a distinction between "effects" and "meanings." Limbaugh and company see games as having social and psychological "effects" (or in some formulations, as constituting "risk factors" that increase the likelihood of violent and antisocial conduct). Their critics argue that gamers produce meanings through game play and related activities. Effects are seen as emerging more or less spontaneously, with little conscious effort, and are not accessible to self-examination. Meanings emerge through an active process of interpretation; they reflect our conscious engagement; they can be articulated into words; and they can be critically examined. New meanings take shape around what we already know and what we already think, and thus, each player will come away from a game with a different experience and interpretation. Often, reformers in the "effects" tradition argue that children are particularly susceptible to confusions between fantasy and reality. A focus on meaning, on the other hand, would emphasize the knowledge and competencies possessed by game players, starting with their mastery over the aesthetic conventions that distinguish games from real-world experience. . . .

The Limbaugh decision was reversed by higher courts, and the St. Louis ordinance seems to be dead for the moment. Yet, similar city and state regulations are being proposed and contested. We have not heard the end of this debate. Often, these policy discussions filter down into decisions being made in our schools, such as how to draft digital policies (which may allow or exclude the use of games in computer labs or dorm rooms) or whether game playing constitutes a warning sign of antisocial personalities. . . .

Games as Teaching Machines?

The Effects Model

David Grossman, a retired military psychologist and West Point instructor, argues that video games are teaching kids to kill in more or less the same ways that the military trains soldiers.[1] He identifies "brutalization, classical conditioning, operant conditioning, and role modeling" as the basic mechanisms by which boot camps prepare raw recruits for the battlefield. Each of these methods, he suggests, have their parallels in the ways players interact with computer games. Kids are "brutalized" by overexposure to representations of violence at an age when they cannot yet distinguish between representation and reality. They are "conditioned" by being consistently rewarded for in-game violence. Soldiers in boot camp rehearse what they are going to do on the battlefield until it becomes second nature. Similarly, Grossman claims, "Every time a child plays an interactive point-and-shoot video game, he is learning the exact same conditioned reflex and motor skills." Such "practice" helped prepare school shooters for the real-world violence they would commit: "This young man did exactly what he was conditioned to do: he reflexively pulled the trigger, shooting accurately just like all those times he played video games. This process is extraordinarily powerful and frightening. The result is ever more homemade pseudo-sociopaths who kill reflexively and show no remorse. Our children are learning to kill and learning to like it." Finally, Grossman argues, soldiers learn by mimicking powerful role models and players learn by imitating the behaviors they see modeled on the screen. Indeed, given the first-person framing of such games, they are pulling the trigger themselves from the minute the game starts.

So, where is meaning, interpretation, evaluation, or expression in Grossman's model? Grossman assumes almost no conscious cognitive activity on the part of the gamers, who have all of the self-consciousness of Pavlov's dogs. He reverts to a behaviorist model of education that has long been discredited among schooling experts. Grossman sees games as shaping our reflexes, our impulses, our emotions, almost without regard to our previous knowledge and experience. And it is precisely because such conditioning escapes any conscious policing that Grossman believes games represent such a powerful mechanism for reshaping our behavior.

Educational psychologist Eugene Provenzo adopts a similar position: "The computer or video game is a teaching machine. Here is the logic: highly skilled players learn the lessons of the game through practice. As a result, they learn the lesson of the machine and its software—and thus achieve a higher score. They are behaviorally reinforced as they play the game and thus they are being taught."[2] Again, the model is one of stimulus/response, not conscious reflection.

Grossman reaffirms the distaste many educators feel for the contents of popular culture and cagily exploits liberal discomfort with the military mindset. Many teachers feel angry that time spent playing games often comes at the expense of what they would see as more educationally or culturally beneficial activities. Yet, if we think critically about the claims Grossman is making, they would seem to be at odds with our own classroom experiences and with what we know about how education works.

As a teacher, I may fantasize about being able to decide exactly what I want my students to know and to transmit that information to them with sufficient skill and precision so that every student in the room learns exactly what I want. But real-world education doesn't work that way. Each student pays attention to some parts of the lesson and ignores or forgets others. Each has their own motivations for learning. Previous understandings and experiences color how they interpret my words. Some students may disregard my words altogether. There is a huge difference between education and indoctrination.

Add to that the fact that consumers don't sit down in front of their game consoles to learn a lesson. Their attention is even more fragmented; their goals are even more personal; they aren't really going to be tested on what they learn. And they tend to dismiss anything they encounter in fantasy or entertainment that is not consistent with what they believe to be true about the real world. The military uses the games as part of a specific curriculum with clearly defined goals, in a context where students actively want to learn and have a clear need for the information and skills being transmitted. Soldiers have signed up to defend their country with their lives, so there are clear consequences for not mastering those skills. Grossman's model only works if we assume that players are not capable of rational thought, ignore critical differences in how and why people play games, and remove training or education from any meaningful cultural context.

The Meanings Model

Humanistic researchers have also made the case that games can be powerful teaching tools. In his recent book *What Video Games Have to Teach Us about Learning and Literacy*, James Gee describes game players as active problem solvers who see mistakes as opportunities for learning and who are constantly searching newer, better solutions to obstacles and challenges.[3] Players are encouraged to constantly form and test hypotheses about the game world. Players are pushed to the outer limits of their abilities but rarely, in a good game, beyond them. Increasingly, games are designed to be played successfully by players with very different goals and skill sets.

For Gee, the most powerful dimension of game playing is what he calls "projective identity," which refers to the way that role-playing enables us to experience the world from alternative perspectives. Terminology here is key: identity is projected (chosen or at least accepted by the player, actively constructed through game play) rather than imposed. Gee, for example, discusses *Ethnic Cleansing*, a game designed by Aryan Nations to foster white supremacy. For many students, he notes, playing the game will encourage critical thinking about the roots of racism and reaffirm their own commitments to social justice rather than provoking race hatred. Whether the game's ideas are persuasive depends on the players' backgrounds, experiences, and previous commitments. Games, like other media, are most powerful when they reinforce our existing beliefs, least effective when they challenge our values.

While Provenzo worries about players being forced to conform to machine logic, Gee suggests that our active participation enables us to map our own goals and agendas into the game space. To some degree, they are talking about games of different technological generations—the simple early games that amount to little more than digital shooting galleries versus the more robust and expansive universes created by more recent game genres. To some degree, they are adopting very different models of the kinds of learning that occurs through games.

Another humanistic researcher, Kurt Squire, has been studying what kinds of things game players might learn about social studies through playing *Civilization III* (the third game in Sid Meier's best-selling *Civilization* series) in classroom environments.[4] His work provides a vivid account of how game-based learning builds upon player's existing beliefs and takes shape within a cultural context. Students can win the game several different ways, roughly lining up with political, scientific, military, cultural, or economic victories. Players seek out geographical resources, manage economies, plan the growth of their civilization, and engage in diplomacy with other nation-states. Squire's research has focused on students performing well below grade-level expectations. They largely hated social studies, which they saw as propaganda. Several minority students were not interested in playing the game—until they realized that it was possible to win the game playing as an African or Native American civilization. These kids took great joy in studying hypothetical history, exploring the conditions under which colonial conquests might have played out differently. Squire's study showed that teachers played an important role in learning, directing students' attention, shaping questions, and helping them interpret events. An important part of the teacher's role was to set the tone of the activity—to frame game play as an investigation into alternative history as opposed to just learning directly from the game.

Squire asks what meanings these students take from playing games and what factors—in the game, in the player, and in the classroom environment—shape the interpretations they form. These kids are taught to explore their environment, make connections between distinct developments, form interpretations based on making choices and playing out their consequences, and map those lessons onto their understanding of the real world. Might something similar be occurring when players engage with violent video games? Might they be setting their own goals, working through their own emotional questions, forming their own interpretations, talking about them with their friends, and testing them against their observations of the real world?

As we move games into the classroom, teachers can play a vital role in helping students to become more conscious about the assumptions shaping their simulations. Yet, such issues crop up spontaneously online, where gamers gather to talk strategy or share game playing experiences. Just as classroom culture plays a key role in shaping how learning occurs, the social interactions between players, what we call meta-gaming, is a central factor shaping the meanings they ascribe to the represented actions. . . . Sociologist Talmadge Wright has logged many hours observing how online communities interact with violent video games, concluding that meta-gaming provides a context for thinking about rules and rule-breaking.[5] There are really two games taking place simultaneously—one, the explicit conflict and combat on the screen, the other, the implicit cooperation and comradeship between the players. Two players may be fighting to death on-screen and growing closer as friends off-screen. Within the "magic circle,"[6] then, we can let go of one set of constraints on our actions because we have bought into another set of constraints—the rules of society give way to the rules of the game. Social expectations are reaffirmed through the social contract governing play even as they are symbolically cast aside within the transgressive fantasies represented within the games.

Comparative media studies graduate student Zhan Li researched the online communities that grew up around *America's Army*, an online game developed as part of the U.S. Military's recruitment efforts.[7] Li even interviewed players as the first bombs were being dropped on

Baghdad. Veterans and current GIs were often critical of the casual and playful attitudes with which nonmilitary people play the game. For the veterans, playing the game represented a place to come together and talk about the way that war had impacted their lives. Many discussions surrounded the design choices the military made in order to promote official standards of behavior—such as preventing players from fragging teammates in the back or rewarding them for ethical and valorous behavior. The military had built the game to get young people excited about military service. They had created something more—a place where civilians and service folk could discuss the serious experience of real-life war.

Games do represent powerful tools for learning—if we understand learning in a more active, meaning-driven sense. The problem comes when we make too easy an assumption about what is being learned just by looking at the surface features of the games. As Gerard Jones notes in his book *Killing Monsters,* media reformers tend to be incredibly literal-minded in reading game images while players are not. He writes: "In focusing so intently on the literal, we overlook the emotional meaning of stories and images. . . . Young people who reject violence, guns, and bigotry in every form can sift through the literal contents of a movie, game, or song and still embrace the emotional power at its heart."[8]

Meaningful Violence?

Not every gamer thinks deeply about their play experiences, nor does every designer reflect upon the meanings attached to violence in their works. Most contemporary games do little to encourage players to reflect upon and converse about the nature of violence. If anything, the assumption that game play is meaningless discourages rather than fosters such reflection.

Media reformers often fail to make even the most basic distinctions about different kinds of representations of violence.[9] For example, the American Academy of Pediatrics reported that 100 percent of all animated feature films produced in the United States between 1937 and 1999 portrayed violence.[10] For this statistic to be true, the researcher must define violence so broadly as to be meaningless. Does the violence that occurs when hunters shoot Bambi's mother mean the same thing as the violence that occurs when giant robots smash each other in a

Japanese anime movie, for example? What percentage of books taught in English classes would be deemed violent by these same criteria? The reform groups are battling a monolith, "media violence," rather than helping our culture to make meaningful distinctions between different ways of representing violence.

In its 2002 decision striking down an Indianapolis law regulating youth access to violent games, the 7th Circuit Federal Court of Appeals noted: "Violence has always been and remains a central interest of humankind and a recurrent, even obsessive theme of culture both high and low. It engages the interest of children from an early age, as anyone familiar with the classic fairy tales collected by Grimm, Andersen, and Perrault are aware. To shield children right up to the age of 18 from exposure to violent descriptions and images would not only be quixotic, but deforming; it would leave them unequipped to cope with the world as we know it."[11]

Historically, cultures have used stories to make sense of senseless acts of violence. Telling stories about violence can, in effect, remove some of its sting and help us comprehend acts that shatter our normal frames of meaning. When culture warriors and media reformers cite examples of violent entertainment, they are almost always drawn to works that are explicitly struggling with the meaning of violence, works that have won critical acclaim or cult status in part because they break with the formulas through which our culture normally employs violence. They rarely cite banal, formulaic, or aesthetically uninteresting works, though such works abound in the marketplace. It is as if the reformers are responding to the work's own invitations to struggle with the costs and consequences of violence, yet their literal-minded critiques suggest an unwillingness to deal with those works with any degree of nuance. These works are condemned for what they depict, not examined for what they have to say.

Like all developing media, the earliest games relied on fairly simple-minded and formulaic representations of violence. Many games were little more than shooting galleries where players were encouraged to blast everything that moves. As game designers have discovered and mastered their medium, they have become increasingly reflective about the player's experience of violent fantasy. Many current games are designed to be ethical testing grounds; the discussions around such games provide a context for reflection on the nature of violence.

The Columbine shootings and their aftermath provoked soul-searching within the games industry—more than might meet the eye to someone watching shifts in games content from the outside. As game designers have grappled with their own ethical responsibilities, they have increasingly struggled to find ways to introduce some moral framework or some notion of consequence into their work. Because these designers work within industrial constraints and well-defined genres, these changes are subtle, not necessarily the kinds of changes that generate headlines or win the approval of reform groups. Yet, they impact the game play and have sparked debate among designers, critics, and players.

Toward More Reflective Game Design

Sims designer Will Wright argues that games are perhaps the only medium that allows us to experience guilt over the actions of fictional characters.[12] In a movie, because we do not control what occurs, we can always pull back and condemn the character or the artist when they cross social taboos, but in playing a game, we choose what happens to the characters. In the right circumstances, we can be encouraged to examine our own values by seeing what we are willing to do within virtual space. Wright's own contribution has been to introduce a rhetoric of mourning into the video game. In *The Sims,* if a character dies, the surviving characters grieve over their loss. Such images are powerful reminders that death has human costs.

Wright has compared *The Sims* to a dollhouse within which we can reenact domestic rituals and dramas. As such, he evokes a much older tradition of doll play. In nineteenth-century America, doll funerals were a recognized part of the culture of doll play, a way children worked through their anxieties about infant mortality or later, about the massive deaths caused by the Civil War.[13] Today, players use *The Sims* as a psychological workshop, testing the limits of the simulation (often by acting out violent fantasies among the residents) but also using the simulation to imitate real-world social interactions. As *The Sims* has moved online, it has become a social space where players debate alternative understandings of everyday life. Some see the fantasy world as freeing them from constraints and consequences. Others see the online game as a social community that must define and preserve a social contract. These issues have come to a head as some players have banded together into organized crime families seeking to rule territories, while others have become law enforcers trying to protect their fledgling communities.

As games' representations and simulations become more sophisticated, enabling players to set their own goals within richly detailed and highly responsive environments, the opportunities for ethical reflection have grown. *Morrowind*, a fantasy role-playing game, gives characters memories across their family line. Christopher Weaver, founder of Bethesda Softworks, which produced the game, explains that he wanted to show the "interconnectedness of lives" in a society governed by strong loyalties to families or clans: "The underlying social message being that one may not know the effect of their actions upon the future, but one must guide their present actions with an awareness of such potential ramifications."[14]

Grand Theft Auto 3 is one of the most controversial games on the market today because of its vivid representations of violence.[15] Yet, it also represents a technical breakthrough in game design that may lead to more meaningful representations of violence in games. The protagonist has escaped from prison. What kind of life is he going to build for himself? The player interacts with more than sixty distinctive characters and must choose between a range of possible alliances with various gangs and crime syndicates. Every object responds as it would in the real world; the player can exercise enormous flexibility in where they can go and what they can do in this environment. Some of what happens is outrageous and offensive, but this open-ended structure puts the burden on the user to make choices and explore their consequences. Every risk you take comes with a price. Violence leaves physical marks. Early on, players act out, seeing how much damage and mayhem they can inflict, but more experienced players tell me they often see how long they can go without breaking any laws, viewing this as a harder and more interesting challenge. A richer game might offer a broader range of options—including allowing the player to go straight, get a job, and settle into the community.

Peter Molyneux designs games that encourage ethical reflection. In *Black & White*, the player functions as a godlike entity, controlling the fates of smaller creatures. Your moral decisions to help or abuse your creatures map themselves directly onto the game world: malicious actions make the environment darker and more gnarly; virtuous actions make the world flower and glisten. Most players find it hard to be purely good or purely evil; most enter into ethical gray areas, and in so doing, start to ask some core philosophical and theological questions. His newest game, *Fable,* takes its protagonist from adolescence to old age, and every choice along the way has consequences in terms of the kind of person you will become and the kind of world you will inhabit. By living an accelerated lifetime within the game world, teens get to see the long-term impact of their choices on their own lives and those of people around them.

Fostering Games Literacy

If design innovations are producing games that support more reflection and discussion, media literacy efforts can expand the frameworks and vocabulary players bring to those discussions. Around the country, people are beginning to experiment with both classroom and after-school programs designed to foster games literacy. The best such programs combine critical analysis of existing commercial games with media production projects that allow students to re-imagine and re-invent game content. What kids learn is that current commercial games tell a remarkably narrow range of stories and adopt an even narrower range of perspectives on the depicted events. Rethinking game genres can encourage greater diversity and, in doing so, introduce new contexts for thinking about game violence.

OnRamp Arts, a Los Angeles–based nonprofit arts organization, conducted an after-school violence prevention workshop for students at Belmont High School, a 90 percent Latino public school in downtown Los Angeles. Students critiqued existing games, trying to develop a vocabulary for talking about the ways they represented the world. Students created digital superhero characters (like a rock-playing guerilla fighter, a man who transforms into a low-rider, or a peace-loving mermaid), which reflected their own cultural identities and built digital models of their homes and communities as a means of thinking about game space. Students studied their family histories and turned immigration stories into game missions, puzzles, and systems. In other words, they imagined games that might more fully express their own perspectives and experiences.

In the second phase, students, teachers, and local artists worked together to create a Web game, *Tropical America.* Because so many of the kids working on the project were first- or second-generation immigrants, the project increasingly came to focus on the conquest and colonization of the Americas. Jessica Irish, one of the project's directors, said that the greatest debate centered around what kind of role the protagonist should play. Through resolving that question, students came away with a more powerful understanding of the meaning and motivation of violence in games.

In *Tropical America,* the player assumes the role of the sole survivor of a 1981 massacre in El Salvador, attempting to investigate what happened to this village and why. In the process, you explore some five hundred years of the history of the colonization of Latin America, examining issues of racial genocide, cultural dominance, and the erasure of history. Winners of the game become "Heroes of the Americas," and in the process they uncover the name of another victim of the actual slaughter. Students had to master the history themselves, distilling it down to core events and concepts, and determine what images or activities might best express the essence of those ideas. They enhanced the game play with an encyclopedia that allowed players to learn more about the historical references and provided a space where meta-gaming could occur. Rather than romanticizing violence, the kids dealt with the political violence and human suffering that led their parents to flee from Latin America.

Conclusion

Rethinking the debates about media violence in terms of meanings rather than effects has pushed us in two important directions: on the one hand, it has helped us to see the ways that game designers and players are rethinking the consequences of violence within existing commercial games. These shifts in thinking may be invisible as long as the debate is framed in terms of the presence or absence of violence rather than in terms of what the violence means and what features of the game shape our responses to it. On the other hand, a focus on meaning rather than effects has helped us to identify some pedagogical interventions that can help our students develop the skills and vocabulary needed to think more deeply about the violence they encounter in the culture around them. Through media literacy efforts like OnRamp Arts' *Tropical America* project, teachers, students, and local artists are working together to envision alternative ways of representing violence in games and in the process, to critique the limitations of current commercial games. Students are encouraged to think about the media from the inside out: assuming the role of media-makers and thinking about their own ethical choices. . . .

14

The Chinese Columbine

*How One Tragedy Ignited the Chinese
Government's Simmering Fears of
Youth Culture and the Internet*

*"The Chinese Columbine" emerged from my first visit to Bei-
jing, during which I spoke at several universities, met with media industry leaders, and visited the Great Wall and other tourist sites. For much
of my trip, I was accompanied by my colleague Jing Wang, who studies
the impact of advertising on contemporary Chinese culture. Everywhere
I went that week, people wanted to talk about the tragic fire that had
killed dozens of youth who had been locked inside a cyber cafe overnight.
I was struck by the contrast between the American response to the Littleton shootings (which tended to blame media influences) and the Chinese response to this incident (which tended to search for explanations
in terms of the dramatic social changes the country was undergoing).*

"The Chinese Columbine" first appeared in Technology Review *in
April 2002.*

In early June, two boys, aged thirteen and fourteen, set fire to a Beijing
Internet cafe in retaliation for having been kicked out by the manager
earlier that evening, killing more than two dozen patrons and injuring
another thirteen. The Chinese government responded quickly, shutting
down more than fifty thousand cyber cafes nationwide for two or more
months of inspection and re-licensing—an act that has tremendous implications. In a 2000 study, Cheskin researchers found that roughly a
third of the more than 30 million Internet users in China relied on cyber
cafes as their primary means of getting online.

These events occurred shortly before I arrived in Beijing to study the
dramatic media changes reshaping China. As an American who had

been intimately involved in the public policy debates following Columbine, I was fascinated to see how this controversy about youth access to digital media would play out in China.

Even a cursory glance at the history of communications technology shows a recurring pattern. Urban youths become early adopters of new media, carving out a social space that serves their own subcultural needs, which immediately becomes the subject of adult concern. A single tragedy sparks a full-scale moral panic, which governments then leverage to their own advantage. From a distance, it's clear that the Chinese government is using the cyber cafe fire to limit Internet access.

Most Western discussions of the Internet and China describe the rise of digital access and consumer culture as liberating forces that cultivate democratic aspirations behind the repressive government's back. MIT professor Jing Wang notes, however, that the expansion of consumerism has been actively promoted *by* the government throughout the last decade. Embracing a rhetoric of "one nation, two systems," the state has encouraged a shorter work week, recreational activities, entrepreneurship, and more material goods per citizen. The goal has been to facilitate economic and technological change without promoting political destabilization.

A society once characterized by limited choice now confronts a multitude of consumer options and aggressive advertising campaigns. The first billboard I saw in Beijing contained the word "dotcom." A few blocks away from Tiananmen Square, a mob of people stopped in the street and stared at a massive television screen broadcasting the World Cup punctuated by a host of consumer-electronics commercials. Red-tented Coca-Cola stands in the Forbidden City; traditional night markets flanking Starbucks—old economic and social systems are breaking down faster than new ones can emerge, resulting in a culture riddled with contradictions, a state policy characterized by mixed signals, and a public charged by both anxiety and anticipation.

And China's urban youth have stood at the center of these changes. In fact, three-quarters of all Internet users in China are under thirty. Many urban teens don't remember a time without rampant consumerism. A few years in age between siblings translate into dramatic differences in cultural experiences. Fairly or unfairly, these urban youths embody their nation's hopes and fears about the future.

Consequently, youth Internet access has been a core focus of China's emerging digital policy.

On the one hand, the government sees the high-tech sector as central to China's long-term economic interests, especially since joining the World Trade Organization last year. For example, the Shanghai schools now require all nine-year-olds to learn basic Internet skills.

On the other hand, anti-computer rhetoric proliferates. Parents worry that their kids stay out all night at the local cyber cafes and fall behind in their studies. In a country that places high value on family and community, the Internet is also perceived as socially isolating. One distinguished Chinese news anchor claimed that the Internet was preventing young people from developing a meaningful relationship with television, costing broadcasters a generation of potential consumers. The impact of Western "media trash" is feared not only by state authorities but also by members of the public, anxious to preserve cultural traditions virtually eradicated by the Cultural Revolution and only now regaining ground.

Seeking to protect youth from pornography, violence, superstition, and "pernicious information" (i.e., Western news), the state imposed strict new policies several years ago. No one under sixteen can enter an Internet cafe unless accompanied by a teacher, and sixteen- to eighteen-year-olds can only go online after school hours or during vacations. Cafe owners are held legally responsible for the material their patrons access. The computers are directly linked to police headquarters, and an alarm rings when patrons access an inappropriate or prohibited Web site.

Of course, these restrictions only apply to "legal" Internet cafes. By some estimates, 50 to 90 percent of the cyber cafes in Beijing operate underground and have become the center of a thriving youth culture where teens come to play video games, watch porn, and access Western news. The Lanjisu Cyber Cafe, the unlicensed operation where the tragedy occurred, offered a typical discount—students could go online all night for roughly $1.50. When the cafe had reached full capacity, they simply locked their doors. When the outer door burst into flames, the patrons had no way to escape.

Where does blame lie? Could our own culture warriors have resisted pointing out that the two boys involved were gamers? Could liberals have resisted observing the inconsistency of draconian social regulations combined with neglect of illegal operations? Doubtful.

Asked about whether media influences contributed to their misconduct, many Chinese acknowledge some concern. Yet, they were reluctant to find systemic causes for such an unprecedented act, noting the low rate of juvenile crime overall. Most Chinese explanations focus on the boys' broken and tragic home lives. Additionally, they had been treated with indifference by school authorities and neglected by their neighbors. These troubled boys rapidly became poster children for the breakdown of social ties within the dwindling courtyard communities, which many see as symptomatic of urban China's modernization and privatization.

The fires and the resulting crackdown can both be read as complex social and political reactions to rapid change. Whether understood as a product of the breakdown of traditional culture and community or of the uneven regulation of the emerging cyberculture, the incident reveals points of tension in the way that China is dealing with the combined forces of modernization, westernization, and commercialization. In such a charged context, the Chinese government has become increasingly reactive. Unable to respond to all trouble spots, officials shift attention abruptly, literally and metaphorically putting out fires where they must and turning a blind eye when they can. The government was certainly using the fires as a pretext to reign in the emerging cyberculture, but it was also reassuring the public that it was ready to confront and master its own future shock.

I wonder, how differently would this issue have played itself out in the United States?

15

"The Monsters Next Door"

A Father-Son Dialogue about Buffy, Moral Panic, and Generational Differences

Henry Jenkins III and Henry G. Jenkins IV

When I went to Washington, DC, to testify before the Senate Commerce Committee about youth and media violence, I was struck by the fact that my son was the only young person in the room when the senators and moral reformers were making their pronunciations about what was wrong with contemporary youth culture. I had ended my remarks to the Commerce Committee with a call to "listen to our children." And I had been motivated to speak, in part, by the frontline reports of school repression that Jon Katz had posted in his "Voices from the Hellmouth" column at Slashdot. *After the hearings, I visited schools, public and private, across the country, trying to understand how students, teachers, and parents were making sense of the messages they were receiving about media violence. What I saw again and again was that many adults did not know how to talk to youth about the media they were consuming.*

I started looking through the advice literature for parents. While it often talked about fostering a pleasure in reading, say, it had no advice for how to shape your children's relationship to media beyond what I call "just say no to Nintendo" talk. It is assumed that nothing good can come from popular culture, so the advice is always to minimize exposure. But this was very different from the way the media was consumed within my own family. My wife and I were both fans, and we had encouraged our son to play with pop culture; we often had discussions as a family about the media we consumed, and we had through this process taught our son to become a sharp critic of popular culture. In fact, we did our job so well that my son has gone on to study media at the

University of Arizona. It was my son who received the invitation to submit this essay to a book an undergraduate mentor was editing about Buffy the Vampire Slayer, *and we decided together to use the piece as a means of modeling the ways that parents and youth could talk together about the media they consumed.*

This essay was written at a time when my son was a freshman visiting home for the Thanksgiving holiday. We wrote the sections sequentially: one writing a few paragraphs and the other responding. Unfortunately, the essay was bumped from the anthology and so it appears in print for the first time here.

"The Monsters Next Door" is one of several dialogic pieces that grew out of my involvement in the debates on media violence. For another example, see "I'm Gonna Git Medieval on Your Ass! A Conversation on Media and Violence," with James Cain, in Helaine Posner, ed., Cultures of Violence *(Amherst: University of Massachusetts Art Museum, 2002).*

Henry Jenkins III: Television, Neil Postman warns, is a "total disclosure" medium, which exposes children to adult secrets: "For in speaking, we may always whisper so that the child will not hear. Or we may use words they may not understand. But television cannot whisper. . . . By definition, adulthood means mysteries solved and secrets uncovered. If from the start the children know the mysteries and the secrets, how shall we tell them apart from anyone else?"[1] Yet, adults are not the only ones who "whisper" in order to preserve their "secrets." Television may enable adults to better understand their own children through encounters with programs, such as *Buffy the Vampire Slayer,* which grant them access to anxieties, fears, and aspirations that are also often hidden behind bedroom doors.

The moral panic following the Columbine massacre in Littleton, Colorado, revealed a communication breakdown between adults and adolescents, as adults acted out of fear of their own children and out of ignorance of the cultural materials so important to them. Often, adults expressed concern that the Internet was a new space of "secrets," "of covert communications closed to adult supervision."[2] At the same time, the various government investigations made little effort to actually include youth in their hearings. This whole experience indicates the need for new forms of communication between an emerging youth culture and an anxious parent society.

In this dialogic essay, we will explore ways that *Buffy* might enable conversations about (and across) generational differences, starting with how a shared mythology places both participants on a more or less equal footing, allowing parents and children to get some distance from old fights. Discussing television characters can encourage a process of introspection and speculation, which often opens up fresh ways of thinking and talking together. Sometimes you can hide behind the characters; sometimes they can help you find ways to bring thoughts and feelings into the open.[3]

If, in the aftermath of the Littleton shootings, the news media often pathologized youth as "the monsters next door," *Buffy* reversed the polarities, playfully demonizing adults and their will to control teens.[4] Yet the series also presents several figures—most notably Spike and Giles—who mediate between adults and teens. We will use the episodes "Gingerbread," "Band Candy," "Becoming," and "Fool for Love" as points of departure for a far-reaching discussion about the moral panic over Columbine. *Buffy* entered the Columbine story when the WB Network delayed the airing of "Graduation Day" because executives felt it might inspire or condone high school violence. At the same time, the "Hellmouth" analogy was widely applied to the more painful aspects of contemporary high school that some—most notably *Slashdot* columnist Jon Katz—felt had fueled school violence.[5] What *Buffy* can tell us about Columbine doesn't begin and end with its literal representations of youth wielding weapons. By focusing attention on tensions within high school culture and within the family, *Buffy* presents us with an emotional context for Columbine and its aftermath. The culture-war discourse following Columbine displaced attention from school culture onto media violence. To focus on episodes like "Graduation Day" here would be simply to amplify the confusion. Instead, we will examine episodes that address the rather different ways teens and parents understand the line separating adolescence and adulthood. In some cases, this means looking at episodes such as "Band Candy" and "Gingerbread" that foreground adult-teen conflicts; in others, episodes such as "Becomings" and "Fool for Love" that explore how teens make choices that help to define their adult identities.

Henry IV: When I first heard that Kristy Swanson's farcical 1992 comedy, *Buffy the Vampire Slayer*, would be made into a TV show I was underwhelmed. The movie had been released when I was in junior high school and, even at the time, had struck me as simplistic. "The show's cheesy," my friends told me midway through the first season. "[The writers] wouldn't know a teenager if one shook their hand." For three years I dutifully avoided the show, cringing when a culturally inept freshman would show up raving about Sarah Michelle Gellar. During that time I began watching *Dawson's Creek* on a weekly basis, but never once would I stay tuned for the Slayer. That is, until my parents started watching. My parents and I have always been close and media has been one core thing we've had in common. Since the days of *Pee Wee's Playhouse* we've had some common series interests, something to sit down and watch together. So it rather surprised me that they were watching such a juvenile show. Curious to know what they, well-educated media scholars, were getting out of such a series, I watched one night and found myself really responding to the human characters and their repartee. As I stayed up all night watching the better part of the first season on tape, I found that most of the episodes had a point. Even when Xander's teacher turned out to be a praying mantis, even when he was overcome by a hyena, the overblown monster metaphors stood in for experiences I could relate to. Coming back to my friends and telling them I liked *Buffy* meant dangling my head over the social chopping block. It was, after all, uncool to be sixteen at sixteen. But the more I stuck my neck out on the issue the more I found that I wasn't alone. Some of my best friends were silenced *Buffy* fans ecstatic to share their favorite moments with me. I was rather glad, then, that I'd taken the time to understand my parents' culture.

The way parents, teachers, and administrators have reacted to the tragedy at Columbine by shutting out youth culture and shutting down youth privacy is evidence to me of just how little the two sides communicate. *Buffy the Vampire Slayer* is a show about teenagers written by Gen-Xers at an adult reading level. The characters are not all shallow teens and beauty queens, as I once believed, but also the middle-aged men and women they must deal with in their lives—the monsters and the mentors. The fact that the series opening and the "previously ons" are narrated by Giles, Buffy's father figure, suggests that the series could be seen from multiple points of view. It's as much my parents' story as my own. In this essay my father and I will attempt to reconcile these two sets of characters in relation to ourselves as well as to the children and adults we see around us. We will suggest a social relevancy readily found in the stories *Buffy* tells and, implicitly, model the kinds of discussions between adults and teens that might help prevent tragic culture wars and everyday miscommunication from occurring.

"Gingerbread": The Witch-Hunt

Henry IV: Writer Jane Espenson's powerful third-season barbecuing of censorship politics, "Gingerbread," seems like a point-by-point laundry list of the major battles following Columbine: various well-known civil cases, the congressional hearings, and national parental overreaction. Kids wind up dead and the concerned adult community chooses the entire Wiccan culture as a scapegoat for their aggressions—burning books, searching lockers, shutting down the Internet, locking their kids in their rooms and throwing away the key, the very same things I saw happening around me. But what amazes me is that the episode was in no way inspired by Columbine. "Gingerbread" was filmed over four months prior to the massacre. So how could she have so eloquently captured the voice of America's patronized youth?

Henry III: Columbine was the immediate catalyst of the moral panic, but the moral panic did not start at Columbine.[6] The anthropologist Mary Douglas has written about witch-hunts in traditional societies. A witch-hunt may be triggered by an unspeakable and incomprehensible tragedy, but it quickly gets directed against the "usual suspects."[7] Many people may be accused, but the accusations that stick build on existing fault lines in the community. Giles offers a similar explanation in "Gingerbread" when he describes the empathy demons as working on our darkest fears to transform peaceful communities into mobs of vigilantes. If we were not already afraid, such demons—real or metaphorical—could not create such dark mischief. The real-world moral panic erupted around two fault lines: first, the increased visibility of youth culture at a time when our society is just starting to absorb a new demographic bubble as large as the baby boom itself, and second, a considerable generation gap in terms of access and comfort with digital technologies. These concerns surfaced in popular culture well before we were fully conscious of the growing tensions between adults and teens. Many of the works that came under attack (*The Basketball Diaries, Kids,* Marilyn Manson, *Buffy*) articulated youth perspectives on the growing conflicts between parents and children. Politicians such as William Bennett and Joseph Lieberman sought to demarcate the line between "meaningful" and "gratuitous" media violence along ideological and generational lines. You know, *The Basketball Diaries* was bad violence, *Clear and Present Danger* good violence. The congressional hearings may have focused on the entertainment industry, but on the local level, the focus was on kids and their culture.

Henry IV: The parents in this story, much like their real-life counterparts, ignore the unique qualities, strengths, and weaknesses of their own children when judging what restrictions those children should confront. In the episode, Willow's mother notices her daughter's new hairdo. "I got it cut last August," Willow reminds her. Mom hasn't so much as looked at her since August. When they speak, Mrs. Rosenberg stares at a church program, the coffee table, the floor, and even Willow's shoes. But she's almost never able to face her daughter directly. My parents and I argue all the time. But usually our conflicts end in some sort of helpful discussion. Some of my friends have not been so lucky. Several of them have not only been sent out of the room but out on the street. One of my great nemeses in high school often slept in the school music building rather than fighting for the opportunity to sleep in her own bed. She was viewed as very promiscuous because she so often slept over at her boyfriend's house. Most of us never understood that, to her, this was as much necessity as luxury. She relied on the charity of her friends just to eat.

Henry III: Willow's mother never asks her any meaningful questions, because she thinks she already knows the answers. As Willow protests, "The last time we had a conversation more than three minutes long was about the patriarchal bias of the Mister Roger's Show." Mrs. Rosenberg is a painful caricature of the academic parent. Confronted by fears about her daughter's involvement in witchcraft, she explains: "Identification with mythical icons is perfectly typical for your age group. It's a classic adolescent response to the pressures of incipient adulthood." Once she has labeled and categorized her daughter, she doesn't need to listen to what Willow has to say. If the daughter has a different perspective, she's "delusional." If she stands up for her culture, she's "acting out." And if she continues to defy her mother, she's grounded.

Henry IV: Willow's response is one of disbelief. How can her mother believe surveys in an anthropology textbook over the girl standing right in front of her? How can she ignore the special circumstances Willow faces, the traits that make her an individual? "I'm not a part of some age group," she explains. "I'm me. Willow group." The kids at school have never seen Willow as fitting in with them. In their minds she's an alien, an exception to every rule. She's a Jewish kid growing up in an all-blonde California beach town. She's a girl who likes technology—a bumbling, stumbling lab rat in purple overalls. Yet her mother sticks her in the same group as those who torment her. Kids don't like to tell their parents about getting thrown around or humiliated at school. I can say from some experience, it hurts bad enough just trying to tell your friends. Willow faces enough pressure trying to live up to the standards Cordelia and the other girls set for her. So she alienates her mother, tries to factor her out of the equation. And then she can't understand how her mother could be so uninformed.

Henry III: The episode shows us three very different adult responses to moral panic. Mrs. Rosenberg overintellectualizes, because she is so removed from Willow's life. Joyce Summers starts out the episode trying to bond with her daughter, taking a bag lunch and Thermos on patrol. Buffy finds her mother intrusive. When her mother shows up in the lunchroom, Buffy protests, "This hall is about school and you're about home. Mix them and my world dissolves." Joyce can't keep her daughter's secrets and pulls the whole community into her campaign to restore adult control over Sunnydale. In her parents' meeting address, she moves from an abstract concern about "monsters" step-by-step closer to her daughter's own world, "witches and slayers." Her campaign to protect the "children" becomes a war against her own daughter and her daughter's friends.

Henry IV: Joyce won't let Buffy go. Everywhere Buffy turns, everything she says or does or even thinks, Big Mother is watching. Joyce is being difficult. But then she commits the ultimate act of betrayal. Buffy has told her a secret in confidence and she shares what she's learned with everyone else in ways that will adversely affect her daughter's happiness. This is why teenagers don't tell their parents anything. They have nightmares that their trust will be betrayed in just such a manner. But unlike a bad friend who betrays your trust, you can't say goodbye to your parents. You have to come home again and try even harder to keep your parents out the next time.

Henry III: The third perspective is embodied in Principal Snyder. Snyder has always been an authoritarian, but public opinion has held him in check. When the parents panic, he orders a locker search: "This is a glorious day for principals everywhere. No pathetic whining about student's rights. Just a long row of lockers and a man with a key." Public demands to get rid the library of "offensive" literature provide a pretext to settle old scores with Giles. Principals around the country used Columbine in precisely this way; to crack down on kids who annoyed them.

Henry IV: Isn't it funny how much Snyder's official decisions satisfy his personal desires? How anyone who crosses him soon runs out of funding for their students or is subject to police investigation? Clearly he views himself as an uber-parent, a vocal upholder of adult authority rather than an aid to students. On this front the show couldn't be more realistic. A school system near my college banned all of their students from wearing heavy coats two winters ago. Not only couldn't the kids wear black trench coats, they couldn't wear Orioles jackets or Old Navy polar fleeces. Many of the parents complained that their kids had caught pneumonia. But the principal stood by his decision. In many ways Snyder has been polished up for television.

Henry III: Student rights often get violated because teachers and administrators want to make our schools more "secure," but "Gingerbread" suggests that once we turn our schools into a police state, all teens feel threatened. Cordelia acts smug about what happens to Michael, the local Goth, whom she calls "a poster child for yuck," but by the episode's end, her parents have confiscated *her* black dresses and *her* scented candles. When the lockers are searched, Willow feels at risk because of her "witch stuff" while Xander worries, "It's Nazi Germany and I've got *Playboys* in my locker."

Henry IV: So what about Giles? He's an adult. But he's not scary at all. He hangs out with the kids. He attends birthday parties for them. He dresses up in ridiculous costumes and has them over for Halloween. He stands out in every shot of the Scoobys as "the tall one in the suit." But most importantly, he gives them the adult authority they need to win their battles. He can fight the battles Buffy can't—the ones in the real world. I think I'd like to have him around. What's his role in the story?

Henry III: Giles embodies the good teacher who shares the risks with his students. When Snyder cracks down, he attacks Giles and his suspect books, leaving him to confront his students' problems armed only with "a dictionary and *My Friend Flicka*." When the parents burn their children at the stake, Giles's books are the kindling. Giles remembers what it was like to be a teen outcast and feels personally implicated when his students are threatened.

"Band Candy": The Teen Within

Henry III: "Band Candy" is another episode where the "monsters next door" are the adults, not the teens. It opens with anxieties about adult control. Having run away from home, Buffy finds herself under tight scrutiny from both Giles and her mother. Yet, she is even more frightened and confused when adult control breaks down. Demonic band candy causes adults to revert into their adolescent identities and run wild in the streets. As Buffy explains, "They are acting like a bunch of us. . . . No vampire has ever been that scary." What does she find so terrifying?

Henry IV: Many seventeen-year-olds want to be grown up and powerful, like their parents. But few of them want their parents to be adolescent and powerless, like them. Teenagers perceive themselves as being midway through a difficult learning process. They feel burdened by the expectations of overnight growth placed upon them even as they pressure themselves hardest of all. If they admit that they're young and needy they lose all power, control, and credibility in making their own decisions. But to do what's necessary to get out of their parents' house they need to force themselves to grow up faster than they're ready and, if they don't meet society's deadlines, to bluff about it and pretend that they're more secure than they are. Let's not underestimate the degree to which many teenagers depend on their parents as pillars of support. They put food on the table and in the refrigerator. They make sure you can get to school. And even if you lost all of your other friends and had no one, they would still be there. When you take the parents away, maturity is rammed down teenager's throats faster than they know how to swallow it and they throw up all over the freshman dorms at college. "Band Candy" is a story about sudden graduation that tells teenagers to know their limits and remember who they come home to at night.

Henry III: If "Gingerbread" shows what happens when the adult will to control teens gets out of control, "Band Candy" suggests that adults may, actually, desire the freedom and license they would deny their children. Teachers want to cut classes. Mothers want to make out and drink Kahlua with their boyfriends. The watcher wants to form his own rock band and picks fights with the cops. The town doctor strips off his shirt and leaps into the mosh pit. And Snyder is just another geek who can't get a date. Oz suggests that this is "a sobering mirror" for the teen characters, but do you think that is fair? Buffy or Willow don't act like that!

Henry IV: Parents are never there for their teenage daughter's greatest triumphs. When a girl is being pressured to have sex with her boyfriend and she says no, mom and dad are still at home with the lights on, worrying and completely unaware. When she gives a stellar report in school, they are at work, locked carefully outside of the classroom. Even if she tells them at dinner, "I did an awesome job," it will only sound like bragging. But when she gets suspended for drinking in the girl's room, they couldn't be more involved. Teenagers need autonomy so they shut their parents out of their private affairs whenever possible. In "Band Candy," when the adults revert back into teenagers, they don't actually become mirrors of their children. They become mirrors of the way they *see* their children. Joyce wants to have a lot of promiscuous sex because she thinks that's what Buffy must experience behind her back. She's heard the previous season about Buffy giving her virginity to a much older "school tutor" and, rightly or wrongly, has a very low opinion of her sexual maturity. Becoming a teenager (for her) means embracing her fears of her daughter's sexual independence. She doesn't realize that this is completely unnecessary and that Buffy isn't nearly as bad as she imagines.

Henry III: I was really moved by Joyce's description of returning to adolescence as an awakening: "You know, like having a kid and getting married and everything was a dream and now things are back like they are supposed to be." For Joyce, the band candy represents a chance to reclaim aspects of herself she sacrificed in order to fit into the adult world. No wonder the adults seem so greedy to get their hands on more and more of it! I don't know of any adults who really, deep down inside, feel totally grown up. For me, it isn't that I want to drag race or smash store windows (things I didn't do when I was a teen), only that I want to return to a time when I didn't have to make all of the decisions or face all the risks. Yet, I feel anything but nostalgic about my own high school years. Confronted with the reality of what many teens face every day, most of us would run like hell!

Henry IV: I think Joyce would eventually choose to go back to the adult world. When you're an adult you can still laugh. You can still lust. You can still run. But you can do other stuff too. You get the "final say" in all disagreements. That's why adulthood will always win out in your mind. But it's not that bad being young. I'm not sure I'd trade up if I could. Not with all I'd lose. No, high school's only hell on exam weeks.

Henry III: Maybe adults project our transgressive fantasies onto adolescence, imagining an escape from the frustrations of adult life. It is especially telling that the purpose of putting adults under the seductive spell of the band candy is so that they will forget about their own children, so the mayor and his minions can serve up the town's babies to the demon. Pushed to its logical extreme, the desire to reclaim adolescence becomes a desire to take over our children's lives. As Buffy notes: "I guess it is easier to live my life if I am not there."

Of course, my own fascination with *Buffy* is surely motivated by a mixture of nostalgia for the camaraderie of the Scooby gang (a social closeness I never enjoyed in high school) and satisfaction when the series skewers some painful aspect of my own adolescent experience. Am I watching this series as a utopian experience of a high school life I never had or because it acknowledges high school to be the dystopia I remember it to be? A little of both.

"Becoming": You Can't Go Home Again

Henry IV: I once heard that the choices you make in high school affect the person you grow up to be. Some of these choices are obvious.

Consider the college application process, for example. Many decisions we make in high school are less dramatic. Will we cancel a sleepover with our best friend to make time for a girl we barely know? Buy a soda or watch our weight? Choose the sausage roll or the falafel? The red pill or the blue pill? Xander made just such a choice. Willow had just awoken from a coma. Xander's rival for her affections, the better-looking and smoother-talking Oz, was kneeling by her bedside. Xander had to make a decision very quickly. Would he push in and comfort his friend, assuming the credit he deserved for drawing her out of the coma? Or would he do the responsible thing and leave in search of a doctor, allowing Oz to have a moment alone with her? "Becoming" is all about the choices that will determine who we grow up to be; the big and the small, the ones we anticipate and the ones we never do. Indeed, all of the characters make choices: Angel to guide Buffy and later to kill every man on earth, Snyder to ruin an innocent girl's life, Joyce not to listen to her daughter, Giles to submit to his fantasies of Jenny Calendar. These choices shape the way audiences will see the characters. Joyce, until that point sympathetic, is cast in a negative light for believing the police over her own daughter. For the next season her image will continue to decline, passing through her "scandal" youth in "Band Candy" and culminating in her "Gingerbread" bonfire. In choosing to fetch a doctor Xander submits to the reality that he never will get the girl.

Henry III: Parents often think they see the choices so clearly—do this and you are never going to get into college. And we are often mystified when teens opt out of our binaries, choosing options we never offered them. We are starting to imagine how our children are going to survive without us. Or we become convinced our children are going to live in the basement apartment for the rest of their lives. So, we go back and forth between wanting to push them out of the nest and wanting to hold them close. Every choice becomes make or break, just as Buffy's choices have the potential to suck the whole world into hell. Most of the time, when everyone backs down from a fight, not a whole lot has changed, but sometimes, we say things that are impossible to take back. That's the place Joyce and Buffy reach in this episode: a point of no return. Joyce tells Buffy that if she walks out the door, she can never come back, and Buffy takes her at her word. We've had some pretty brutal fights. I'm happy we've never reached that juncture. The scene scares me because I can see how easy it would be to be pushed to that point and not know how to pull back.

Henry IV: The scene starts out with a relatively small choice, or at least a quick one. A vampire attacks Buffy's mother. Will she stake the vampire (and reveal her secret identity) or let her mother die (and always regret it)? Buffy saves her mother's life and thus upsets her so deeply that it breaks the family apart forever. No longer will Joyce look at Buffy as her "teenage daughter." She's now become something impossibly different—a "monster daughter." Joyce is disturbed by her daughter's abnormality, by their difference from the rest of their white suburban neighborhood. She tries to reason with Buffy, to show her that she's just made some sort of a silly mistake. "Honey," she asks. "Are you sure you're the Slayer?" and "Have you ever tried not being the Slayer?" Buffy has just come out of the closet. Joyce must have had all of these plans for Buffy—a happy married life with a handsome and affluent doctor—that have been called into question by these changes. In Joyce's view, Buffy's slaying is just an intriguing but poor habit—a challenge for her to overcome. When Buffy protests that she has to save the world, the mother clings firmly to her authority. "You will not leave this house," she says. World be damned. Joyce never will understand or accept her daughter's alternative lifestyle. Her daughter is just more queer than she'd like her to be.

Henry III: Your references to queerness are right on target. This is a coming-out sequence, and Joyce has to shift her perception of her daughter and of herself before she can accept Buffy's revelations. Joyce has tried very hard to be the ideal mother, especially since her divorce; she has sought to be aware of Buffy's interests and get to know her friends. Suddenly, she learns how little she knows: "Open your eyes, Mom. What do you think has been going on for the past two years, the fights, the weird occurrences. How many times have you washed blood out of my clothing and you still haven't figured it out."

Each line counts; each phrase Joyce utters represents a mental shift. Joyce struggles to hold onto something, anything, as her world crumbles around her. Her first response is one of denial: "Honey, are you sure?"; then, a desire for change: "Have you tried not being a slayer?"; then, an attempt to locate causes and to separate herself from the problem: "It's because you didn't have a strong father figure." Joyce appeals to outside authority—the police—in order to restore adult control. Her daughter can't be responsible for the fate of the world. She isn't ready.

Her responses are banal, predictable, and oh so familiar. They are things we've sworn we would never say and found ourselves saying anyway. Joyce knows they are inadequate even as she says them but what else can she say? She draws a line and forces Buffy to cross it. After that line, their relationship can never be the same. Either she doesn't mean it and she has lost all credibility or she does and she has permanently shattered her family. Joyce knows this is a permanent choice; she has reached this point before with her husband. Buffy has no option. Suddenly, Joyce is what stands between her and her mission. She will slash through her mother just as she will stab her soul mate, because this is what she must do to save the world. Joyce feels like she has to do something, even if it is wrong—and when we reach that point, we usually do all the wrong things.

Henry IV: Interestingly enough, the episode is written in such a way that teenagers can look ahead to adulthood and imagine what the conflict might be like if the shoe were on the other foot. It helps us to overcome the disadvantage in perspective we have as young people—the "You can see inside of me but I can't see inside of you" paradigm. This is, in part, because Joyce is treated well. Even though her perspective is often portrayed with outright buffoonery (anyone who has seen the show should get a good laugh out of "Have you ever tried not being the Slayer?"), a certain amount of realism seeps through. Would you understand if your parents came to you and confided, "You know, son, I'm actually the Green Hornet." You'd think it was a very upsetting joke. I suppose in Joyce's case she thinks it's a plea for attention. Once she loses control Joyce is no more worldly than she was as a teenager. The anxiety and desperation she's learned to stuff down inside comes roaring out like a fart at a dinner party. She's almost adolescent.

On the other hand, Buffy was born forty. The power and responsibility other teenagers seek is dumped on her in unmanageable quantities. She will always be the Slayer. No more, no less. She's future-free. And that places her in a category somewhat removed from the other teenagers. No matter how young her body might look she will never know what it's like to be sixteen.

Kind of like Spike and Angel—who don't fit into normal categories of teenager and adult either. Angel was born in the 1700s. He could have been Benjamin Franklin's babysitter. If maturity was directly correlated with age, Joyce would have to bow at his feet. But instead he's getting it on with her daughter. Spike and the other vampires serve as impartial commentators, mediators between the age groups. He's never raised children. He's never walked the streets as an adult or held a grown-up job. He's always been treated like a mature college student, a young man still coming into his own. If teenagers are stuck in an awkward phase between childhood and adulthood, this is ever so much worse for vampires. They simply get more and more worldly without ever receiving the respect they deserve. A fifth-season episode, "Fool for Love," details Spike's transformation from mental child to mental man, from frightened adolescence to commanding maturity. I wonder, how will I become a writer? Will it come in a beautiful instant of transformation, a moment that opens my eyes to the world? Or will it come slowly and painfully over years and years of waiting and trying? Will I know when I'm an adult? In "Fool for Love," we follow Spike upon his quest—spanning centuries—for enlightenment and self-esteem. We see teenager and adult reconciled as two ends of a single life process.

"Fool for Love": Portrait of a Vampire as a Young Man

Henry IV: Buffy's trouble is that she must visit the crime scenes night after night. She's always checking the dead body for puncture wounds, seeing the dead rise from their graves. And worst of all, she often has to kill them again. Everyone she knows dies—even the people she tries hardest to protect. So when she herself gets stabbed while on nightly patrol she has no trouble imagining the worst. "At least none of my vital organs got kabobbed," she quips the next day. But the expression on her face tells all. She can no longer say: "I'm strong. I'm unique. It won't happen to me." She must face the inevitability that it not only can but will.

The natural response to feeling threatened is to take action. When you feel ugly you go on a diet. When you feel violated you crave retribution. So Buffy tries to improve herself—to polish away any flaws in her fighting style. She goes to Spike, killer of two Slayers, for advice on personal survival. "It's not about memorizing a list of moves," he tells her. Through the course of the episode he tells his tale—of the lust, the kill, the glory—but in the end she learns nothing. For her there is no sure method of preventing death, no way she can prepare. She can always reach for her weapon and cling tightly to her friends, as he suggests, but she had been all ready at the time of her assault. Death is a reality in her life—an intangible but unyielding force beneath her feet, stained in her clothes.

Henry III: One of the reasons it's dangerous to allow political leaders to use the term "children" when they really mean adolescents is that our culture has so romanticized the myth of childhood innocence. We see childhood as a simple time, without anger or anxiety, protected from violence. As they move from parental protection toward autonomy, teens confront enormous anxiety. Since Columbine, concern about media violence has all but displaced any focus on real-world violence. It is as if we felt it was more important to shelter teens from violent images than to protect them from emotional and physical violence in their real-world environment. Adults looked everywhere and anywhere to understand the cause of these murders; most of the teens I've met have no trouble understanding where that rage came from.

Harris and Klebold may have been drawn toward violent images but those media images didn't turn them into killers. Violence begins much closer to home. Consider, for example, one of the high school football players whom *Time* interviewed: "Columbine is a clean, good place except for those rejects. Most kids didn't want them there. . . . Sure we teased them. But what do you expect with kids who come to school with weirdo hairdos and horns on their hats? It's not just jocks; the whole school's disgusted with them. They're a bunch of homos, grabbing each other's private parts."[8] His language is one of banal homophobia; he expects his opinions to be unquestioningly embraced both by other teens and by adult authorities. We will never know what Harris and Klebold's sexuality was. It doesn't matter. Homophobia impacts every American teen insofar as it makes them feel fear or shame over the ways they are different from their classmates. I remember being devastated by those kinds of remarks in high school. I was ridiculed, spat on, called names, and beaten up in the locker room. Years later, I ran into one of my tormentors at our high school reunion and he said he didn't really know why he picked on me. Everyone else was picking on me and he was afraid if he didn't, they would start picking on him. Confronted with that homophobia, some teens commit suicide and others turn their guns on their tormentors.

"Fool for Love" explains what turns a sensitive young man toward violence and why Spike seems to always want to take on the world. One of the most honest moments in the episode comes when Spike calls Angel a "poofter," the nineteenth-century equivalent of a faggot. Even Angel is startled by how quickly he becomes enraged by that particular epithet.

Henry IV: When Willow met her vampire twin in "Doppelgang land" she was rather taken aback by some aspects of her persona. "I'm rotten and I'm skanky. And I think I'm kinda gay." The vampire's strong sexuality embarrassed Willow, making her hide behind her boyfriend. "It's a good thing who you are as a vampire isn't a reflection of who you are as a person," she notes. Willow, of course, really is bisexual. Her vampire side has simply allowed her to break free of her inhibitions and realize her passions sooner than she would have on her own. But is there a power inherent in becoming a vampire that fills you with artificial, chemical, or magical self-confidence? Or is the difference more cultural than clinical? Vampires are already freaks of society. They have fangs, live in darkness, and kill cows to drink rather than eat. As they're constantly drinking from the necks of strangers, they get over feeling shy pretty quickly. Spike worked much this way. In life he was a soft-spoken poet, tragically in love with a woman who despised him. He was so sheltered that he wouldn't even take note of the vampires overrunning the city. "That's what the police are for," he explains. "I prefer placing my energies into creating things of beauty." When Cicely very cruelly rejects him, he runs away. He tries so hard to offer the world beauty and receives nothing but hatred in return. The object of his inspiration becomes his source of greatest despair, depriving him of dreams.

Henry III: Dru seems to understand Spike's bruised feelings, saying the things he needs to hear: "I see you, a man surrounded by fools who cannot see his strengths, his vision, his glory. Your wealth is in the spirit and the imagination. You walk in worlds the others can't even begin to imagine." I am reminded of another contemporary story about a wounded intellectual who comes to discover his specialness, Harry Potter. This is a story we need to be told over and over, because the best minds of each generation undergo such ostracization. After Columbine, teachers, parents, and administrators often pushed those kids further away, pathologizing their imaginations, while comforting the "muggles."

Henry IV: When Spike crosses over moments later, the experience is so new to his virgin skin that he appears to be caught in the throngs of ecstasy. When next we see him, everything is different. His hair is shorter and better kept. He's been working out. And most importantly he has the kind of security and self-confidence that's impossible to fake. Spike is becoming a "man." When he accuses Angel of being a poofter it's with the greatest of pleasure. Spike's been bullied his whole life for being too queer (even though he's very obviously passionate about women). To turn around and slam someone else with a homophobic joke of his own is to beat the world at its own game, to assert his new-found position at the top of the social food chain. Two beautiful women are following him around. He's having some adventure. The whole thing gives him a new lease on death.

Henry III: Spike refuses to allow Buffy to trivialize this moment: "Becoming a vampire is a profound and powerful experience. I felt this new strength coursing through me. Nearly killed me but it made me feel alive for the very first time." Look at the expression on Spike's face when he realizes what Dru is offering. Up until her fang face transformation, he probably read it as a sexual encounter. After Cicely questions his manhood, he is prepared to lose his virginity on the spot. Others have run away from vampires in horror, but Spike embraces the monstrous with intellectual curiosity. Spike is searching out new experiences.

Henry IV: When he first hears about the Slayer, he falls madly in love with the entire idea. To him, the Slayer is the alpha dog—the great bully that all vampires must fear. Spike no longer allows himself to be ordered around. He already is the new alpha dog of his own reality. Defeating the woman would be his way of proving independence (and, as importantly, his masculine prowess) to all vampires everywhere. Just as Buffy tries to overcome her failings as a warrior, Spike must overcome his failings as a man. After killing the Slayer, the first thing he does is make love to Druscilla in a puddle of the fallen champion's blood—desecrating the body, allowing his masculinity to proclaim its victory. Perhaps it was the most adult thing he could think to do.

As the decades have passed Spike has continued to invest a great deal in his sexuality. He's the quickest of the characters to jump into bed with someone. He clearly craves a good fight—comes out to whoop someone for the sheer enjoyment of seeing them fall. But there's no mistaking a part of the old William poet child that remains. He still uses an almost impossibly sharp and refined sense of wit and sarcasm as his primary tool for quieting potential pretenders to the throne. And as he remarks to Buffy near the end of "Becoming," "I want to save the world!" Simply the great vision he has to kill the Slayer—the optimism of the challenger beating the odds—suggests a romantic underside to his personality. When Buffy massacres him at the end of their conversation by quoting Cicely, he falls to the earth. No matter how hard he's fought to obliterate any sign of William, he can't entirely hide the remnants of a soul—his intellectual mind, willful naiveté, natural romantic impulses. He can never kill William. He can only hide him, a secret identity.

Henry III: I take exception to your suggestion that Spike's hypermasculine behavior makes him more "adult." His posturing reflects a great deal of anxiety. It is pretty conventional to represent vampires as frozen culturally at the moment of their transformation. They dress in archaic clothing and speak antiquated language. They are ghosts of the past still walking among us. But Spike hadn't fully defined himself yet. Across the flashbacks, he tries on one identity after another. He takes on a working-class accent. Hoping to escape the sting of "William the Bloody," he changes his name to "Spike." Or in the 1970s, he punks out. Now a Goth, he wears a black leather trench coat and blackens his nails. No matter how many years he's walked the planet, Spike is still trying to figure out who he is and still nursing the wounds of his youth. In "Becomings," he acknowledges that a lot of being a vampire is a performance: "We like to talk big. Vampires do. I'm going to destroy the world. It's just tough guy talk, strutting around with your friends over a pint of blood." To me, the moment of real maturity comes when he comes upon Buffy crying on her back porch. He is ready to put aside his anger and allow himself to be caring again. He sees her as another person in pain. Spike's gawky gentleness speaks volumes about his relative inexperience in dealing with human emotion. All the rest of it is just posturing.

Henry IV: You're using the adult definition of adult. I'm using the adolescent definition. There's only a passing resemblance. To be grown up at seventeen is to act nineteen. The mature boys I went to high school with had three traits in common: cars, cell phones, and private entrances to their bedrooms. Some of them were intelligent and in touch with their romantic desires. But some of them were among the biggest blowholes I've ever met. Regardless, all they needed to do to ascend the social ladder was to have money, self-confidence, and a strong upper body. A lot like Angel (and eventually Spike). The Williams I've known have taken a much broader range of forms. One suffered a nervous breakdown his junior year and never was the same after. Another guy had so little emotional control that when he lost his temper he picked a chair up and threw it at a girl, nearly spearing her. One was so shy that she could barely have a conversation without going into conniption fits of blushing and hiding behind her hair. Just like William is frail and sheltered, they too had fatal flaws. Some were incredibly mature, some were total children. But, like the "mature" kids, they weren't judged by their intellectual ability so much as their sexual prowess. I think we are simply dealing with a difference in the way teenagers and adults use language.

Henry III: This sequence really makes your case that Spike is a mediating figure between teens and adults. Buffy is feeling enormously vulnerable; she has just learned about Joyce's health problems. Consider how different the scene would have been if it had been either Giles or Xander who came to comfort her. Giles would have offered too much protection and Xander would have needed more help than he could offer. But, Spike promises a more complex and ambiguous kind of comfort. Spike understands more of the world than Xander and yet is less willing to take charge of her life than Giles would have been.

Final Thoughts

Henry III: As I traveled the country speaking to various groups about adolescence and popular culture after Columbine, I was often asked how parents can open better communications with their children. I have suggested that speaking with them about shared television programs might be a good start. *Buffy* is a particularly rich series for fostering such discussions, because it so consistently raises issues about the relationship between adults and adolescents and because it consciously seeks to heal the scars we carry with us from high school. There are so many more episodes we could have, perhaps should have discussed here, ranging from the representation of teen's involvement with digital media in "I Robot . . . You Jane" to the radical rethinking of the nature of family in "Family" or the series of episodes depicting Buffy's attempt to deal with the shock of Joyce's death. Almost every week, *Buffy* gives parents and teens something to discuss. My son and I have tried to use the series as, in Oz's words, a "sobering mirror" that enables us to reflect on our feelings, values, and relationships.

Henry IV: Well, not that sobering! I actually find it very positive. I've learned a lot from television about people in all kinds of situations far removed from my own. I've never been forty. I can't look back on it. It's a real problem that the younger you are the fewer experiences you have in common with your parents. They are, in a sense, alien. Even if the adults can speak to the kids knowingly—and that's a real if—the kids can only talk back abstractly. But if a good novel can transport you to ancient Rome or King Arthur's court then a good television show can take you into your parent's world. When I was growing up I couldn't always go to work with my dad. But by learning about office politics on TV I could more easily decipher his dinnertime rants. If your dad says "I have problems too," it isn't inherently clear what those problems are or whether he's exaggerating. You aren't born knowing. You've got to learn. With time and experience you will. But in the meantime you still have to coexist with your parents, and television, by illustrating their concerns, makes it so much easier to know where to start. No one would suggest that television in and of itself is sufficient communication. It just bridges the information gap so communication can go both ways.

Henry III: The fact this exchange is going to be published made it much harder for me to be totally open, and much harder for me to accept my son's ideas without trying to reshape them. I remain too conscious of how this essay is going to be judged. Critical dialogue works best when it is conducted in private and neither side feels exposed. Yet, even in this somewhat artificial context, I have developed greater respect for my son. Though I see us sharing many common values, my son is also developing his own voice. Sometimes we agree. Sometimes we disagree. Sometimes we are watching the same program and seeing very different things. Through the years, I have learned to value his insights and to trust his judgments by testing them out on the hypothetical situations provided by television. I have also found such exchanges an important occasion for sharing things that matter to me.

Cultural studies has often framed itself as the study of everyday life. It will only truly achieve its potential for social change if it learns to move beyond academic discourse and into more mundane contexts; we need to develop new modes of theory and criticism that can be applied in our ordinary interactions with each other. Otherwise, the media effects community will provide the common-sense categories through which parents make sense of their children's media consumption.

Notes

NOTES TO THE INTRODUCTION

1. James Paul Gee, *Situated Language and Learning: A Critique of Traditional Schooling* (New York: Routledge, 2004); David Buckingham, *After the Death of Childhood: Growing Up in the Age of Electronic Media* (London: Polity Press, 2000).

2. Rosemary J. Coombe, *The Cultural Life of Intellectual Properties: Authorship, Appropriation, and the Law* (Durham, NC: Duke University Press, 1998).

3. Steve Duncombe, *Notes from the Underground: Zines and the Politics of Alternative Culture* (London: Verso, 1997).

4. Kurt Lancaster, *Interacting with Babylon 5: Fan Performances in a Media Universe* (Austin: University of Texas Press, 2001).

5. Robert V. Kozinets, "Utopian Enterprise: Articulating the Meanings of *Star Trek*'s Culture of Consumption," *Journal of Consumer Research* 28 (June 2001): 67–88.

6. Geraldine Bloustein, *Girl-Making: A Cross-Cultural Analysis of the Processes of Growing Up Female* (Sydney: Bergham Books, 2004).

7. Thomas McLaughlin, *Street Smarts and Critical Theory: Listening to the Vernacular* (Madison: University of Wisconsin Press, 1996).

8. David A. Brewer, *The Afterlife of Character, 1726–1825* (Philadelphia: University of Pennsylvania Press, 2005); Carolyn Sigler, *Alternative Alices: Visions and Revisions of Lewis Carroll's Alice Books* (Lexington: University Press of Kentucky, 1977).

9. Ien Ang, *Watching Dallas: Soap Opera and the Melodramatic Imagination* (London: Methuen, 1985); Janice Radway, *Reading the Romance: Women, Patriarchy, and Popular Literature* (Chapel Hill: University of North Carolina Press, 1984); John Tulloch, *Doctor Who: The Unfolding Text* (London: St. Martin's, 1983); David Morley, *The Nationwide Audience: Structure and Decoding* (London: British Film Institute, 1980); John Fiske, *Television Culture* (London: Methuen, 1987).

10. Camille Bacon-Smith, *Enterprising Women: Television Fandom and the Creation of Popular Myth* (Philadelphia: University of Pennsylvania Press, 1991);

Constance Penley, *NASA/Trek: Popular Science and Sex in America* (London: Verso, 1997).

11. Tom Wolfe, *New Journalism* (New York: Harper Collins, 1973).

12. Matt Hills, *Fan Cultures* (London: Routledge, 2002). See also my conversation with Matt Hill, reproduced in Chapter 1 of this book.

NOTES TO CHAPTER 1

1. Janet Staiger, *Perverse Spectators: The Practices of Film Reception* (New York: New York University Press, 2000), 54.

2. Janice Radway, *Reading the Romance: Women, Patriarchy, and Popular Literature* (Chapel Hill: University of North Carolina Press, 1984).

3. Camille Bacon-Smith, *Enterprising Women: Television Fandom and the Creation of Popular Myth* (Philadelphia: University of Pennsylvania Press, 1991).

4. Richard Burt, *Unspeakable Shaxxxspeares* (London: Macmillan, 1998), 15.

5. Thomas McLaughlin, *Street Smarts and Critical Theory: Listening to the Vernacular* (Madison: University of Wisconsin Press, 1996).

6. David Giles, *Illusions of Immortality: A Psychology of Fame and Celebrity* (London: Macmillan, 2000), 135.

7. Lawrence Grossberg, "Is There a Fan in the House? The Affective Sensibility of Fandom," in *The Adoring Audience,* ed. Lisa A. Lewis (London: Routledge, 1992), 57.

8. Pierre Bourdieu, *Distinction: A Social Critique of the Judgement of Taste* (Cambridge, MA: Harvard University Press, 1987).

9. For more on Clive Barker and the aesthetics of horror, see Henry Jenkins, "Monstrous Beauty and Mutant Aesthetics: Rethinking Matthew Barney's Relationship to the Horror Genre," in *The Wow Climax: Exploring Popular Art* (New York: New York University Press, 2006).

10. John Tulloch, *Watching Television Audiences: Cultural Theories and Methods* (London: Arnold, 2000)

11. Matt Hills, "The 'Common Sense' of Cultural Studies: Qualitative Audience Research and the Role of Theory in(-)Determining Method," *Diagesis* 5 (Winter 1999): 6–15.

12. David Morley, *Family Television: Cultural Power and Domestic Leisure* (London: Routledge, 1988).

13. John Hartley, *Popular Reality: Journalism, Modernity, Popular Culture* (London: Arnold, 1996).

14. Ian Craib, *Experiencing Identity* (New York: Sage, 1998).

NOTES TO CHAPTER 2

1. Charles Leerhsen, "*Star Trek*'s Nine Lives," *Newsweek*, December 22, 1986, p. 66.

2. Michel de Certeau, *The Practice of Everyday Life* (Berkeley: University of California Press, 1984), 174.

3. No scholarly treatment of *Star Trek* fan culture can avoid these pitfalls, if only because making such a work accessible to an academic audience requires a translation of fan discourse into other terms that may never be fully adequate to the original. I come to both *Star Trek* and fan fiction as a fan first and a scholar second. My participation as a fan long precedes my academic interest in it. I have sought, where possible, to employ fan terms and to quote fans directly in discussing their goals and orientation toward the program and their own writing. I have shared drafts of this essay with fans and have incorporated their comments into the revision process. I have allowed them the dignity of being quoted from their carefully crafted, well-considered published work rather than from a spontaneous interview that would be more controlled by the researcher than by the informant. I leave it to my readers to determine whether this approach allows for a less-mediated reflection of fan culture than previous academic treatments of this subject.

4. E. P. Thompson, "The Moral Economy of the English Crowd in the 18th Century," *Past and Present* 50 (1971): 76–136.

5. Elizabeth Osbourne, letter to *Treklink* 9 (1987): 3–4.

6. The terms "letterzine" and "fictionzine" are derived from fan discourse. The two types of fanzines relate to each other in complex ways. Although there are undoubtedly some fans who read only one type of publication, many read both. Some letterzines, *Treklink* for instance, function as consumer guides and sounding boards for debates about the fictionzines.

7. Sondra Marshak and Myrna Culbreath, *Star Trek: The New Voyages* (New York: Bantam Books, 1978).

8. Media fan writing builds upon a much older tradition of "zine" publication within literary science fiction culture, dating back to the mid-1930s. For discussions of this earlier tradition, see Lester Del Rey, *The World of Science Fiction* (New York: Ballantine, 1979); Harry Warner, *All Our Yesterdays* (New York: Advent, 1969); and Sam Moskowitz, *The Immortal Storm* (New York: ASFO Press, 1954). These earlier fanzines differ from media fanzines in a number of significant ways: they were dominated by male fans; they published primarily essays or original fiction that borrowed generic elements of science fiction but not specific characters and situations; they were focused upon literary rather than media science fiction; and they were far fewer in number and enjoyed smaller circulation than media zines. Media fans borrow traditional formats from these earlier zines, but give them a new focus and a new function;

they were met with considerable hostility by the older literary science fiction community, though a number of media fans participate in traditional zine publishing as well as media-oriented ventures. Roberta Pearson has suggested to me that an interesting parallel to media fanzine publication may be the fan writings surrounding Sherlock Holmes, which date back to the beginning of this century. I do not at this time know enough about these publications to assess their possible relationship to Trek fan publishing.

9. Camille Bacon-Smith, "Spock among the Women," *New York Times Book Review,* November 16, 1986, pp. 1, 26, 28.

10. David Bleich, "Gender Interests in Reading and Language," in *Gender and Reading: Essays on Readers, Texts and Contexts,* ed. Elizabeth A. Flynn and P. P. Schweickart (Baltimore: Johns Hopkins University Press, 1986), 239.

11. Mary Ellen Brown and Linda Barwick, "Fables and Endless Generations: Soap Opera and Women's Culture," paper presented at a meeting of the Society for Cinema Studies, Montreal, May 1987.

12. Cheris Kramarae, *Women and Men Speaking* (Rowley, MS: Newbury House, 1981).

13. Carroll Smith-Rosenberg, *Disorderly Conduct: Gender in Victorian America* (New York: Alfred A. Knopf, 1985), 45.

14. Judith Spector, "Science Fiction and the Sex War: A Womb of One's Own," *Gender Studies: New Directions in Feminist Criticism,* ed. Judith Spector (Bowling Green, OH: Bowling Green State University Press, 1986), 163.

15. S. E. Whitfield and Gene Roddenberry, *The Making of Star Trek* (New York: Ballantine, 1968).

16. Pamela Rose, "Women in the Federation," in *The Best of Trek 2,* ed. W. Irwin and G. B. Love (New York: New American Library, 1977); Yoni Lay, letter to *Comlink* 28 (1986): 15.

17. Lay, letter to *Comlink,* 15.

18. Jane Land, *Kista* (Larchmont, NY: Author, c. 1984), p. 1; Catherine A. Siebert, "Journey's End at Lover's Meeting," *Slaysu* 1 (1980): 33.

19. Siebert, "Journey's End at Lover's Meeting," 33.

20. Karen Bates, *Starweaver Two* (Missouri Valley, IA: Ankar Press, 1982); *Nuages One* and *Nuages Two* (Tucson, AZ: Checkmate Press, 1982 and 1984).

21. Although a wide range of fanzines were considered in researching this essay, I have decided, for the purposes of clarity, to draw my examples largely from the work of a limited number of fan writers. While no selection could accurately reflect the full range of fan writing, I felt that Bates, Land, Lorrah, and Siebert had all achieved some success within the fan community, suggesting that they exemplified, at least to some fans, the types of writing that were desirable and reflected basic tendencies within the form. Further, these writers have produced a large enough body of work to allow some commentary about their overall project rather than localized discussions of individual stories. I have

also, wherever possible, focused my discussion around works still currently in circulation and therefore available to other researchers interested in exploring this topic. No slight is intended to the large number of other fan writers who also met these criteria and who, in some cases, are even better known within the fan community.

22. Jane Land, *Demeter* (Larchmont, NY: Author, 1987).

23. Tania Modleski, *Loving with a Vengeance: Mass-Produced Fantasies for Women* (Hamden, CT: Archon Books, 1982).

24. Jacqueline Lichtenberg, personal communication, August 1987.

25. I am indebted to K. C. D'Alessandro and Mary Carbine for probing questions that refined my thoughts on this particular issue.

26. Bethann, "The Measure of Love," *Grup* 5 (n.d.): 54.

27. Kendra Hunter, "Characterization Rape," in *The Best of Trek* 2, p. 78.

28. Janice Radway, *Reading the Romance: Women, Patriarchy, and Popular Literature* (Chapel Hill: University of North Carolina Press, 1984), 149.

29. Hunter, "Characterization Rape," 78.

30. Joan Verba, "Editor's Corner," *Treklink* 6 (c. 1985): 2.

31. Jean Lorrah, *Full Moon Rising* (Bronx, NY: Author, 1976), 9–10.

32. Tim Blaes, letter to *Treklink* 9 (1987): 6.

33. Siebert, "By Any Other Name," *Slaysu* 4 (1982): 44–45.

34. Thompson, "The Moral Economy of the English Crowd in the 18th Century," 78.

35. Shari Schnuelle, letter to *Socia trek* 4 (1987): 9.

36. Hunter, "Characterization Rape," 77.

37. Ibid., 83.

38. Jean Lorrah, introduction to *The Vulcan Academy Murders* (Bronx, NY: 1984).

39. Leslie Thompson, "*Star Trek* Mysteries—Solved!" *The Best of Trek*, ed. Walter Irwin and G. B. Love (New York: New American Library, 1974), 208.

40. The area of Kirk/Spock fiction falls beyond the project of this particular paper, raising issues similar to yet more complex than those posed here. My reason for discussing it here is because of the light its controversial reception sheds on the norms of fan fiction and the various ways fan readers and writers situate themselves toward the primary text. For a more detailed discussion of this particular type of fan writing, see Patricia Frazer Lamb and Diana Veith, "Romantic Myth, Transcendence, and *Star Trek* Zines," in *Erotic Universe: Sexuality and Fantastic Literature,* ed. Donald Palumbo (New York: Greenwood Press, 1986), 235–56, who argue that K/S stories, far from representing a cultural expression of the gay community, constitute another way of feminizing the original series text and of addressing feminist concerns within the domain of a popular culture that offers little space for heroic action by women.

41. Thera Snaider, letter to *Treklink* 8 (1987): 10.

42. M. Chandler, letter to *Treklink* 8 (1987): p. 10.

43. Regina Moore, letter to *Treklink* 4 (1986): 7.

44. Slusher, personal communication, 1986.

45. Land, *Demeter*, ii.

46. Ian Spelling, Robert Lofficier, and Jean-Marie Lofficier, "William Shatner, Captain's Log: *Star Trek V*," *Starlog* (May 1987): 40.

NOTES TO CHAPTER 3

1. Franklin Hummel, "Where None Have Gone Before," *Gaylactic Gayzette* (May 1991): 2. I am indebted to John Campbell for his extensive assistance in recruiting members of the Gaylaxians to participate in the interviews for this chapter. Interviews were conducted both in informal settings (members' homes) as well as more formal ones (my office), depending on the size and the needs of the groups. As it evolved, the groups were segregated by gender.

2. For more information on the Gaylaxian Network, see Franklin Hummel, "SF Comes to Boston: Gaylaxians at the World Science Fiction Convention," *New York Native*, October 23, 1989, p. 26.

3. Gaylaxians International recruitment flier.

4. John Hartley, *Tele-ology: Studies in Television* (New York: Routledge, Chapman and Hall, 1992), 5.

5. Ibid., 7.

6. Susan Sackett, executive assistant to Gene Roddenberry, letter to Franklin Hummel, March 12, 1991.

7. Mark A. Altman, "Tackling Gay Rights," *Cinefantastique* (October 1992): 74.

8. Franklin Hummel, Director, Gaylactic Network, letter to Gene Roddenberry, May 1, 1991.

9. The nineteenth-century word *Uranian* was coined by early German homosexual emancipationist Karl Ulrichs and used popularly through the First World War to refer to homosexuals. As Eric Garber and Lyn Paleo note, "It refers to Aphrodite Urania, whom Plato had identified as the patron Goddess of homosexuality in his Symposium." Eric Garber and Lyn Paleo, *Uranian Worlds: A Guide to Alternative Sexuality in Science Fiction, Fantasy and Horror* (Boston: G. K. Hall, 1990), 1.

10. Hummel, letter to Roddenberry, May 1, 1991.

11. The analogy John and other Gaylaxians draw between the black civil rights movement of the 1960s and the queer civil rights movement of the 1990s is a controversial one. But it is hardly unique to these fans. This analogy has been part of the discursive context surrounding Bill Clinton's efforts to end the American military's ban on gay and lesbian enlistment.

12. Sackett, letter to Hummel, March 12, 1991. Roddenberry has, at various times, acknowledged that he saw his inclusion of Uhura on the original series as a contribution to the civil rights movement, that he had added Chekhov in response to a *Pravda* editorial calling for an acknowledgement of Soviet accomplishments in space, and that he introduced the blind character, Geordi, on *Star Trek: The Next Generation* as a response to the many disabled fans he had encountered through the years. Given such a pattern, it was not unreasonable for the Gaylaxians to anticipate a similar gesture toward gay, lesbian, and bisexual viewers.

13. Hummel, "Where None Have Gone Before," 12.

14. Edward Gross, *The Making of The Next Generation* (Las Vegas: Pioneer Books), as reprinted in *Gaylactic Gayzette,* May 1991.

15. David Gerrold, letter to Frank Hummel, November 23, 1986.

16. Steve K., "Gays and Lesbians in the 24th Century: *Star Trek—The Next Generation,*" *The Lavender Dragon* 1, no. 3 (August 1991): 1.

17. Theresa M., "*Star Trek: The Next Generation* Throws Us a Bone," *The Lavender Dragon* 2, no. 2 (April 1992) 1.

18. "*Star Trek*: The Next Genderation," *The Advocate,* August 27, 1991, p. 74.

19. Richard Arnold, letter to J. DeSort, Jr., March 10, 1991.

20. Richard Arnold, letter to J. DeSort, Jr., September 10, 1989.

21. Ibid.

22. Mark A. Perigard, "Invisible, Again," *Bay Windows,* February 7, 1991, p. 8.

23. Arnold, letter to DeSort, March 10, 1991.

24. Ibid.

25. Altman, "Tackling Gay Rights," 72. Note that Berman and the other producers have never made similar arguments in their public statements about the controversy, always suggesting other reasons for their failure to introduce gay, lesbian, or bisexual characters into the series.

26. Patricia Clark, "Star Trek: The Next Genderation," *The Advocate,* August 27, 1991, p. 8.

27. Ibid.

28. Ibid.

29. Ruth Rosen, "Star Trek Is on Another Bold Journey," *Los Angeles Times,* October 30, 1991.

30. John Perry, "To Boldly Go . . . These Are the Not-So-Gay Voyages of the Starship Enterprise," *Washington Blade,* September 20, 1991, p. 36.

31. Altman, "Tackling Gay Rights," 74.

32. Gene Roddenberry, *Star Trek: The Motion Picture* (New York: Pocket Books, 1979), 22.

33. Ibid.

34. D. A. Miller, "Anal *Rope*," in *Inside/Out: Lesbian Theories, Gay Theories*, ed. Diana Fuss (New York: Routledge, Chapman and Hall, 1991), 124. For other useful discussions of this subject, see Danae Clarke, "Commodity Lesbianism," *Camera Obscura* 25, no. 6 (January–May 1991): 181–202; Eve Kosofsky Sedgwick, *Epistemology of the Closet* (Berkeley: University of California Press, 1990).

35. Altman, "Tackling Gay Rights," 73.

36. Ibid., 74.

37. Christine M. Conran, letter to Gene Roddenberry, May 23, 1991.

38. Altman, "Tackling Gay Rights," 74.

39. Jonathan Frakes: "I don't think they were gutsy enough to take it where they should have. Soren should have been more obviously male." Rick Berman: "We were either going to cast with non-masculine men or non-feminine females. We knew we had to go one way or the other. We read both men and women for the roles and decided to go with women. It might have been interesting to go with men, but that was the choice we made." Brannon Braga: "If it would have been a man playing the role would he have kissed him? I think Jonathan would have because he's a gutsy guy." "Episode Guide," *Cinefantastique* (October 1992): 78. Gays might find some solace in the fact that it clearly takes more "guts" to be a homosexual than a heterosexual.

40. Email posting, name withheld.

41. Altman, "Tackling Gay Rights," 74.

42. Ibid.

43. Steve K., "Gays and Lesbians in the 24th Century," 2.

44. Miller, "Anal *Rope*," 125.

45. The Gaylaxians note, for example, a similar pattern in the introduction and development of Ensign Ro in *Star Trek: The Next Generation*'s fifth season: Ro, like Yar, drew on iconography associated with butch lesbians, and appearing in the midst of the letter-writing campaign was read as the long-promised queer character. Within a few episodes of her introduction, however, the program involved her in a plot where the *Enterprise* crew loses its memory and Riker and Ro become lovers. As one Gaylaxian explained during a panel discussion of the series at Gaylaxicon, "Oops! I forgot I was a Lesbian!"

NOTES TO CHAPTER 5

1. Ien Ang, *Watching Dallas: Soap Opera and the Melodramatic Imagination* (London: Methuen, 1985).

2. For examples of science fiction stories that explore the potential ramifications of the computer net, see Orson Scott Card's *Ender's Game*, William Gibson's *Neuromancer*, and Norman Spinrad's *Little Heroes*.

3. The gender balance on the net has gradually shifted, but the technological sphere continues to be a highly masculine space. Female participation is reported to be much higher on commercially accessible networks such as Prodigy and Compuserve.

4. As with other writing on media audiences, this essay is at least implicitly autobiographical. My discovery of *Twin Peaks* coincided with my introduction to the potentials of email and computer net discussion groups. I fell for both of them hard. The experience of "lurking" on the net (i.e., acting as a voyeur rather than an active contributor to the virtual community) shaped my responses to the series and became a central part of what *Twin Peaks* meant to me. In writing this essay, I therefore commemorate this moment as well as try to recapture and communicate something of what it meant to those of us who were part of that reception community. I therefore dedicate this essay to the men and women who shared with me the experience of alt.tv.twinpeaks. I also wish to thank members of the Narrative Intelligence reading group at MIT, especially Marc Davis and Amy Bruckman, who have encouraged me to bring my insights as a humanist to the previously unfamiliar realm of contemporary American technoculture.

5. According to one news story posted on the net, *Twin Peaks* had become the most video-taped program on network television during the time of its airing, with about 830,000 recording it each week. Most netters claimed that they watched the episodes multiple times during the week between their initial airing and the appearance of a new episode.

6. See my *Textual Poachers: Television Fans and Participatory Culture* (New York: Routledge, 1992).

7. For a fuller account of computer net discussions of *Star Trek,* see John Tulloch and Henry Jenkins, *Science Fiction Audiences: Watching Doctor Who and Star Trek* (London: Routledge, 1995).

8. My use of the term "emotional realism" is derived from Ien Ang.

9. Once the murder was solved in the series, Jennifer Lynch's shocked response to her father's narrative makes more sense, given the incestuous relationship posited between Leland Palmer and his daughter.

10. Although "Lynch" proved to be a fraud in this case, the fans' demise was not totally far-fetched. It is well established that some soap producers do tap into the net to monitor audience response to their plot lines, while producer Joe Straczynski made extensive use of net communications to build audience interest in the airing of his science fiction television pilot *Babylon 5.* At least one contributor to the net did seem to have personal contact with Mark Frost, who occasionally leaked information to the group.

11. A team of MIT students (Douglas D. Keller, David Kung, Rich Payne) surveyed participants on alt.tv.twinpeaks in March 1993 as part of their work for my American Television course. Asked about the qualities they associated

with the "average *Twin Peaks* fan," the respondents offered descriptions that stressed their own exceptional qualities, particularly their intellectual abilities:

> The average *Twin Peaks* fan is intelligent, odd, quirky, over analytical and does not watch *Full House* or *Family Matters*.

> *Twin Peaks* required a great deal of patience and intelligence to watch . . . and the average American has neither in abundance.

> Fairly intellectual . . . also creative.

> High IQ, patient attention span.

> Exactly the same core audience for *Star Trek, Doctor Who* and *Master-piece Theatre*.

> The die-hard *TP* watchers are probably white, male, middleclass or higher, college-educated in the liberal arts, like jazz and Thai food.

> A strange and wonderful person with hidden personality traits that make him or her relate to the weirdness on the show. Probably a fan of *Star Trek, Picket Fences, Northern Exposure*. Probably doesn't even watch a lot of TV.

> Most people found it took too much thought to stay involved in the show. For instance, both my mother and sister didn't like the show. They are both average intelligence. To them *TP* was just an annoyingly confusing blur of images. But everyone I know who likes the show is above average intelligence.

Here, the program's exceptional qualities, the demands it made on the spectator's activity, allows fans to assert their own intellectual superiority to the bulk of the viewing public, stressing traits that are particularly valued within the computer net subculture. *Twin Peaks,* they explained, was "not a show for passive people." Many cited the fact that the program did not sustain strong ratings and was cancelled as evidence of their discriminating taste and departure from the cultural mainstreams: "Heaven forbid that Americans think about anything."

NOTES TO CHAPTER 6

1. Pierre Levy, *Collective Intelligence: Mankind's Emerging World in Cyberspace* (Cambridge: Perseus, 1997), 217.

2. The phrase "imagined community" comes from Benedict Anderson, *Imagined Communities: Reflections on the Origin and Spread of Nationalism* (New York: Verso, 1991). Anderson argues that we feel strong affiliations with nation-states even though they are too large for us to have personal contacts with all

of the other citizens and cites the role media plays in providing the social ce-
ment between these scattered populations. Levy (*Collective Intelligence*, 125) introduces the concept of an "imaging community" to describe how a sense of affiliation emerges from an active process of self-definition and reciprocal knowledge
transfer.

3. A fuller account of Gernsbeck's role in the development of science fiction
fandom can be found in Andrew Ross, *Strange Weather: Culture, Science and
Technology in the Age of Limits* (New York: Verso, 1991). For a fuller account
of contemporary literary SF fandom, see Camille Bacon-Smith, *Science Fiction
Culture* (Philadelphia: University of Pennsylvania Press, 2000).

4. John Tulloch and Henry Jenkins, *Science Fiction Audiences: Watching
Doctor Who and Star Trek* (London: Routledge, 1995).

5. Sherry Turkle, *The Second Self: Computers and the Human Spirit* (New
York: Touchstone, 1984), provides some glimpse of the centrality of science fic-
tion in that early hacker culture, as does my study of *Star Trek* fans at MIT in
Tulloch and Jenkins, *Science Fiction Audiences*.

6. Susan J. Clerc, "Estrogen Brigades and 'Big Tits' Threads: Media Fandom
Online and Off," in *Wired Women: Gender and New Realities in Cyberspace*,
ed. Lynn Cherney and Elizabeth Reba Weise (Seattle: Seal, 1996).

7. Nancy Baym, "Talking about Soaps: Communication Practices in a Computer-Mediated Culture," in *Theorizing Fandom: Fans, Subculture, and Identity*, ed. Cheryl Harris and Alison Alexander (New York: Hampton Press,
1998).

8. Levy, *Collective Intelligence*, 20.

9. Baym, "Talking about Soaps," 115–16.

10. Ibid., 127.

11. Matthew Hills, *Fan Cultures* (London: Routledge, 2002).

12. For a useful discussion of the ways that the net is challenging traditional
forms of expertise, see Peter Walsh, "That Withered Paradigm: The Web, the
Expert and the Information Hegemony," http://media-in-transition.mit.edu.

13. Hills, *Fan Cultures*, 78–79.

14. Ibid.

15. For an overview of anime and its fans, see Susan J. Napier, *Anime from
Akira to Princess Mononoke: Experiencing Contemporary Japanese Animation*
(New York: Palgrave, 2001).

16. The phrase "week-end only world" is discussed in the concluding chapter of Henry Jenkins, *Textual Poachers: Television Fans and Participatory Culture* (New York: Routledge, 1992).

17. Andre McDonald, "Uncertain Utopia: Science Fiction Media Fandom and
Computer-Mediated Communication," in *Theorizing Fandom: Fans, Subculture,
and Identity*, ed. Cheryl Harris and Alison Alexander (New York: Hampton
Press, 1998).

18. Nancy Baym, *Tune In, Log On: Soaps, Fandom and Online Community* (New York: Corwin, 1999).

19. Stephen Duncombe, *Notes from Underground: Zines and the Politics of Alternative Culture* (New York: Verso, 1997).

20. For a fuller discussion of fan video practices, see *Textual Poachers*. For a larger context on amateur media production, see Patricia R. Zimmermann, *Reel Families: A Social History of Amateur Film* (Indianapolis: Indiana University Press, 1995).

21. Henry Jenkins, "Quentin Tarantino's Star Wars? Digital Cinema, Media Convergence and Participatory Culture," in *Dfilm*, ed. Bart Cheever and Nick Constant (Cambridge, MA: MIT Press, 2001).

22. Levy, *Collective Intelligence*, 121.

23. Ibid., 123.

24. Kurt Lancaster, *Interacting with Babylon 5: Fan Performances in a Media Universe* (Austin: University of Texas Press, 2001).

25. Levy, *Collective Intelligence*, 125.

26. Amelie Hastie, "Proliferating Television in the Market and in the Know," paper presented at the "Console-ing Passions" conference, Bristol, UK, July 6, 2001.

27. Lancaster, *Interacting with Babylon 5*, 26. See also Alan Wexelblat, "An Auteur in the Age of the Internet," in *Hop on Pop: The Politics and Pleasures of Popular Culture*, ed. Henry Jenkins, Tara McPherson, and Jane Shattuc (Durham, NC: Duke University Press, 2002).

28. Allison McCracken, "Bronzers for a Smut-filled Environment: Reading Fans Reading Sexual Identity at Buffy.com," paper presented at the "Console-ing Passions" conference, Bristol, UK, July 6, 2001.

29. David Spitz, "Contested Codes: Toward a Social History of Napster" (Masters thesis, Comparative Media Studies Program, MIT, June 2001).

30. See, for example, Eileen Meehan, "Holy Commodity Fetish, Batman!": The Political Economy of a Political Intertext" in *The Many Lives of the Batman: Critical Approaches to a Superhero and His Media,* ed. Roberta Pearson and William Uricchio (New York: Routledge, 1991).

31. This formulation of the issue was inspired by Sara Gwenllian Jones, "Conflicts of Interest? The Folkloric and Legal Status of Cult TV Characters in Online Fan Culture," paper presented at the Society for Cinema Studies Conference, Washington, DC, May 26, 2001.

32. Levy, *Collective Intelligence*, 237.

33. For example, see Amy Jo Kim, *Community Building on the Web: Secret Strategies for Successful Online Communities* (Berkeley: Peachpit Press, 2000).

34. Jupiter Communication, as cited in "Just Exactly What Is Viral Marketing?" http:marketsherpa.co.uk.

35. Don Peppers, "Introduction," in Seth Godon, *Permission Marketing: Turning Strangers into Friends, and Friends into Customers* (New York: Simon and Schuster, 1999), 12.

36. Robert V. Kozinets, "Utopian Enterprise: Articulating the Meanings of *Star Trek*'s Culture of Consumption," *Journal of Consumer Research* (June 2001): http://www.journals.uchicago.edu/JCR/journal/.

37. See, for example, Elizabeth Kolbert, "Pimps and Dragons: How an Online World Survived a Social Breakdown," *New Yorker*, May 28, 2001.

38. Kurt Squire, "Wars Galaxies: A Case Study in Participatory Design," *Joystick 101*, www.joystick101.org, forthcoming.

39. Personal interview, April 2001.

40. Mark Dery, *Culture Jamming: Hacking, Slashing and Sniping in the Empire of Signs* (Open Magazine Pamphlet Series, 1993), http://web.nwe.ufl.edu/~mlaffey/cultjam1.html.

For elaboration on the concept of culture jamming, see also Gareth Branwyn, *Jamming the Media: A Citizens Guide for Reclaiming the Tools of Communication* (San Francisco: Chronicle, 1997); and David Cox, "Notes on Culture Jamming," http:www.syntac.net/hoax/manifesti/notes.php.

41. For a useful overview of media activism in this period, see Douglas Rushkoff, *Media Virus! Hidden Agendas in Popular Culture* (New York: Ballantine, 1996).

42. Philip Hayward, "Situating Cyberspace: The Popularization of Virtual Reality," in *Future Visions: New Technologies of the Screen*, ed. Philip Haywood and Tana Wollen (London: British Film Institute).

43. Dery, *Culture Jamming*.

44. Levy, *Collective Intelligence*, 171.

45. Ibid., 36–37.

NOTES TO CHAPTER 7

1. Todd Gitlin, *Media Unlimited: How the Torrent of Images and Sounds Overwhelms Our Lives* (New York: Metropolitan, 2002).

2. Jeff Yang, Dina Gan, Terry Hong, and the Staff of *A. Magazine*, eds., *Eastern Standard Time: A Guide to Asian Influence on American Culture from Astro Boy to Zen Buddhism* (Boston: Houghton Mifflin, 1997).

3. For the most thorough discussion of the Bert and Bin Laden story, see http://www.lindqvist.com/index.php?katID=7&lang=eng&incl=bert.php.

4. Grant McCracken, *Plenitude,* published online as a work in progress at http://www.cultureby.com/books/plenit/cxc_trilogy_plenitude.html.

5. Henry Jenkins, *Convergence Culture: Where Old and New Media Collide* (New York: New York University Press, 2006).

6. Ulf Hannerz, "Cosmopolitans and Locals in World Culture," in *Global Culture: Nationalism, Globalization, and Modernity,* ed. Mike Featherstone (London: Sage, 1990), 237.

7. For another take on what I am calling pop cosmopolitanism, see Martin Roberts, "Notes on the Global Underground: Subcultural Elites, Cospicious Cosmopolitanism," paper presented at "Globalization, Identity and the Arts" conference, University of Manitoba, Winnipeg, Canada, 2000.

8. Matt Hills, "Transcultural Otaku: Japanese Representations of Fandom and Representations of Japan in Anime/Manga Fan Cultures," paper presented at "Media-in-Transition 2: Globalization and Convergence" conference at Massachusetts Institute of Technology, Cambridge, MA, 2002.

9. Ramaswami Harindranath, "Reviving 'Cultural Imperialism': International Audiences, Global Capitalism and the Transnational Elite," in *Planet TV,* ed. Lisa Parks and Shanti Kumar (New York: New York University Press, 2003), 156.

10. For overviews of the debates on media imperialism, see John Tomlinson, *Cultural Imperialism* (Baltimore: Johns Hopkins University Press, 1991); David Howe, "Commodities and Cultural Borders," in *Cross-Cultural Consumption: Global Markets, Local Realities,* ed. David Howes (London: Routledge, 1996); Tamar Liebes and Elihu Katz, *The Export of Meaning: Cross-Cultural Readings of Dallas* (Oxford: Oxford University Press, 1990); Mike Featherstone, "Localism, Globalism and Cultural Identity," in *Global/Local: Cultural Production and the Transnational Imaginary,* ed. Rob Wilson and Wimal Dissanayake (Durham, NC: Duke University Press, 1996).

11. Janet Wasko, Mark Phillips, and Eileen R. Meehan, eds., *Dazzled by Disney? The Global Disney Audiences Project* (London: Leicester University Press, 2001).

12. Rana Foroohar, "Hurray for Globowood: As Motion-Picture Funding, Talent and Audiences Go Global, Hollywood is No Longer a Place, but a State of Mind," *Newsweek International,* May 27, 2002; Christina Klein, "The Globalization of Hollywood," paper presented at the Modern Language Association conference, New York, 2002.

13. Arjun Appadurai, *Modernity at Large: The Cultural Dimensions of Globalization* (Minneapolis: University of Minnesota Press, 1996), 4.

14. Mike Levin, "Independent Distributors and Specialty Labels Move Product in the U.S. by Such International Artists as Shakira,"

15. Koichi Twauchi, *Recentering Globalization: Popular Culture and Japanese Transnationalism* (Durham, NC: Duke University Press, 2002), 25–27.

16. Anne Allison, "A Challenge to Hollywood: Japanese Character Goods Hit the U.S.," *Japanese Studies* 20, no.1 (2002): 67–88.

17. Anne Allison, "The Cultural Politics of Pokemon Capitalism," paper

presented at "Media-in-Transition 2: Globalization and Convergence" conference, Massachusetts Institute of Technology, Cambridge, MA, 2002.

18. Wasko, Phillips, and Meehan, eds., *Dazzled by Disney?*

19. Heather Hendershott, *Saturday Morning Censors* (Durham, NC: Duke University Press, 1998).

20. Kaoru Hoketsu, *Iron Chef: The Official Book* (Berkeley: Berkeley Publishing Group, 2001).

21. Alison James, "Cooking the Books: Global or Local Identities in Contemporary British Food Cultures?" in *Cross-Cultural Consumption: Global Markets, Local Realities,* ed. David Howes (London: Routledge, 1996).

22. Don Kaplan, "Iron Chef to America," *New York Post,* May 18, 2001.

23. Charlie McCollum, "Iron Chef USA: Something's Lost During Translation," *San Jose Mercury,* November 16, 2001. For other negative reactions to the Americanization of the series, see Tim Goodman, "Iron Chef USA Is an Abomination: UPN Remake Is an Insult to Food Fans," *San Francisco Chronicle,* November 16, 2001; Douglas Levy, "Iron Chef," *Oakland Press Online Edition,* November 16, 2001.

24. Hannerz, "Cosmopolitans and Locals in World Culture," 250.

25. Aswin Punathambekar, "Bollywood Bytes: A Story of How I Found an Online Adda" (unpublished manuscript).

26. On the role of ethnic groceries in preserving diasporic traditions, see Hamid Naficy, *The Making of Exile Cultures: Iranian Television in Los Angeles* (Minneapolis: University of Minnesota Press, 1992).

27. Nabeel Zuberi, *Sounds English: Transnational Popular Music* (Chicago: University of Chicago Press, 2002); Sanjay Sharma, John Hutnyk, and Ashwani Sharma, eds., *Dis-Orienting Rhythms: The Politics of the New Asian Dance Music* (London: Zed, 1996); George Lipsitz, *Dangerous Crossroads: Popular Music, Postmodernism, and the Politics of Place* (London: Verso, 1994).

28. Sunaina Marr Maira, *Desis in the House: Indian American Youth Culture in New York City* (Philadelphia: Temple University Press, 2002).

29. Sandhya Shukla, "Building Diaspora and Nation: The 1991 Cultural Festival of India," *Cultural Studies* 11, no. 2 (1997): 296–315; Anandam P. Kavoori and Christina A. Joseph, "Why the Dancing Diasporic Desi Men Cross-Dressed," *Jump Cut,* no.45 (Fall 2002), available online at http://www.ejumpcut .org/archive/jcas.2002/kavoori/index.html.

30. "Bollywood Goes Global," *Newsweek International,* February 28, 2000.

31. Cynthia Littleton, "Nair, CWM Bring Family Values to ABC for Comedy," *Hollywood Reporter,* December 5, 2002; Michael Fleming, "Monsoon Forecast for Broadway," *Variety,* December 15, 2002; John Lahr, "Whirlwind: How the Filmmaker Mira Nair Makes People See the World Her Way," *New Yorker,* December 9, 2002.

32. "Bright Launch," *The Hindu,* June 28, 2002; "Indian Summer: Raising the Curtain on Bombay Dreams," *Theatregoer,* June 2002.

33. Foroohar, "Hurray for Globowood."

34. Abhijeet Chatterjee, "Leela Is a Hollywood Production with the Soul of a Hindi Film," *Rediff.com,* January 2 2001, http://www.rediff,com/entertai/2001/jan/021leela.htm

35. Sunaina Maira, "Henna and Hip Hop: The Politics of Cultural Production and the Work of Cultural Studies," *Journal of Asian American Studies* 3, no. 3 (2000): 329–69.

36. Hills, "Transcultural Otaku."

37. Sean Leonard, personal correspondence, February 2003.

38. On Manga fandom, see Frederik Schodt, *Dreamland Japan: Writings on Modern Manga* (Berkeley: Stone Bridge, 1996); Sharon Kinsella, *Adult Manga: Culture and Power in Contemporary Japanese Society* (Honolulu: University of Hawaii Press, 2000); Patrick Macias and Carl Gustav Horn, eds., *Japan Edge: The Insider's Guide to Japanese Pop Subculture* (San Francisco: Cadence Books, 1999).

39. Sean Leonard, personal correspondence, February 2003.

40. "Anime Airwaves," *Wizard* (March 2003): 102.

41. Douglas Wolk, "Manga, Anime Invade the U.S.: Japanese Comics and Animation Work Together to Attract Readers," *Publisher's Weekly,* March 12, 2001; Sachiko Sakimaki, "Manga Mania: Cartoonists Eye America," *Washington Post,* September 5, 2002; Mie Sakamoto, "Shonen Jump Manga Takes Giant Leap into U.S. Market," *Japan Economic Newswire,* January 5, 2003.

42. Susan Napier, *Anime from Akira to Princess Mononoke: Experiencing Japanese Animation* (New York: Palgrave, 2001), 242. See also Annilee Newitz, "Anime Otaku: Japanese Animation Fans Outside Japan," *Bad Subjects* 13, http://eserver.org/bs/13/Newitz.html; Joseph Tobin, "An American Otaku or, a Boy's Virtual Life on the Net," in *Digital Diversions: Youth Culture in the Age of Multimedia,* ed. Julian Sefton-Green (London: University College of London Press, 1998).

43. Hannerz, "Cosmopolitans and Locals in World Culture," 240.

44. For useful overviews on the literature about hybridity, see Jan Nederveen Pieterse, "Globalization as Hybridization," in *Global Modernities,* ed. Michael Featherstone (New York: Sage, 1995); Nestor Garcia Canclini, *Consumers and Citizens: Globalization and Multicultural Conflicts* (Minneapolis: University of Minnesota Press, 2001).

45. Christina Klein, "*Crouching Tiger, Hidden Dragon*: A Diasporic Reading," *Cinema Journal* 43, no. 4 (2004): 18–42.

46. Ang Lee and James Schamus, as quoted in *The Guardian,* November 7, 2000, online at http://film.guardian.co.uk/interview/interviewpages/0,6737,

394698,00.html. Elsewhere, Schamus explained: "We wanted to make a quin-tessentially Chinese film that could speak to worldwide audiences in much the same way that Hollywood makes quintessentially American films that speak to worldwide audiences. The film embraces its international audiences, I hope, with the same amount of generosity that Hollywood films often have toward world-wide audiences. So, rather than making a kind of Hollywood version of a Chinese movie, I think we ended up making a Chinese version of an international block-buster." A.C. Basoli, "Kung Fu Writing: A Conversation with James Schamus," available online at http://www.moviemaker.com/hop/o1/scrn-Schamus.html.

47. Rene A. Guzman, "Manga Revises Marvel Heroes," *San Antonio Ex-press-News,* January 23, 2002.

48. "Tsunami Splash," *Wizard* (March 2003): 100.

49. Available online at http://whatisthematrix.warnerbros.com/rl_cmp/ani matrix_trailer_640.html.

50. Olivia Barker, "The Asianization of America But Eastern Influences Do Not Mean Asian-Americans Are Insiders," *USA Today,* March 22, 2001.

51. Renalto Rosaldo, *Culture and Truth* (Boston: Beacon, 1992).

NOTES TO CHAPTER II

1. John Michael, *Anxious Intellectuals: Academic Professionals, Public Intel-lectuals, and Enlightenment Values* (Durham, NC: Duke University Press, 2000).

2. Brad King and John Borland, *Dungeons and Dreamers: The Rise of Com-puter Game Culture from Geek to Chic* (New York: McGraw-Hill, 2003).

3. John Borland, "Star Wars and the Fracas over Fan Films," *Cnet News .com,* May 2, 2005, http://news.com.com/Star+Wars+and+the+fracas+over+fan +films/2008-7337_3-5690595.html.

4. Atikus XI—The Lawyer of Doom, "A Conversation with Dr. Henry Jenk-ins," *Penny Arcade,* http://www.penny-arcade.com/lodjenkins.php.

NOTE TO CHAPTER 12

1. National Organization of Women, Action Alert, "Speak Out Against Grand Theft Auto III," January 25, 2002, http://www.asmainegoes.com/ubb/ Forum/HTML/009958.html.

NOTES TO CHAPTER 13

1. David Grossman, "Teaching Kids to Kill," *Phi Kappa Phi National Forum* (2000), available online at http://www.killology.org/article_teachkid.htm.

2. Eugene Provenzo, "Children and Hyperreality: The Loss of the Real in

Contemporary Childhood and Adolescence," paper presented at the University of Chicago Cultural Policy Center conference, Chicago, 2002, available online at http://culturalpolicy.uchicago.edu/conf2001/papers/provenzo.html.

3. James Gee, *What Video Games Have to Tell Us about Learning and Literacy* (New York: Palgrave, 2000).

4. Kurt Squire, "Replaying History: Learning World History through Playing *Civilization III*" (Ph.D. dissertation, Indiana University School of Education, 2004).

5. Talmadge Wright, "Creative Player Actions in FPS Online Video Games: Playing Counter-Strike," *Game Studies* (December 2002), available online at http://www.gamestudies.org/0202/wright/.

6. Katie Salens and Eric Zimmerman, *Rules of Play: Game Design Fundamentals* (Cambridge, MA: MIT Press, 2003).

7. Zhan Li, "The Potential of America's Army: The Video Game as Civilian-Military Public Sphere" (master's thesis, Comparative Media Studies Program, Massachusetts Institute of Technology, 2003).

8. Gerard Jones, *Killing Monsters: Why Children Need Fantasy, Super Heroes, and Make-Believe Violence* (New York: Basic, 2002), 11.

9. Marjorie Heins, Brief Amica Curiae of Thirty Media Scholars, submitted to the U.S. Court of Appeals, Eight Circuit, *Interactive Digital Software Association et al. v. St. Louis County et al.*, archived at http://fepproject.org/courtbriefs/stlouissummary.html.

10. American Academy of Pediatrics, Committee on Public Education, *Policy Statement on Media Violence* (2001), archived at http://aappolicy.aappublications.org/cgi/content/full/pediatrics;108/4/1222.

11. Judge Richard Posner, U.S. Court of Appeals, *American Amusement Machine Association et al. v. Teri Kendrick et al.*, as quoted at http://www.fepproject.org/courtbriefs/kendricksummary.html.

12. Will Wright, personal communication, May 2002.

13. Miriam Formanek-Brunnel, "The Politics of Dollhood in Nineteenth-Century America," in *The Children's Culture Reader*, ed. Henry Jenkins (New York: New York University Press, 1998), 363–81.

14. Christopher Weaver, personal communication, May 2002.

15. Henry Jenkins, "Coming Up Next! Ambushed on *Donahue*," *Salon* (September 2002), reprinted as Chapter 12 of this volume.

NOTES TO CHAPTER 15

1. Neil Postman, *The Disappearance of Childhood* (New York: Vintage, 1994), 88.

2. For an alternative perspective on teen's use of the net, see Henry Jenkins, "The Kids Are Alright Online," *Technology Review* (January–February 2001):

121; and Henry Jenkins, "Empowering Children in the Digital Age: Towards a Radical Media Pedagogy," *Radical Teacher* (Spring 1997): 30–35.

3. Several other authors have used *Buffy* as a springboard for adult–teen discussions. See, for example, Steven C. Slotzman, "Vampires and Those Who Slay Them: Using the Television Program *Buffy the Vampire Slayer* in Adolescent Therapy and Psychodynamic Education," *Academic Psychiatry* 24, no. 1 (Spring 2000): 49–55; and Richard Campbell with Caitlin Campbell, "Demons, Aliens, Teens, and Television," *Television Quarterly* (Winter 2001), accessed at http://www.slayage.tv/essays/slayage2/campbell.htm.

4. "The Monsters Next Door," *Time,* May 3, 1999, 22–36.

5. Jon Katz, "Voices from the Hellmouth," *Slashdot* 24 (April 1999) and subsequent issues. Katz is currently developing a book based on these columns.

6. For a useful overview of the concept of moral panic as it has been developed in cultural studies, see Martin Barker and Julian Petley, eds., *Ill Effects: The Media/Violence Debate* (London: Routledge, 1997).

7. Mary Douglas, *Risk and Blame* (London: Routledge, 1994).

8. "The Columbine Tapes," *Time,* December 20, 1999, 40–51.

Index

About the Author

The founder and director of MIT's Comparative Media Studies Program, Henry Jenkins is the author or editor of ten books on various aspects of media and popular culture, including *Textual Poachers: Television Fans and Participatory Culture*; *From Barbie to Mortal Kombat: Gender and Computer Games*; *The Children's Culture Reader*; and *Hop on Pop: The Politics and Pleasures of Popular Culture*. His career so far has included testifying before the U.S. Senate Commerce Committee hearing into Marketing Violence for Youth following the Columbine shootings; promoting media literacy education before the Federal Communications Commission; speaking to the Governor's Board of the World Economic Forum about intellectual property and grassroots creativity; heading the Education Arcade, which promotes the educational uses of computer and video games; writing monthly columns for *Technology Review* and *Computer Games* magazines; and consulting with leading media companies about consumer relations.